The Project Approach
for All Learners

The Project Approach for All Learners

A Hands-On Guide for Inclusive Early Childhood Classrooms

by

Sallee J. Beneke, Ph.D.
St. Ambrose University
Davenport, Iowa

Michaelene M. Ostrosky, Ph.D.
University of Illinois at Urbana-Champaign

and

Lilian G. Katz, Ph.D.
University of Illinois at Urbana-Champaign

·P·A·U·L·H·
BROOKES
PUBLISHING CO®

Baltimore • London • Sydney

Paul H. Brookes Publishing Co.
Post Office Box 10624
Baltimore, Maryland 21285-0624
USA

www.brookespublishing.com

Typeset by Absolute Service, Inc., Towson, Maryland.
Manufactured in the United States of America by
Versa Press, Inc., East Peoria, Illinois.

Cover photo © iStockphoto.com.

Library of Congress Cataloging-in-Publication Data

ISBN-13: 978-1-68125-228-5
ISBN-10: 1-68125-228-7
EPUB: 978-1-68125-318-3
PDF: 978-1-68125-319-0
Library of Congress Cataloging in Publication Control Number: 2018020630

British Library Cataloguing in Publication data are available from the British Library.

2022 2021 2020 2019 2018
10   9   8   7   6   5   4   3   2   1

Contents

About the Online Materials and Videos

Purchasers of this book may download, print, and/or photocopy the forms and checklists for educational use. Likewise, training materials and PowerPoints are available for download. These materials are available at www.brookespublishing.com/downloads with (case-sensitive) keycode: 23neOsC8j.

Purchasers may also watch the videos mentioned throughout the book at the link provided above. These videos show real teachers in their classrooms, modeling the book's key strategies.

VIDEO CONTENT

Chapter 3

Video 3.1 Pretending with the teacher

Video 3.2 Creating the teacher planning web

Video 3.3 Adding to the web with a child

Video 3.4 Revisiting the web

Video 3.5 Sketching and dictating from memory

Chapter 4

Video 4.1 Drawing plans for a bookshelf

Video 4.2 Moving shelves to play library

Video 4.3 Using the real shelves as a reference

Video 4.4 Discovering a possible support for the top

Video 4.5 Researching how to make a library

Video 4.6 Discovering bar codes and numbers on books

Video 4.7 Discussing bar codes at the snack table

Video 4.8 Making a book of photos of the library

Video 4.9 Modeling observational drawing

Video 4.10 Sketching at the library

Video 4.11 Developing the survey

Video 4.12 Beginning to survey in other classrooms

Video 4.13 Figuring out materials

Video 4.14 Prompting children to make predictions

About the Authors

Sallee J. Beneke, Ph.D., Professor, Director of the Master's in Early Childhood Education Program, St. Ambrose University, Davenport, Iowa

Dr. Beneke's educational background and research focus on the potential of the Project Approach to support high-quality inclusion in early childhood education. Professor Beneke's interests are inspired by the many years she spent teaching in inclusive classrooms, administering early childhood education programs, providing professional development to teachers in the field, and studying curriculum and instruction as well as special education. She is committed to responsive teaching that engages the interest and motivation of all learners in early childhood settings.

Michaelene M. Ostrosky, Ph.D., Grayce Wicall Gauthier Professor of Education, Department Head of Special Education, University of Illinois at Urbana-Champaign, Champaign, Illinois

Throughout her career, Dr. Ostrosky has been involved in research and dissemination on the inclusion of children with disabilities, social-emotional competence, and challenging behavior. Professor Ostrosky is a former editor of *Young Exceptional Children (YEC)* and is the co-editor of several *YEC* monographs. She coauthored *The Making Friends Program: Supporting Acceptance in Your K–2 Classroom* (Paul H. Brookes Publishing Co., 2016), which supports the acceptance of individuals with disabilities.

Lilian G. Katz, Ph.D., Professor Emerita, Children's Research Center, University of Illinois at Urbana-Champaign, Champaign, Illinois

Dr. Katz is an international leader in early childhood education who played a major role in bringing project work to the attention of U.S. teachers. She taught at the University of Illinois at Urbana-Champaign for more than 3 decades and directed the ERIC Clearinghouse on Elementary and Early Childhood Education (ERIC/EECE) for more than 30 years. Professor Katz has lectured in all 50 states and in 43 countries. Dr. Katz has authored more than 150 publications, and she founded two journals: *Early Childhood Research Quarterly* and *Early Childhood Research & Practice.*

Foreword

The Project Approach for All Learners: A Hands-On Guide for Inclusive Early Childhood Classrooms is a book that educators of young children will use often. It is the go-to source for teachers who want to use the Project Approach but have been hesitant to try it. It also is a wonderful supplement for teachers who are veterans of the approach. The heart of the book is the 52-step Project Approach Implementation Checklist, which supports the teacher through the three phases of the Project Approach. The checklist provides clear guidelines for every step. In addition, it encourages teachers to monitor their implementation by evaluating what is working and to make adaptations as needed to meet children's learning needs and interests. It supports teachers in maintaining fidelity in their implementation of the Project Approach.

Users will find many positive outcomes for both teachers and students in using this approach. First, the goals of the Project Approach are to empower children to become curious, purposeful, thoughtful, collaborative learners within the context of studying a project and representing their findings. Learning is an adventure and a process that leads to authentic knowledge in content areas such as math, literacy, and social studies. Learning is not restricted to the topic of the project but becomes a way for children to examine the world in which they live. Through the Project Approach, children will gain generalizable skills that will help them to continue to learn about other topics.

Second, the Project Approach provides flexibility in the ways information is presented to children; it supports accommodations that promote engagement by all children, ultimately supporting success for all children. At the center of the Project Approach is the concept of universal design for learning (UDL), which calls for learning using multiple means of engagement, representation, and action and expression. Children can play diverse roles in the Project Approach that build on their strengths and extend their skills, demonstrating their learning in many different ways. It is not a "cookie-cutter" approach but one that can be individualized as needed. It can be used in classrooms with dual language learners, children with disabilities or developmental delays, and children with challenging behavior, as well as with children who are typical learners and children who are gifted learners.

Third, the Project Approach, as noted by the authors, is not a curriculum; it is a versatile teaching and learning approach that can be "woven into the fabric of the daily schedule" (p. 3) and supplement a curriculum required by the school district or program. Teachers can integrate early learning standards throughout their project so that by the project's culmination, they can document children's mastery of standards in content areas of math, language arts, and social studies. The checklist creates manageable steps and phases for the approach.

Fourth, the Project Approach is consistent with precepts of early learning—that it be developmentally matched to the skills of the children, that it incorporate responsive teaching, and that it rely on children's social interaction and cooperative efforts for learning. In effect, it can create a community of children working together to explore the project and to engage in shared discussion, problem solving, and collaboration. The Project Approach also supports opportunities to resolve different points of view. Children participate in these efforts through center play, dramatic play, storytelling, drawing, construction, and other forms of two- and three-dimensional representation using everyday classroom materials. Projects may include field trips, or the field can be brought to the classroom by hosting guest experts and bringing in specially selected artifacts related to the project.

Finally, the Project Approach helps teachers to develop new insights about their role and to strengthen their disposition to be flexible and responsive to children's ideas and interests. Examples include advocating that teachers slow down to listen to children and to use open-ended questions to expand and extend conversations with children. Teachers can use the Project Approach to emphasize the strengths of each child and provide each child with multiple opportunities over time to participate in activities. In doing so, teachers have many opportunities to establish in children an intellectual disposition by helping them to wonder about their world by prompting them to question, to seek answers, to hypothesize, to experiment, and to draw conclusions.

The Project Approach concepts are well illustrated through three engaging projects described throughout the book; these sample projects present the creative ways in which teachers and children became involved in each project and move from start to finish. The examples allow the readers to visualize and imagine how they might support children conducting a project in their own classroom. After establishing the history and current relevance of the Project Approach in Chapter 1 and the key role of the teacher in Chapter 2, the authors describe how to implement the approach in Chapters 3, 4, and 5. How to identify and explore a sustainable topic during Phase I is clearly discussed in Chapter 3 (see Figure 3.2: Task Sheet: Identifying Topics for Projects). Chapter 4 provides many pictures, figures, and video clips that illustrate successful use of strategies used by children for learning more about their topic during Phase II. For example, the reader can see a word wall, a web created by children and their teacher, children's use of clipboards for drawing and collecting survey data, and examples of thought-provoking questions. Chapter 5 addresses ways for teachers to help children create visual organizers, share what they know, and plan for ways to create a group representation of the project as well as a culminating event during which they celebrate their project work. Again, Chapter 5 is filled with photographs and examples to support Phase III. Chapter 6 provides advice on how to sustain future project work and how to demonstrate the ways in which the Project Approach also accomplishes child mastery of early learning standards (see Table 6.1: Mathematics standards met during the Dog Project). The authors describe strategies for linking the Project Approach with required curriculum, for developing administrative support, and for building a community of practice with other teachers.

In summary, Beneke, Ostrosky, and Katz have expanded on their earlier work and created a book that "does it all" for teachers of young children who wish to be creative and to support children's curiosity and love of learning. It expands the Project Approach to include all children, ensuring that as the world becomes increasingly diverse in language, culture, and abilities, the Project Approach will work. Finally, and importantly, it provides a role for families and ways to include them in supporting their child's learning so that learning extends beyond the classroom to home and the community.

Susan A. Fowler, Ph.D.
University of Illinois at Urbana-Champaign

Preface

Some teachers in early childhood classrooms struggle to find ways to engage each and every child in interesting, motivating, and educational ways. When one considers the broad diversity of abilities that might be present in a preschool classroom, the task of engaging every child can be especially daunting. Imagine having students who range in age from 3 to 5 years old, whose home language might not be English, and who have a variety of strengths (including some children who are reading chapter books, some who can speak three languages, and some who have advanced numeracy skills) and weaknesses (including some children who have limited social skills, some who have speech delays, and some who have significant fine and gross motor disabilities). The addition of the Project Approach to early childhood curricula can help achieve the goal of engaging each and every child because, through project work, teachers identify a topic of potentially high interest to their particular group of students and they facilitate an in-depth study of the topic through firsthand investigation and research.

Although teachers may be enthusiastic about using the Project Approach, they sometimes struggle to implement it with fidelity, in part because they are not sure how to do it. In addition, in our research, we found that some teachers did not believe the Project Approach was appropriate for children with disabilities because they thought that it was not structured enough or might not provide enough opportunities for children to work on areas where they lacked skills. We wrote this book to provide a practical tool that will help teachers understand *how* to implement the three phases of the Project Approach. The book also highlights research demonstrating how effective the approach is for children with disabilities and their peers in inclusive classrooms. Finally, it offers strategies for supporting children's successful inclusion in project work.

Each chapter begins with a vignette that cues readers in to the content that is covered in that chapter. Likewise, the chapters include real-life examples of projects that were conducted through the Illinois Early Learning Project. The book features three main projects, the Dog Project, the Garden Project, and the Library Project, each of which is explored through a discussion of their implementation process, samples of their planning tools, and visuals including photographs and children's drawings. Readers can learn more about the projects discussed in this book by visiting the Illinois Early Learning Project web site at https://illinoisearlylearning .org/resources/pa/projects/.

To further aid in educators' implementation of the Project Approach, the Implementation Checklist is the centerpiece of the book; it is referenced frequently throughout the book as readers come to understand its purpose and how to use it. Readers are also provided with concrete examples of how other early childhood teachers have used the checklist in their search to become skillful Project Approach implementers. The content of Chapters 3, 4, and 5 parallels the items on the checklist. Appendix A includes completed Implementation Checklists for the Dog Project, the Garden Project, and the Library Project. Educators can use these samples to guide their own use of the implementation tool.

Appendix B features training activities and discussion questions to further support educators' understanding of project work and their ability to implement it in their own classrooms. The sets of activities are aligned with the chapter content and might be implemented by educators with their peers, by an administrator, by a group of educators, or by a trainer in a professional development session. Finally, the book's online resources include download-able forms, PowerPoints, and video examples. The videos, which are referenced throughout the book, illustrate strategies being implemented by a real teacher in the classroom and serve to bring key concepts to life. References to videos are called out in the text by a "play" icon, which also appears next to this paragraph.

Each coauthor brings a unique perspective to this book. Lilian Katz has been a champion of emergent curriculum for young children throughout her career. *Engaging Children's Minds: The Project Approach* (Katz & Chard, 1989) sparked a renewed interest in project work in the United States and around the world. Michaelene Ostrosky has spent her career focused on the inclusion of young children in early childhood settings, studying and writing about methods for sup-porting the social development and friendships of children with and without disabilities. As a classroom teacher, Sallee Beneke was struck by the potential of the Project Approach to support learners with a wide range of abilities. During her doctoral studies in special education at the University of Illinois, Sallee immersed herself in exploring the potential of the Project Approach to support the development of *all* young children in inclusive classrooms. This search to blend the Project Approach and inclusive education brought Lilian, Micki, and Sallee together, and one outcome from this collaboration is this book. We hope that you benefit from our collabora-tion and, in turn, that many children with a range of abilities benefit as you implement project work in early childhood settings in ways that interest, motivate, and educate all of the young minds whom you teach.

REFERENCE

Katz, L. G., & Chard, S. C. (1989). *Engaging children's minds: The Project Approach.* Stamford, CT: Ablex.

Acknowledgments

Many teachers, administrators, children, colleagues, friends, and family members contributed to this book through their enthusiasm, support, thoughtful suggestions, and the models they provided through their own work! We see traces of their influence in the adjustments we made to the Project Approach Implementation Checklist, the examples we selected to share, and the way that we organized the chapters in this book. We cannot thank them enough for their contributions, both big and small.

In particular, we wish to thank the teachers who provided in-depth documentation of their project work for us to use as examples throughout this book. Special thanks are extended to Karissa Utz from Jefferson Early Childhood Center in East Moline, Illinois; Laura DeLuca, Kim Burd, and Danielle Lavin from the John L. Hensey Elementary School in Washington, Illinois; and Andromahi Harrison from the St. Ambrose University Children's Campus in Davenport, Iowa. The documentation of their project work helped bring our writing about the Project Approach to life and, we hope, will help other early childhood educators see that it is doable.

Thanks also to the many preservice students and children who helped us remember the excitement and joy of engaging in project work for the first time. Observing you and hearing about your experiences with project work inspired us to persevere in completing this book.

Many thanks go to the veteran project implementers who provided feedback on the Project Approach Implementation Checklist. In particular, our sincere thanks go to Lynn Lubben, Androhami Harrison, and Abbey Wildemuth from the St. Ambrose University Children's Campus, who provided feedback and used the checklist to help preservice teachers participate in their first project. Their suggestions made the final version of the Project Approach Implementation Checklist better than we had initially imagined.

We also extend our gratitude to Kathy Althoff and Sandy Lerner-Schwartz, who allowed us to spend weeks in their classrooms observing and who agreed to let us coach them using the first version of the Project Approach Implementation Checklist. Many of the insights regarding project implementation that we share in this book were inspired by Kathy and Sandy's work.

For the past 6 years, we have provided draft versions of the Project Approach Implementation Checklist to participants in the Summer Institute on the Project Approach at St. Ambrose University and to participants who attended our early childhood and early childhood special education conference presentations. Thanks to the many individuals who went back to their classrooms, used the checklist to support their project work, and then gave us feedback on the usefulness of the checklist and offered suggestions for change.

We are grateful to the many state consultants and trainers who used earlier versions of the Project Approach Implementation Checklist to support the teachers with whom they work and then provided us with feedback on this process. In particular, we want to thank the consultants from the Grant Wood, Great Prairie, and Green Hills Iowa Area Education Agencies. Your insights were invaluable.

Many of the resources included in this book were originally prepared for the Illinois Projects in Practice web site, now a section of the Illinois Early Learning Project web site (https://illinoisearlylearning.org/pa/). A huge shout-out to our colleagues in the Department of Special Education at the University of Illinois at Urbana-Champaign who have faithfully supported this web site for more than 12 years. In particular, we extend our thanks to Jean Mendoza for her excellent contributions to the site and her thoughtful editing and Bernadette Laumann for her steady support and leadership. We also want to thank Bernie's predecessor, Karen Smith, for her enthusiastic support in getting real-life projects in practice out for others to see.

We offer our sincere thanks to Susan Fowler and Amy Santos, our colleagues at the University of Illinois' Department of Special Education, who supported the idea that the Project Approach could provide a path to more fully include children with disabilities in early childhood classrooms. Their suggestions enhanced the content provided in the Project Approach Implementation Checklist and gave us fuel for thought regarding the benefits of project work for learners with a range of abilities. Colleagues at St. Ambrose University also deserve our gratitude. Thanks to Dr. Tom Carpenter for his encouragement and enthusiasm for this approach to teaching. Thanks also to Deb Brownson, Director of the St. Ambrose Children's Campus. Her steadfast dedication and belief in the power of the Project Approach have helped her teachers provide a model of excellence and a beacon for others who want to know more about this approach. Finally, we thank our families, who have listened to us talk about this book for many, many months and have shared our enthusiasm as the final product became a reality.

To early childhood professionals
who regularly and fearlessly encourage young
children's curiosity about the world around them

Getting Started
With the Project
Approach

Ms. Carly watched with interest as a group of preschool children from Ms. Tamara's class worked on constructing a semi-truck using cardboard boxes and found objects. She was amazed at their persistence and was especially impressed by the participation of children at varying developmental levels. Everyone seemed to have a way to help. Alex, a child on the autism spectrum, was busily working on taping boxes together alongside two other children. Ms. Carly knew this construction was the result of a project in which the children were engaged. She wished she knew how to get a project going in her own class. She had been to a workshop on the Project Approach once and had attempted to get a project started, but it had fizzled out soon after it began. The children just did not seem interested in pursuing it. Ms. Carly wished she knew more about how to begin and sustain project work. She wanted to foster the level of inclusion she observed among the children in Ms. Tamara's class, but she did not know where to turn for support.

This chapter includes an overview of the Project Approach and introduces the Project Approach Implementation Checklist that is at the heart of this guide. The 52-item checklist is designed to support teachers who are new to implementing the Project Approach by prompting them to include important elements of the approach in each of the three major phases of a project. For teachers who already have experience implementing the Project Approach, the suggestions and examples provided here can help ensure implementation with fidelity. Our collective experiences have shown that when project work is not implemented correctly, teachers, like Ms. Carly, often struggle. We also provide an overview of the goals teachers can set and reach when they implement the Project Approach and explore the potential of the Project Approach as a context for universal design for learning. Finally, the chapter closes with an examination of the evidence base for the Project Approach and a brief overview of its historical roots.

GETTING TO KNOW THE PROJECT APPROACH

Many teachers have heard of the Project Approach, but they often have only a vague idea of what it entails. They may have misunderstandings or misperceptions about the goals of project work or how projects work. For example, they may believe the goal of a project is to come up with an amazing product, such as a mural or a three-dimensional construction, or they may think it is necessary to have transportation to a field site in order to do a project. In this guide, we clarify these misperceptions.

What Is the Project Approach?

Young children are naturally curious, and the Project Approach is a way of teaching that capitalizes on this common trait. In project work, the teacher identifies a topic of potentially high interest to the children in the class and facilitates an in-depth study of the topic through firsthand investigation and research. Essentially, the teacher strengthens children's interest in a topic by involving them in project work. As they engage in project work, children learn about how the world around them works and develop confidence in their ability to figure things out. They learn how to work collaboratively with their peers, as they seek and find answers to their questions. They gradually develop confidence in their own abilities and build perseverance. Rather than focusing predominantly on academic achievement, the Project Approach strengthens children's intellectual dispositions, such as analyzing, predicting, hypothesizing, and explaining, and the skills involved in each of these dispositions.

> As they engage in project work, children learn about how the world around them works and develop confidence in their ability to figure things out.

Three phases provide a framework for inquiry-based learning, which is at the heart of project work. In Phase I, teachers introduce the topic and provide the children with opportunities to share what they already know about it through activities such as storytelling, dramatic play, and drawing. Teachers identify aspects of the topic that the children are curious to learn more about. In Phase II, teachers provide the children with activities that allow them to satisfy their curiosity, such as interviews with guest experts, field trips, experiments, and examinations of artifacts. When the children have satisfied their curiosity, teachers introduce Phase III, which provides opportunities for children to reflect on and share what they have learned and experienced.

Although children need instruction in certain skills and subjects (e.g., counting, naming colors, tying shoes), their development is strengthened when they are provided with experiences that encourage their intellectual capabilities. Notably, project work can be incorporated into an existing curriculum, although it does not typically constitute the entire curriculum. For younger children, project work is typically woven into the fabric of the daily schedule. For example, new materials or concepts might be introduced at circle time, opportunities to investigate or represent new understanding might be incorporated into choice time, and opportunities to reflect on or summarize what has been learned might be a focus of class discussions. Academic skills in numeracy, literacy, and social-emotional competence can be reinforced within project work.

The content of projects varies depending on the topic a particular group of children and their teacher are interested in investigating and children's strengths and needs. The Project Approach provides a context that supports the abilities of *all* children, including children with special needs (Beneke & Ostrosky, 2015). It provides opportunities for children to use their strengths and build new knowledge and skills.

> The Project Approach provides a context that supports the abilities of *all* children, including children with special needs. It provides opportunities for children to use their strengths and build new knowledge and skills.

Project Approach Implementation Checklist

This book offers support to new implementers of the Project Approach and to those already familiar with the approach. A teacher who is new to the Project Approach can read the book in its entirety and follow along on the checklist, whereas experienced teachers may simply choose to review a section of the book referred to in the checklist. The 52-item Project Approach Implementation Checklist (or "Implementation Checklist") is included as this chapter's appendix. It contains items focusing on the three phases of projects, which we refer to as Phases I, II, and III. Chapters 3, 4, and 5 correspond to the sequence of the items in the Implementation Checklist and provide in-depth explanations and examples for each item listed.

The items in the Implementation Checklist were originally developed by Sallee Beneke (the first author of this book) as part of her dissertation research to assist teachers in inclusive early childhood classrooms who were attempting to implement the Project Approach but did not have a mentor or coach available on a daily basis to support their implementation (Beneke & Ostrosky, 2015). The teachers used the checklist as a source of ideas for implementation and as a basis for discussion with each other and with Dr. Beneke during weekly meetings.

Educators can use the Implementation Checklist to support their implementation of the Project Approach. Before beginning a project, educators should review the items in the Phase I section. They can use it to stimulate ideas and make notes about possible Phase I activities in the blank spaces in the right-hand column. As educators implement the project, they should revisit the checklist regularly to record how each checklist item was implemented over the course of the project. It is helpful to include dates because they can be used later to document the development of the project. For each checklist item, educators should record Yes, No, or N/A (not applicable) to indicate whether or not that checklist item was met. It can be helpful to review the activities that have been implemented with a coach, mentor, or teaching partner(s) as a basis for discussing what has gone well, what has been challenging, and what might be next steps in implementing the Project Approach.

A teacher does not have to implement every item on the checklist to engage children in the Project Approach because not every aspect of project work is used in every project. For example, a project on babies might begin spontaneously with a child's announcement that his mother is expecting. Therefore, there is no need for the teacher to plan an introduction to the topic. Or, in a project on farms, a teacher might want to arrange a field trip to a farm, but in a project on worms, fieldwork can be done right on the school or center playground. However, the more items that are implemented, the more likely it is that the project will be successful during each phase. Checklist items were initially developed by Dr. Beneke, with input from the other authors of this book, based on their many years of experience implementing the Project Approach, training others to use the checklist, and working in a variety of early childhood settings. Revisions to the checklist were based on the collective wisdom of the authors and many colleagues who have implemented and coached others on the Project Approach. Numerous teachers who are experts in the approach reviewed and commented on the checklist before it was finalized. The coauthors of this guide provided input into the development of checklist items. The Implementation Checklist is included as this chapter's appendix. Three sample completed checklists can be found in Appendix A.

Importance of Fidelity of Implementation

Fidelity of implementation is defined as "the implementation of a practice or program as intended by the researchers or developers" (IRIS Center, 2018a, p. 1). As educators who have written about, trained others in implementation of, and conducted research on the Project Approach for many years, the authors of this book believe that if implemented with fidelity, project work can effectively help teachers to reach their goals in inclusive early childhood classrooms. However, monitoring and measuring how an intervention is implemented are important for evaluating its outcomes (Harn, Damico, & Stoolmiller, 2017). The Implementation Checklist, in combination with this guide, can help teachers monitor how they implement the Project Approach and help them connect their implementation to child outcomes in a way that reflects progress toward achievement of their teaching goals.

THE PROJECT APPROACH AND TEACHING GOALS

What is important for a young child to learn? What will help a child succeed and live a life in which he or she feels fulfilled and satisfied? The goals of teachers who implement the Project Approach go beyond satisfaction of requirements for age- or grade-level standards. Their goals are for children to become curious, purposeful, thoughtful, collaborative learners who know how to learn more and who can communicate their findings with others. To achieve this goal, teachers need to provide opportunities for children to develop the understanding, skills, dispositions, and feelings that will help them successfully use this knowledge. Teachers can do this most effectively by providing children with opportunities for hands-on learning. However, teachers may encounter challenges to implementing the Project Approach and may need support to overcome these challenges.

Knowledge, Understanding, and Skills

Children rely not only on what they know about a project topic, but also on what they understand about how and when to use that knowledge, how that knowledge connects to other aspects of their lives, and the skills they need to successfully engage in project work. However, children often memorize discrete facts and recite them without fully understanding their significance. For example, a child might learn in a textbook that the bread he sees in the grocery store comes from the bakery. However, that does not mean that he understands *how* the bread comes from the bakery. In a project focused on the bakery, the teacher's goal is to help children acquire not just *knowledge* about the bakery, but also an *understanding* of the many aspects of what goes on inside it. In such a project, the children might:

- Interview the baker
- Visit the bakery
- Sketch aspects of the bakery that catch their interest
- Observe the ingredients and watch them being mixed and then baked into loaves
- Notice the uniforms various bakery workers wear and what they do in their jobs
- Watch as the bread is loaded onto a truck for delivery to the grocery store
- Observe customers exchanging money for baked goods at the cash register

After discussing what they saw on their trip to the bakery, the teacher might invite the children to suggest what they would like to make to show what they learned on their trip. With the teacher's support, the children might decide to construct their own bakery in the dramatic play area in their classroom, which could include a large oven constructed from cardboard boxes and other art materials, a check-out area with cash registers, and uniforms. With the teacher's support, the children might also measure and mix ingredients, knead dough, and bake their own loaves of bread. Finally, they might dictate and illustrate a report that tells the story of a loaf of bread, and they might survey their families to find out where they buy their bread or what types of bread they buy.

Children who have been involved in this type of learning experience can develop a deep understanding about how the bakery works, and in the course of acquiring this understanding, they may use many skills (e.g., wondering, asking questions, counting, comparing, measuring, noticing, describing, drawing, pretending, labeling, cutting, taping). A learning experience in which children can fully satisfy their curiosity helps them develop confidence in their own ability to figure out how the world around them works. They feel engaged with the learning process and are motivated to figure out how many other elements of their world work.

Dispositions and Feelings

Strengthening positive dispositions and discouraging negative dispositions are important goals for all teachers. A disposition is a habit of mind or "a tendency to exhibit frequently, consciously, and voluntarily a pattern of behavior that is directed to a broad goal" (Katz, 1993, p. 2). Dispositions are important as educational goals because they impact the likelihood that a child will make effective use of the knowledge, understanding, or skills that he or she has learned. For example, a child might have the disposition to be curious, persistent, and a risk-taker, which could positively affect the chances that the child will apply what he or she has been taught. If the child was a member of the class that was investigating the bakery, he or she might offer questions, make predictions, and volunteer to help peers with the class construction. However, the disposition to be short-tempered, argumentative, or impatient might have the opposite effect. A child with these dispositions might not gain as much from the project on the bakery because the child might be preoccupied with his or her own negative feelings. Part of the teacher's role is to encourage and nurture positive dispositions.

Project work can have a positive impact on children's feelings about themselves as learners. Children who feel confident in their own ability to figure things out are more likely to take risks and tackle challenging problems (Dweck, Walton, & Cohen, 2014).

> The teacher's goal is to ensure that children feel that their opinions and ideas are valued and respected by others and that they will value and respect the opinions and ideas of others.

The teacher's goals for a child are that the child will feel that his or her opinions and ideas are valued and respected by others and that the child will value and respect the opinions and ideas of others. The child will feel that he or she has something to offer to other children and to adults and that he or she has something to gain from them as well. The child will begin to develop the expectation that learning is a lifelong way of being and that there is always something new to learn.

Standards of Experience and Hands-On Learning

Educators and the population in general typically discuss educational goals in terms of standards. In particular, various educational authorities and responsible governmental agencies tend to develop, promote, and require standards of learning. Yet, as this book explores, it is more developmentally and educationally appropriate to develop an agreement on the standards of the experiences we believe children should have. For example, children should have many experiences with learning-related skills, such as taking responsibility, working cooperatively with others, working independently, and organizing materials (Katz, 2012; McClelland, Acock, & Morrison, 2006). The Project Approach includes standards of experiences, such as developing questions about relevant topics, working hard to seek answers to those questions, and spending thoughtful and strong energies to find ways to explain, share, and demonstrate those questions and the answers to them.

These experiences in project work are obtained through direct hands-on investigation and representation. Children learn answers to their questions by examining artifacts with all their senses (e.g., kneading dough, smelling it, watching it rise), by looking closely to identify details to draw and use in pretend play, by exploring how things work through hypothesizing, and by experimenting to answer questions. Classrooms in which children learn through child-initiated experiences have been found to promote later academic success (Marcon, 2002).

Challenges to Meeting Teaching Goals Through the Project Approach

Teachers in U.S. schools often struggle with the tension between implementing what they know to be best practices or developmentally appropriate methods of teaching and the expectations of the school system for which they work. This dualism may be particularly true for early childhood educators whose preservice training often includes an emphasis on responsive teaching and early development. For example, Blank, Damjanovic, Peixoto da Silva, and Weber (2014) found that teachers who were initiating the Project Approach as a new practice in their schools felt uncomfortable because they were teaching in a way that was different from the status quo. Blank et al. (2014) found that teachers' success in implementing the approach hinged on the presence of professional learning communities because the teachers needed space to communicate problems, brainstorm ideas, and consider various initiatives with others. Professional learning communities provide teachers with opportunities "to learn deeply with colleagues about an identified topic, to develop shared meaning, and identify shared purposes related to the topic" (Hord, 2009, p. 40). For more information on professional learning communities in early childhood education, see *Reflecting in Communities of Practice: A Workbook for Early Childhood Educators* by Curtis, Lebo, Cividanes, and Carter (2013).

In addition, before they can fully comprehend the potential of the Project Approach to support young children and help them learn, teachers need to be able to support the dynamic *processes* of the project (e.g., questioning, predicting, representing) (Clark, 2006). The process of questioning involves encouraging children to articulate what they want to find out about the topic. In situations where children are not able to articulate these questions, it is up to teachers to determine what the children are curious about based on observations of children's play. Teachers can involve children in the process of predicting answers to their questions throughout the project. Then, through investigation, children can determine whether their predictions were accurate. The process of representing also takes place throughout the project. Similarly, project work provides a context for individual children and groups of children to represent their understanding of the project though the arts (e.g., drawing, dramatizing, storytelling, singing). In our experience, teachers often want to implement projects, but they struggle with *how* to implement the processes that support good project work. We have found that the further situated a teacher's current practices and beliefs about curriculum are from the project work, the more difficult it is for the teacher to make a full transition to that approach without support. Teachers may attend a 1- or 2-day training on the Project Approach, but they typically do not have the professional development resources or support needed to help them guide the development of a project. The Implementation Checklist featured in this book provides vital assistance in this regard.

> The Project Approach Implementation Checklist featured in this book provides vital assistance in professional development.

THE PROJECT APPROACH AND UNIVERSAL DESIGN FOR LEARNING

Young children come to school with a wide variety of interests and "abilities to see, hear, attend, write, read, count, understand English, transition from one activity to another, manage physical tasks, care for their own needs, engage in learning activities, and remember" (Beneke & Ostrosky, 2016, p. 1403). These interests and abilities are influenced by their previous experiences. In the past, when children's abilities were not considered typical for their age, children were grouped by ability or label with the intention of providing them with an education that would best meet their special educational needs. However, the inclusion of children with disabilities in classrooms with their typically developing peers is considered recommended practice for all children. Universal design for learning (UDL) is one way to ensure all children in inclusive settings have access to the learning environments, educational routines and activities, and general education curriculum (Division for Early Childhood & National Association for the Education of Young Children, 2009). UDL is a scientifically valid framework for guiding educational practice that:

> (A) provides flexibility in the ways information is presented, in the ways students respond or demonstrate knowledge and skills, and in the ways students are engaged; and

> (B) reduces barriers in instruction, provides appropriate accommodations, supports and challenges, and maintains high achievement expectations for all students, including students with disabilities and students who are limited English proficient. (Higher Education Opportunity Act of 2008 [PL 89-329])

The National Center on Universal Design for Learning (2017) promotes three overarching principles that guide implementation of UDL: multiple means of engagement, multiple means of representation, and multiple means of action and expression. (For more information on UDL, see the CAST web site at http://www.cast.org/our-work/about-udl.html.)

Potential of the Project Approach to Support Diverse Learners

Instead of starting with a one-size-fits-all curriculum and then making adjustments to accommodate learners based on their labels, UDL requires teachers to plan goals, methods, materials, and assessments that provide *all* learners with equal access to the curriculum from the beginning. The goal is to address learning challenges that act as barriers to full participation. The Project Approach has the potential to provide a UDL. The Project Approach is a good fit with UDL because, in project work, teachers plan based on the interests, knowledge, skills, and abilities of each individual child in their classrooms from the very beginning. One of the strengths of the Project Approach is the potential to provide opportunities for children to use their strengths to participate at the level that best fits their abilities and interests through multiple means of engagement, multiple means of representation, and multiple means of action and expression.

> The Project Approach is a good fit with UDL because, in project work, teachers plan based on the interests, knowledge, skills, and abilities of each individual child in their classrooms from the very beginning.

The term *multiple means of engagement* refers to "how learners get engaged and stay motivated. How they are challenged, excited, or interested. These are affective dimensions" (National Center on Universal Design for Learning, 2014). The Project Approach provides for engagement in many ways. The topic of a project is based on the interests of the children in the class, and once the project is underway, the direction of the project follows the interests of the children as they continue to evolve. The long-term nature of project work is helpful in this regard. It allows skillful teachers to carefully observe and respond to individual as well as group interests over time. It allows children to become experts on the topic of study and provides children with disabilities with more opportunities to consider the roles associated with the topic. For example, this knowledge can help children who do not typically engage in dramatic play join in pretend play with other children.

Teachers can facilitate children's engagement in ongoing activities by exploring each child's interests and experiences with their families, adding topic-related artifacts to the environment, asking children questions about and pointing out attributes of topic-related artifacts, prompting and acknowledging children's participation in project exploration, and featuring each child's contributions and/or work in an ongoing documentation display about the project (see the Garden Project and the Dog Project featured in Chapters 3, 4, and 5).

The term *multiple means of representation* refers to "how we gather facts and categorize what we see, hear, and read" (National Center on Universal Design for Learning, 2014). Projects provide many opportunities for children to learn about the topic under investigation in different ways. Over time, teachers plan and provide sources of information through firsthand exploration, child-friendly reference materials, props for dramatic play, images, discussion, field trips, and visits from guest experts. Teachers can support children in representing their experiences by simplifying or making materials and experiences more complex to support individual learners. They can add topic-related images to dramatic play or block areas, place topic-related tools in the discovery area, and add topic-related artifacts to the classroom for firsthand investigation.

The term *multiple means of action and expression* refers to "how we organize and express our ideas" (National Center on Universal Design for Learning, 2014). In project work, children have many ways to express their growing understanding about the topic across all three phases of the project. They can dictate, paint, draw, sing, pretend, and work on individual and group constructions to communicate their growing understanding about the topic under study.

Teachers can support children in expressing their ideas by helping children notice important attributes of topic-related objects or experiences that they can record, pairing a child with a more competent peer who can help with expressing ideas, providing accessible open-ended media for expression, helping children with limited verbal ability to participate in dictating lists or webbing by describing their interests, and placing topic-related objects in dramatic play and block areas to spark dramatic play. Teachers observe children closely to determine which supports are most effective for which children.

Potential of the Project Approach to Support Dual Language Learners

Dual language learners (DLLs) are children learning two (or more) languages at the same time, as well as children learning a second language while continuing to develop their first (or home) language (Office of Head Start, 2008). Developing two languages during the early childhood years can help children acquire "executive function abilities, such as working memory, impulse control, attention to relevant versus irrelevant task cues, and mental or cognitive flexibility, as well as improved language skills" (Espinosa, 2013, p. 5). However, the time it takes to process input in two languages may cause some DLLs to be a little slower at word retrieval (Espinosa, 2013). Increasing numbers of DLLs now attend preschool programs, and research has shown that attending a high-quality preschool can close gaps in achievement. To support the language acquisition of DLLs, it is effective for teachers to "intentionally activate knowledge and concepts in the home language and then explicitly help the child transfer this knowledge to the new language" (Espinosa, 2015, p. 80). The long-term nature of project work allows teachers many opportunities to help DLLs acquire vocabulary in their home and school languages in a meaningful context.

> The long-term nature of project work allows teachers many opportunities to help DLLs acquire vocabulary in their home and school languages in a meaningful context.

Experts agree that the following strategies support DLLs: knowing students' families and their home contexts, developing positive relationships with each child, relating learning experiences to what children already know and can do, teaching vocabulary, engaging in informal conversations, and teaching skills and facts in meaningful contexts. Each of these strategies is well supported by the Project Approach.

Children's language is inextricably bound with their cultural experiences. The families of DLLs come from a variety of countries, and expectations about how their children will learn and use English are likely to be influenced by cultural experiences in the country of origin. In addition, two families from the same culture are not identical; they will have varying expectations, strengths, and needs. It is important for teachers to get to know and develop relationships with the families of their DLLs. Project work can help with this because families can be consulted about children's interests to help identify useful topics for projects. Families can act as a resource to advise teachers and help in the development of culturally relevant projects. The long-term nature of a project allows teachers time to communicate with families about the project topic. An interpreter or family member who speaks English can help teachers establish and maintain communication about the project.

Project work helps teachers develop positive relationships with individual DLLs, because projects take place in socially and emotionally supportive classroom environments. Project work facilitates friendly, one-on-one conversations between teachers and their students, allowing teachers opportunities to show interest in students' ideas, experiences, and feelings related to the project topic and project experiences.

The three phases of the Project Approach naturally lead to an understanding of what children already know and can do. In Phase I, children communicate what they already know about the topic and represent their knowledge through discussions, dramatic play, and a variety of the arts. Children continue to communicate about and represent their understanding of the topic as the project proceeds through Phase II and culminates in Phase III. This ongoing process gives teachers many opportunities to observe DLLs closely and plan instruction related to what each child is beginning to understand. Teachers can use their insights about children's skills and understanding to plan small group experiences with children who can stimulate each other's language development.

Learning new vocabulary takes place naturally in project work, as children discover new information about the project topic. Whenever possible, teachers should express new vocabulary words in the DLLs' home language so that the acquisition of knowledge is supported. At the same time, as DLLs acquire English vocabulary, they bring their expressive vocabulary into line with their receptive vocabulary (August, Carlo, Dressler, & Snow, 2005). Teachers of DLLs need to *intentionally* and *continually* support bilingualism (Prieto, 2009), and ongoing communication efforts about the project under study are perfect for this purpose. Teachers also can use pictorial cognate charts that feature an image of a project-related object along with the written name of the object in both languages. Cognates are words in two languages that share the same meaning and have similar spelling and pronunciation (e.g., the English word *circle* and the Spanish word *circuló*). In addition, teachers can use a combination of facial expressions, gestures, real-life objects, and pictures to support children's understanding of new vocabulary (Figueras-Daniel & Barnett, 2013).

The primary way in which children develop language at school is through informal teacher–child and child–child conversations (Dickinson & Porche, 2011). Teachers can take advantage of the many informal conversations that take place as children represent and discuss their ideas and experiences during project work to prompt child–child conversations and to reinforce vocabulary in teacher–child conversations.

Young children, including DLLs, are more motivated and engaged when their learning experiences are meaningful. In research on parents' perceptions of the impact of project work on their second-grade children, Souto-Manning and Lee (2005) found that the parents believed that "projects allowed those students who spoke English as a second language to participate in the classroom activities in a personally meaningful manner" (p. 14). Selecting topics for investigation that are familiar to DLLs and that the DLLs can investigate firsthand is likely to provide a context for meaningful learning. Espinosa (2015) recommends that teachers select three to four picture books related to the project topic as anchor texts to use repetitively to foster development of a particular concept and related vocabulary. For example, in a project on hats, the teacher might use *Caps for Sale* (Slobodkina, 1968) and *I Want My Hat Back* (Klassen, 2012) as anchor texts.

EVIDENCE BASE FOR THE PROJECT APPROACH

Evidence of the impact of the Project Approach has grown in the recent years. The evidence includes both formal research studies (Beneke & Ostrosky, 2009, 2015; Chun, Hertzog, Gaffney, & Dymond, 2011; Mitchell, Foulger, Wetzel, & Rathkey, 2009; Souto-Manning & Lee, 2005) and reports from teachers on their experiences (Baldwin, Adams, & Kelly, 2009; Burns & Lewis, 2016; Griebling, Elgas, & Konerman, 2015; Lickey & Powers, 2011; Maple, 2005; McCormick & Twitchell, 2017; Yuen, 2009). The following section summarizes key research on the Project Approach.

Impact on Children's Engagement With Learning Content

Our research revealed that teachers believed the Project Approach increased the interest, motivation, and attention span of diverse learners in their classrooms (Beneke & Ostrosky, 2009). We conducted pre- and posttraining interviews with seven preschool teachers who attended professional development sessions on the Project Approach. Some teachers reported that children's increased engagement led to a reduced need for guidance techniques to manage challenging behavior. Interview data also showed that teachers felt that children were "highly engaged in project work with peers" (Beneke & Ostrosky, 2015, p. 364), which they attributed to the way elements of project activities, such as drawing and surveying to collect and record information related to the project topic, contributed to children's engagement (Beneke & Ostrosky, 2015).

Learning Standards

Researchers have found that project work supports children in meeting grade-level learning standards (Souto-Manning & Lee, 2005), especially when planning is negotiated between students and teachers (Mitchell et al., 2009). Researchers also determined that learning standards were met most effectively when teachers integrated the standards with the children's interests (Mitchell et al., 2009). Mitchell et al. (2009) suggest that a teacher's fluency (i.e., knowledge and familiarity) with the standards is key to connecting the standards and the students' interests and that teachers need to "shift their ideas about planning to embrace co-creating and participating in the learning context *with* children" (p. 345).

Several experienced project implementers share the belief that the Project Approach provides a powerful influence on helping young children master content. For example, over the course of a 4-month preschool Skyscraper Project, teachers "recognized and responded to the mathematics that emerged in the children's play and built on and extended their understandings" (McCormick & Twitchell, 2017, p. 347). The Skyscraper Project arose from teachers' observation of their students' spontaneous play and exploration with blocks. During this project, children investigated and constructed skyscrapers. Teachers believed they were able to teach mathematics content so effectively to the children because the project was "connected to their play, interests, and everyday activity of building" (McCormick & Twitchell, 2017, p. 347). Teachers in a Hong Kong kindergarten class shifted from thematic teaching to project work and found that their project on shoes created a reason for children to "quantify information as they gathered it and to represent quantities with numerals" (Yuen, 2009, p. 29). During the Shoe Project, these kindergartners collected and classified more than 70 pairs of shoes. This project "provided children with reasons to classify and sort, to develop categories for things so they could think about it" (Yuen, 2009, p. 29). Veteran project implementers also shared that "children crave the opportunity to solve math problems related to questions or dilemmas of importance to them" (Burns & Lewis, 2016, p. 143).

Across the phases of a long-term project, children are motivated to take advantage of many opportunities for developing language arts skills. For example, in the Shoe Project, kindergarten children began to represent concepts through drawing and early writing. They were motivated to read "signs, pamphlets, or books to find information and answers to the questions generated in the project" (Yuen, 2009, p. 29). Technical vocabulary expands as children develop "a zeal for word collection and pride in being able to convey new scientific language and vocabulary when writing or speaking on a project discovery" (Burns & Lewis, 2016, p. 143). Writing and book making were important components of a negotiated first-grade project on animal biomes (Mitchell et al., 2009), and children's books about construction provided valuable information about construction and physics in the Skyscraper Project (e.g., a triangle is the strongest shape) (McCormick & Twitchell, 2017).

Teacher and researcher reports indicate that mastery of science content is supported in project work. For example, in the project on biomes, first graders demonstrated investigating and modeling scientific testing, organizing and analyzing data, and communicating results of investigations (Mitchell et al., 2009). Students involved in a project on animals that lived on the school grounds observed habitats, took notes, and drew pictures of animals. They interviewed a naturalist and constructed animal habitats. Their teacher helped them to come up with initial questions and engaged them in continuous conversations about what they were learning, and this led to more questions (Souto-Manning & Lee, 2005). Teachers can evaluate the potential of topics to support children's science learning by using their initial questions about the topic (e.g., "Why do the worms come on the playground when it rains?") as a prompt for them to conduct research about the topic (Baldwin et al., 2009).

Social studies content for young children is covered in a way that is deeper and more meaningful through project work than through formal lessons. For example, one teacher explained that his goal for the kindergarten and first-grade children in a 9-week project on mail was not really for the children to memorize all the parts of the post office, but rather for them to learn "how to be empirical, strive for accuracy, and work cooperatively" (Maple, 2005, p. 137). He wanted them to learn:

> How to observe people, places, things, and events to become active participants in a group that had a common goal and support each other in their search for knowledge and truth. I hoped for them to become citizens of our classroom and school community. (Maple, 2005, p. 137)

This teacher's words reflect his desire to help his children learn how to figure out the world around them and to appreciate the part that people with different occupations play in the quality of their lives.

Project work also provides many opportunities for service learning (Chun et al., 2011; Maple, 2005). For example, as part of a project on water, children in a mixed-age class of 5- to 7-year-olds raised money to help victims of a tsunami in Asia. Researchers found that the children understood the concept of helping others and acquired a model of service through participation in the project (Chun et al., 2011).

The evidence base for the Project Approach has grown in recent years. Research reveals that the Project Approach can increase interest, motivation, and the attention span of diverse learners. The Project Approach has been found to support children in meeting learning standards in the content areas of math, language arts, and social studies and to support children's participation in service learning.

Parent Support for Project Work

In a case study, Souto-Manning and Lee (2005) found that parents of children who had been involved in long-term project work believed it 1) increased motivation, 2) built a sense of community among learners, 3) used children's strengths, and 4) improved academic achievement. Yuen (2009) held parent–teacher meetings over the course of the implementation of her first project. She reported that, at first, the parents of her students were "anxious and lacked confidence in their children's abilities" (p. 30). However, by the end of the project, all 12 parents believed the children had benefited from the project (p. 31). Parents felt the project enhanced their conversations with their children and increased their confidence in dealing with their children's teachers.

Support for Diverse Learners

This guide uses the term *diverse learners* to include children with special needs, children with challenging behaviors, children from environments that put them at risk for academic failure, and DLLs. Teachers and researchers believe that the Project Approach has the potential to support diverse learners in a variety of ways. They believe that individualized education programs and individualized family service plan goals can be met through meaningful naturalistic opportunities provided by projects (Griebling et al., 2015; Harte, 2010; Lickey & Powers, 2011). For example, teachers who implemented their first projects in inclusive classrooms reported that project work increased their ability to include diverse learners in class activities. Analysis of interview data showed that project work 1) increased the interest, motivation, and attention span of their students; 2) provided more opportunities to adapt classroom activities for children with a range of abilities; 3) reduced the need for guidance techniques; and 4) supported academic and social development (Beneke & Ostrosky, 2009). In addition, interview and observational data indicated that project work had a positive impact on children's play levels (i.e., adult–child, onlooker, solitary, parallel, associative, and cooperative) and language (Beneke & Ostrosky, 2015).

Warash, Curtis, Hursh, and Tucci (2008) pointed out that teachers can do project work and also use behavioral approaches in their classrooms. "It is not an either/or issue, but rather an issue that calls for converging theories and teaching methods" (Warash et al., 2008, p. 446). The Project Approach is not the whole curriculum. It can be complementary to direct instruction and to specific strategies that support children with special needs, especially when it helps "children acquire knowledge and skills that allow them to successfully learn from their everyday environment" (Warash et al., 2008, p. 447). For example, Griebling et al. (2015) focused on three children who were involved in a project on trees. One child, a 5-year-old named Joy, received support in the classroom from a "team of specialists, including speech, occupational, and physical therapists who addressed specific IEP [individualized education program] goals for encouraging communication, social interaction, and cognitive development" (Griebling et al., 2015, p. 7). Joy became actively engaged in the project on trees. She was motivated to communicate about aspects of the project, drew pictures related to the project, and engaged enthusiastically with and learned from a small group of peers. Project work emphasizes children's strengths rather than their deficits, which may be a key reason that it supports diverse learners. Having multiple opportunities over time to participate in activities that help learners understand the project may be another reason for its appeal to meet the needs of students with a range of abilities (Beneke & Ostrosky, 2015; Griebling et al., 2015). The Project Approach provides a flexible and rich context for *all* learners, including children identified as gifted (Burns & Lewis, 2016).

> The Project Approach is not the whole curriculum. It can be complementary to direct instruction and to specific strategies that support children with special needs.

HISTORICAL AND THEORETICAL FRAMEWORK OF THE PROJECT APPROACH

Although some believe that the Project Approach began with the publication of *Engaging Children's Minds* (Katz & Chard, 1989), it actually has roots in the work of John Dewey and others from over a century ago. Understanding the historical and theoretical background of the Project Approach provides a valuable vantage point as teachers begin to implement the approach in their own classrooms.

Roots of Project Work in the United States

After the Civil War, many Americans were concerned "about increased industrialization, about a political system that was ineffective, and about what was happening to American society and its children" (Lascarides & Hinitz, 2011, p. 215). Out of this concern, a movement led by social workers, psychologists, and economists, called the *progressive movement*, developed. A major emphasis of the progressive movement was on children and education because children were viewed as the hope for the future. This emphasis led to the progressive education movement.

John Dewey was a leader in the progressive education movement. He was interested in how children learn and championed educational reform aimed at connecting school with the real world and using investigation of real-life topics to drive students' interest in learning and integrating academic skills. Dewey was concerned that, due to industrialization, children were no longer learning about how the world worked through firsthand experience. He believed that the child's role in the educational model of the times was too passive and that, to improve the quality of education, schools should provide the firsthand experiences that had naturally been a part of children's lives in an agrarian society in the past. Dewey believed that the community formed by students and teachers within a school would contribute to the betterment of society as a whole (Dewey, 1899).

Dewey emphasized the connection between knowing and doing through hands-on exploration, which reflects the constructivist influence of Jean Piaget. Piaget believed that teachers learn about the meaning children make of their experiences by observing them interact with the environment and their peers and by asking them open-ended questions. He reasoned that educators could use the information they gather in this way to plan better learning experiences.

While at the University of Chicago (1894 to 1904), Dewey established a laboratory school, which began with 15 students and grew incrementally over the 7 years that it existed. Dewey worked with the staff to develop a curriculum that reflected his philosophical beliefs by helping children integrate the practical application of academic content with learning about the world in which they lived. In explaining this curriculum, he stated:

> The material is not presented as lessons, as something to be learned, but rather as something to be taken up into the child's own experience, through his own activities, in weaving, cooking, shop work, modeling, dramatic play, conversation, discussion, story-telling, etc. . . . The aim, then, is not for the child to go to school as a place apart, but rather in the school so to recapitulate typical phases of his experience outside of school, as to enlarge, enrich, and gradually formulate it. (Dewey, 1899, pp. 98–99)

Although Dewey's laboratory school lasted a relatively short time, it affected the thinking of many educators for years to come.

Dewey left the University of Chicago for a position at Teacher's College at Columbia, which became the "intellectual crossroads of the [progressive] movement" (Cremin, 1964, pp. 175–176). There, Dewey enjoyed a long professional career and published several books about education, including *How We Think* (Dewey, 1910) and *Democracy and Education* (Dewey, 1916). In *How We Think*, Dewey emphasized that routine and random exercises on trivial topics would destroy children's curiosity and that to avoid this, the teacher's role was to support children's curiosity by keeping "alive the sacred spark of wonder and to fan the flame that already glows" (Dewey, 1910, p. 34). In *Democracy and Education*, Dewey focused on the potential of the school to improve society by educating children of all social classes to become socially aware citizens who know how to solve unanticipated problems that the future in an industrialized society might bring. Dewey believed that curious, thoughtful, and intentional problem solvers would be more likely to reach their fullest potential and would therefore improve society (Dewey, 1916).

Dewey's thinking influenced many of his students and colleagues, including William Heard Kilpatrick. Described by Dewey as "the best [student] I ever had" (Kilpatrick, 1909), Kilpatrick studied under Dewey at Columbia. After graduating, Kilpatrick also became a professor at Teacher's College at Columbia and went on to popularize Dewey's educational theories (Beineke, 1998; Cremin, 1964). Kilpatrick was less philosophical than Dewey and more interested in thinking about how Dewey's theories could be translated into a curriculum that would effectively engage children in learning.

In 1918, Kilpatrick published an essay called *The Project Method* in which he explained that Americans desired "that education be considered as life itself and not as mere preparation for later living" (p. 6) and that the process of education is "wholehearted purposeful activity proceeding in a social environment" (p. 4). He theorized that children who approach a task in a wholehearted, purposeful way are more motivated and will ultimately learn more and be more satisfied with the learning experience than children who are coerced into participating in the same task. At the center of this activity was "the project."

Kilpatrick had high expectations for the impact of project work on children, but to achieve this impact, he believed that the teacher must stimulate and educate children's interests. He saw the teacher as a guide who had the "special duty and opportunity" to help children widen their interests and achievement (Kilpatrick, 1918, p. 12). He believed that project work would have a positive impact on children's moral character and consideration for the welfare of others in a group, and he believed that engaging in project work would develop the habits of "give and take" (Kilpatrick, 1918, p. 13).

In Kilpatrick's view, the teacher's goal was to strengthen children's ability to work independently, but that did not mean that the teacher took a laissez-faire approach to teaching. A skillful teacher would not be a slave to the whim of the child, but would guide children in learning to make independent judgments. "The teacher's success—if we believe in democracy—will consist in gradually eliminating himself or herself from the success of the procedure" (Kilpatrick, 1918, p. 13). Kilpatrick (1918) described four types of projects, and he advocated for the first type "where the purpose is to embody some idea or plan in external form, such as building a boat, writing a letter, presenting a play" (p. 16). The other three types of projects involved enjoying an aesthetic experience, solving a problem, or acquiring some knowledge or skill. In Kilpatrick's view, children would likely engage in all four types of projects as they followed their interests to their conclusion.

By the 1950s, the progressive education movement had lost much of its momentum due to the impact of two world wars, the Great Depression, changes in American society, the Cold War, and the fragmentation of its members. By the 1960s, the emphasis in education had shifted from fostering the social, emotional, physical, and intellectual development of the young child to promoting cognitive development or teaching basic academic skills (Spodek & Saracho, 2003).

Project-Based Learning in Reggio Emilia, Italy

While interest in Dewey's ideas declined in the United States, it emerged and blossomed across the sea in Europe, particularly in Britain. However, the best-known site for the lasting development of these ideas is to be found today in Reggio Emilia, Italy. There, Loris Malaguzzi and other educators who guided the development of a city-funded system of infant–toddler and preschool centers were inspired by Dewey, along with Piaget, Vygotsky, Hawkins, Bruner, and Gardner (Gandini, 2008). Over the course of more than 50 years, these centers have evolved to become an international focus of inspiration, discourse, and reflection among visiting educators about what they can do to improve the quality of their own early childhood programs and about what is possible in inclusive early childhood education.

After World War II, many Italian families were eager to make a change from the church-controlled preschools that had flourished under fascism. For a short time following the war, there were spontaneous attempts in some Italian cities to establish parent-run preschools. The earliest preschools in Reggio Emilia began in this way (Edwards, Gandini, & Forman, 2012). Loris Malaguzzi, who would become the leader of the Reggio Emilia early childhood centers, was involved from the start (Barazzoni, 2000).

Malaguzzi's pedagogical leadership was grounded in Dewey's philosophic and theoretical ideas (Lindsay, 2015). According to Malaguzzi, Reggio schools do not have a preplanned curriculum with units and subunits. "Instead, every year each school delineates a series of related projects, some short-range and some long" (Gandini, 2012, p. 61). The teachers then follow the interests of the children related to these identified themes. The adult's role is to intervene as little as possible. Instead, adults observe and document the children closely, work together to respond by setting up situations that support the children's motivation and learning across the domains of development, and help children meet their goals. They use "flexible planning in which initial hypotheses are made about classroom work" (Edwards et al., 2012, p. 380) but are modified in response to ongoing development in the children's work. Reflection and discussion of carefully prepared documentation of children's learning contribute to this planning. Their philosophy reflects Dewey's belief that "good teaching involves continual learning on the part of the teacher" (Tennenbaum, 1951, p. viii).

The educators of the municipal preschools in Reggio Emilia have not rested on their laurels. They continue to push the boundaries of what is recommended practice through study, observation, and discussion. Much has been written about the excellent and seamless system of early childhood education demonstrated in these schools. For more information on Reggio Emilia, see *The Hundred Languages of Children* (Edwards et al., 2012).

The Emergence of the Project Approach

In 1989, Lilian Katz and Sylvia Chard published the first edition of *Engaging Children's Minds: The Project Approach*, a book that sparked renewed interest in project work and proved to be a major influence on early childhood teacher education (Rothenberg, 2000). This was around the same time that American educators were beginning to hear about Reggio Emilia:

> When U.S. early educators first began to hear about Reggio Emilia in the late 1980s, they were immersed in a growing debate about the nature of early childhood as distinct from that of formal elementary schooling. Amid renewed interest in the "Project Approach" (Katz & Chard, 1989), Reggio Emilia's practices resonated with the premises and promise of progressive education. (New, 2007, p. 9)

Katz and Chard provided a framework that could support teachers who wanted to move toward a more child-centered, responsive approach to teaching through long-term projects that would capitalize on children's interests and motivation. The Project Approach "refers to a way of teaching and learning as well as the content of what is taught and learned" (Katz & Chard, 1989, p. 3).

The Project Approach, as outlined by Katz and Chard (1989), and the project work that teachers do in what has come to be called the Reggio Approach, are similar in many ways, because they both stem from a rethinking of early education following experiences of teaching in Europe during World War II. Both are attempts to support hands-on learning by young children that capitalizes on their interests and motivation in a meaningful topic of study. Both emphasize the potential for individualized instruction as a group of children engage in project work with a teacher as a guide. The Project Approach and the project work that is part of the Reggio Approach have much in common, although they differ with regard to topic selection. Topics studied by children in Reggio (e.g., friendship, angels, dinosaurs) are sometimes too abstract to meet the criteria established by Katz and Chard. As readers learn more about selecting topics for projects through Chapter 3 of this book, this difference will become clearer.

CONCLUSION

This chapter introduced the Project Approach, the Project Approach Implementation Checklist, and the relationship of the Project Approach to teaching goals. It also described the potential of the Project Approach to provide learning experiences that can support diverse learners, including DLLs. Finally, the chapter highlighted the evidence base for the Project Approach and the historical and theoretical roots of the approach. This background is important as novice implementers begin project work in their classrooms or as veteran implementers seek to strengthen their project work. Chapter 2 explores the role of the teacher as researcher and introduces two projects that will be followed in depth through the three phases of project work.

Project Approach Implementation Checklist

Phase I		
	Record Yes, No, or N/A	Record notes about the activities and dates that you implemented these items
1. Select a topic based on children's interests, district curriculum, or an unexpected event (e.g., topics of conversations among children, unexpected event such as a new baby, or a neighborhood construction project).		
2. Select a topic that meets the criteria for a topic.		
3. Generate a teacher topic web with co-teacher(s).		
4. Select an aspect of the topic to use as a starting point (e.g., an aspect of the topic that is most likely to interest the children and lend itself to firsthand investigation).		
5. Brainstorm a list of open-ended materials to begin collecting (e.g., papers, boxes, cardboard tubes, lids).		
6. Brainstorm a list of child reference materials to begin collecting (e.g., children's reference books and nonfiction; adult manuals with diagrams and photos; and magazines or brochures).		
7. Begin to collect materials and tools that children may use to gather information.		
8. Brainstorm a list of vocabulary words and/or terms children might learn as a result of participating in the project (e.g., words for topic-related tools, processes, objects, or jobs).		

Phase I		
	Record Yes, No, or N/A	**Record notes about the activities and dates that you implemented these items**
9. Identify an area of wall space at the large group meeting area where ongoing documentation of the project will be displayed on a Project History Board (e.g., low bulletin board or wall area that children can view and reference during class meetings).		
10. Plan and implement an opening event to provoke discussion of the topic (e.g., simple story, topic-related book, presentation of topic-related object, or photograph or poster).		
11. Begin recording children's knowledge of the topic in web format on large paper that is then posted on the Project History Board.		
12. Explain the Project Approach to families (e.g., send home a written explanation, hold an informational meeting, and/or send e-mail informational links).		
13. Notify families that the project is beginning and suggest ways they can be helpful (e.g., contribute materials, props, or expertise).		
14. Provide opportunities for children to reflect on and represent their prior knowledge or experience with the topic (e.g., drawing, painting, sculpting, pretending, or dictating).		
15. Begin to generate a list of possible guest experts and locations for fieldwork.		
16. Hold large- and/or small-group discussions to identify and record children's questions about the topic (e.g., "What do you want to find out?").		

Phase I		
	Record Yes, No, or N/A	**Record notes about the activities and dates that you implemented these items**
17. Select one or two questions and ask children to make predictions about the answers.		
18. Select one or two questions and ask children how they can find out the answers to their questions.		
19. Continue to capture children's questions on an ongoing basis (e.g., large- and/or small-group discussions, opportunities in the natural course of everyday activities).		
20. Display children's web, questions, and samples of Phase I work on the Project History Board (e.g., artwork, photographs, emergent writing).		

Phase II		
	Record Yes, No, or N/A	**Record notes about the activities and dates that you implemented these items**
21. Continue to inform families about the progress of the project on a regular basis (e.g., newsletter stories, notes home, phone calls).		
22. Provide materials that could help children better understand the topic through firsthand exploration (e.g., authentic objects related to the topic such as tools, accessories, components, and/or samples).		
23. Provide topic-related materials that could help children better understand the topic through experimentation (e.g., mixing, touching, cutting, connecting, mashing, cooking, combining, taking apart).		

Phase II		
	Record Yes, No, or N/A	**Record notes about the activities and dates that you implemented these items**
24. Provide topic-related props that could help children better understand the topic through dramatic play in the housekeeping and block areas (e.g., hats, uniforms, equipment, tools, accessories, signs, components, photographs).		
25. Provide open-ended art materials that children could use to represent their growing understanding of the topic (e.g., a variety of papers, cardboard, tape/glue, staplers, cardboard tubes, cardboard boxes, clay, paint).		
26. Prepare teacher- and/or child-made word cards that include illustrations for the class word wall and for the writing area (e.g., children can suggest new topic-related words, child or teacher copies the word onto the card, and child illustrates it).		
27. Teach the children to use drawing as a way to record information.		
28. Read children's books that provide factual information and introduce new vocabulary (e.g., children's reference books, nonfiction books, stories based on factual information).		
29. Teach the children to use clipboards and pens to record their observations.		
30. Teach children how to conduct surveys.		
31. Ask children to draw a plan for three-dimensional constructions they intend to build individually or as part of a small group.		

Phase II		
	Record Yes, No, or N/A	**Record notes about the activities and dates that you implemented these items**
32. Encourage children to take advantage of their peers' help or expertise (e.g., ask a friend who is good at hammering to help you connect the boards, find someone to hold the tape so you can cut it).		
33. Ask open-ended questions to provoke deeper thinking about the topic (e.g., What makes you think so? How could you do that? What else could we try? What do you think will happen if . . . ?).		
34. Regularly invite children to suggest additions to the Project History Board (e.g., new words, graphs, samples, anecdotal notes, quotes, photos, artifacts, drawings).		
35. Provide regular opportunities for children to review and add new knowledge of the topic to the class topic web.		
36. Provide regular opportunities to review the list of questions, record any findings, and add additional questions.		
37. Invite a guest expert or experts to visit the class. Provide them with background on the project and the children's questions.		
38. Provide opportunities for fieldwork (e.g., focused observations of the topic, whether on or off site).		
39. Prepare children to ask questions during fieldwork (e.g., take dictation of each child's question and record it on an index card, provide children with opportunities to practice asking questions).		

Phase II		
	Record Yes, No, or N/A	**Record notes about the activities and dates that you implemented these items**
40. Involve children in a variety of methods to summarize and view their findings (e.g., charting, diagramming, graphing).		
41. Ask children what the group would like to make to show what they have learned about the topic (e.g., large group construction, playscape, mural, other).		
42. Ask children to dictate plans for their group representation (e.g., What exactly do they plan to make? How will they make it? What materials do they think they will need? Who will make what?).		
43. Revisit and invite the children to update their plans for the group representation regularly (e.g., two or three times per week).		
44. Provide time and space for production of the group representation (e.g., at least an hour of uninterrupted choice time, a designated project production area, and/or learning centers set up for small group work on components of the representation).		
45. Provide a variety of open-ended materials that lend themselves to the construction being produced.		
46. Teach children new skills or strategies that will help them accomplish project-related tasks (e.g., writing, tracing, taping, measuring, drilling, nailing, sewing, gluing, and/or folding).		
47. Scaffold when an aspect of producing the representation is beyond children's ability (e.g., sawing thick wood, cutting wire, sewing fabric).		

Phase III		
	Record Yes, No, or N/A	**Record notes about the activities and dates that you implemented these items**
48. Ask children how they would like to celebrate their accomplishments (e.g., open house for families, inviting another class over, displaying their group representation in a public place).		
49. Invite children to help make specific plans for the culminating event (e.g., deciding who will be invited, deciding what will happen at the event, making displays, designing invitations, and/or creating posters).		
50. Support the children's efforts to implement the culminating event (e.g., mail invitations, prepare refreshments, and/or communicate with administration).		
51. Prepare a final documentation display summarizing important events in the project (e.g., How did the project start? What were the children's questions? What were the salient events? What were the challenges? Which children especially benefited from participation in the project? How did the class benefit from participation in the project? What standards were met?).		
52. Summarize and communicate information about the project with families and administrators (e.g., hallway documentation display and/or newsletters or notes to families).		

Defining the Role of the Teacher

Ms. Carly asked Ms. Tamara if she would be willing to answer some of her questions about teaching with project work, and they agreed to meet the next day over lunch. Ms. Carly was curious about what it was like to be the teacher while a project was underway. She wondered if she had the skills she would need to successfully mentor her students during project work. Ms. Tamara reassured Ms. Carly that this way of teaching is fun for her, and that it has allowed to her get to know her students better and to conduct more accurate, authentic assessments. Ms. Tamara stated, "You just have to watch and listen closely, so you pick up on what they already know and what they want to find out. You get lots of opportunities for that in projects. I've found that children who do not typically get involved in group work are involved in our semi project. For example, Alejandro usually avoids social situations, but this morning he volunteered to work with Lisa and Joey on making the cab for the truck. He told them he could hold the steering wheel while they taped it to the cardboard box." Ms. Tamara encouraged Ms. Carly to give project work a try, saying, "I feel like it helps me be a better teacher, and I bet you will feel that way too!" Ms. Tamara offered to lend Ms. Carly a copy of the Implementation Checklist she had just downloaded. She shared, "It really helped me stay on track and avoid forgetting anything." She also invited Ms. Carly to view the class's documentation of their project on the Project History Board.

Project work provides many opportunities for teachers to use their knowledge, skills, and abilities to support the development and learning of every child in their class. Teachers use their knowledge and understanding about individual children (e.g., areas of strength, struggles, interests), as well as the characteristics of the class as a whole, to provide the best possible learning experiences. Teachers become researchers as they assess children's knowledge and skills, and then develop and revise teaching strategies based on those ongoing assessments. Teachers should ask themselves, "What do most of the children already know about this topic? What aspects of the topic are they most likely to be interested in? What information related to the topic is most important for them to learn? What goals do I have for each of the children that might be met by the various kinds of activities in this project? What strengths do children have that they might use as they engage in the many aspects of project work? What changes should I make given what I have seen the children do?" In a way, teachers conduct their own project on what the children in their classes are experiencing. Project work allows teachers the latitude to do this in a way that is as engaging for them as for the children in their rooms. In this chapter, we explore the role of the teacher in project work, and we introduce three authentic projects—the Dog Project, the Garden Project, and the Library Project.

> Project work allows teachers the latitude to conduct their own project based on what the children are experiencing in their classes. This is as engaging for them as for the children.

THE ROLE OF THE TEACHER AND THE PROJECT APPROACH

Teachers are sometimes reluctant to include project work in their curriculum because it seems so different from the way they are accustomed to teaching. However, teachers who learn to implement the Project Approach typically discover that it is interesting and engaging and that it provides a wide range of important learning opportunities for children. Many teachers have told us that after learning to implement the Project Approach, they find themselves excited about getting to school in the morning because they are eager to see what will happen next as the class proceeds with the project. Learning to incorporate project work into the curriculum requires teachers to develop new insights about their role and to strengthen important teaching dispositions. For example, rather than planning in advance what the children will do and what they will learn in a given week, implementing the Project Approach requires flexibility and the frequent adjustment of plans in response to children's interests. It helps when teachers cultivate the disposition to be open to the viewpoints, perspectives, and ideas that emerge from the children, their family members, co-teachers, and other professionals who work in their classrooms. In this section, we look at the process of motivating children to learn by teaching in ways that are responsive to their interests and therefore engage them.

Considering Children's Motivation, Interest, and Engagement

One way that teachers motivate children to engage in project work is to approach the children as individuals who can make good decisions. Teachers respect them as able researchers and trust that all children have an innate drive to learn. Teachers define their role as a facilitator or guide in the implementation of the project, and they know that emphasis on competition or knowing the "right" answers to questions is not conducive to interest and motivation (Dweck, 2006). During project work, children are encouraged to hypothesize, predict, experiment, and learn from their findings and those of their peers. Children do not usually become frustrated by not knowing the answer, but rather, they become motivated and excited to figure out what the answers and findings will be.

Teachers may wonder whether it will be worth the effort to learn yet another approach to teaching. It can be encouraging to teachers who are considering implementing the Project Approach to keep in mind that learning happens within the child, not just in the lessons they attempt to teach. In other words, just because a teacher presented a lesson, there is no guarantee that children learned the expected content or skills from the lesson. Children are more likely to learn when they are motivated and engaged, and teachers can support children's motivation, interest, and engagement in learning through project work.

Teachers can support children's project work by slowing down and staying attuned to them through *active listening*. Active listening involves paying attention not just to what children say, but also to what they are trying to say through both their verbal and nonverbal communication. It helps to get down to the children's eye level and note their facial expressions and body language, as teachers attempt to read children's cues. To understand what a child is communicating, teachers might offer words they believe the child is searching for, or they might paraphrase or ask a child or group a question for clarification. For example, consider the following conversation about taking care of library books that took place between a teacher, Mahi Harrison, and her student, Bianca:

> Mahi: How do we take care of books? So far on our web, we have that we can't rip them.
>
> Bianca: We can't break all the books, because we can't, we can't, so the books is colored in there.
>
> Mahi: [Watching Bianca intently] Tell me again. We can't do something with books because . . .
>
> Bianca: Because they colored.
>
> Mahi: Because we can't color in them?
>
> Bianca: Yeah.

Another way that teachers can improve their ability to actively listen to their students is by providing children with adequate *wait time* to answer questions or to initiate comments or questions. Teachers are accustomed to setting a pace that allows them to cover the content, material, and skills they have planned to teach for the day. They may unintentionally hurry children along to meet this goal. However, many young children, such as dual language learners (DLLs) or children with special needs, are likely to need a longer amount of time to process a question before they can form an answer. A short wait time (1–33 seconds) can produce superficial dialogue in which children produce memorized facts (e.g., "What color is this?" "What number is that?"). However, when teachers provide children with longer wait times (3–55 seconds), more children become involved in discussions, the length of their replies is extended, and the teachers learn more about the children's thinking (Hill, 2016). It is important to remember that some children with disabilities may require wait times longer than 5 seconds to process information, such as a question or instruction (Johnson & Parker, 2013). Using instructional strategies such as active listening and longer wait time requires teachers to pause periodically and reflect on the way they interact with the children in their class, thereby actively working to develop the disposition to slow down and listen.

Teachers also support children's interest and motivation by engaging them in conversations about their ideas, thoughts, and feelings. A teacher might engage an individual child or a group of children in a conversation about a pressing topic of interest (e.g., "Do you have ideas about how you are going to make the baby's bed into a rocking bed?"), or the teacher might use children's ideas as a way to open up a conversation with the whole group (e.g., "Braxton and Taylor were talking, and they have an idea they want to share"). The teacher's goal is to support dialogue among the children in the group and to downplay teacher leadership in the conversation. Developing skills in using questions to extend conversations is exceptionally helpful in project work. For example, a teacher might ask a question to assist other children in understanding a peer's thinking or to get children to consider alternative ideas. Consider the following discussion about babies:

Teacher:	We have done a lot of investigating about babies. We had visits from babies, we visited the hospital to see where babies are born, and we talked with Nurse Paula. What are some of the things we know about babies?
Max:	It might cry.
Teacher:	A baby might cry because it can't go everywhere you go?
Max:	No. If it can't come out of its mommy.
Teacher:	Oh, when they're born. Do they cry before they're born?
Jamal:	No. They cry when they're born.
Max:	Yes they do. A little bit.
Teacher:	Have you ever heard a baby cry before they were born?
Max:	Yeah. Frank and Rosie's.
Teacher:	It seems like we disagree about whether babies cry before they are born. How could we find out the right answer?
Jamal:	Maybe we could ask Nurse Paula.

In this conversation, the teacher asked a "big" question to get the conversation started (i.e., "What are some of the things we know about babies?"), a clarifying question (i.e., "Do they cry before they're born?"), and a question that caused the child to think about alternatives (i.e., "How could we find out the right answer?"). These three types of questions are useful in project work. For example, "big" questions can be used to start discussions intended to interest the children in learning more about the topic. Clarifying questions can be used to stimulate children to develop theories they want to test or investigate, and questions that cause children to think about alternatives can be used to prompt children to plan how they will go about testing or investigating to find the answers.

Teaching Children With a Range of Abilities

The Project Approach provides teachers with a useful context for individualizing instruction for a group of children with a range of abilities. Typical lesson approaches, such as thematic units or a series of lessons from a commercial classroom curriculum, often present plans geared toward children at a particular level of development. Teachers must then take the plans and adapt them for the heterogeneous group in their classrooms. In contrast, plans for project work emerge from and are negotiated between the teacher and the children who will implement them. In Phase I of a project (described in detail in Chapter 3), teachers observe closely and collect data about topics that may interest their students and things that individual children already know or have experienced about the topic. In Phase II (described in Chapter 4), teachers tailor the materials and experiences they bring to the classroom in response to individual questions and abilities of the children in their classrooms. In Phase III (described in Chapter 5), teachers help their students bring the project to a close by celebrating their individual and group accomplishments. Within this framework, the children make many decisions as they plan their next steps together. Children use their strengths and abilities to accomplish their plans, and their teacher supports and scaffolds *all* children so that they can participate fully. In project work, there are many possibilities for children to participate and to use their strengths. For example, a child who has a language delay may not be able to verbally explain how she thinks the class should construct a combine, but she may be able to draw as a way to communicate and share her contributions to the construction plans.

> Within the three-phase framework, children make many decisions as they plan their next steps together. Children use their strengths and abilities to accomplish their plans, and their teacher supports and scaffolds *all* children so that they can participate fully.

A child with an intellectual disability might volunteer to mix the blue and yellow paints to make the green paint that will be used to paint the combine, and a peer who is just learning English might discover opportunities to learn and practice new color names as she works alongside him.

Throughout the project planning process, it is important for teachers to be mindful of factors that affect each child's willingness and ability to fully participate in the project and offer encouragement, support, and accommodations. For example, consider a small group discussion in which the teacher is gathering data on the children's questions (e.g., "What do you want to find out about babies?"). A child who is shy or a non-native language speaker may need to sit in close proximity to the teacher to have the confidence to share his or her ideas. The teacher may need to sign as he or she talks in order to more fully include a child with hearing impairment in the discussion. Having visuals, such as images or objects available, can help support communication and engagement during project discussions. A DLL may need the teacher to verbally label the objects under discussion in both languages so that the child can share his or her interests. Children with developmental delays may need opportunities to participate in the project by pointing to images related to the topic of discussion, rather than engaging in more lengthy conversations about the topic. These children also may need numerous opportunities to explore the topic with as many of their senses as possible. As children play, teachers can observe and infer which aspects of the topic are interesting to them. Teachers might ask themselves questions to better understand the children's interests. For instance, as children play with props and objects related to a project, a teacher might wonder, "Which ones do they choose to play with? Does their facial expression show curiosity or wonder? Does their body language change?" Teachers can then provide children with the language to verbalize their questions or use an augmentative and alternative communication system to offer questions, which can be recorded along with those of the other children in the class.

Teachers may choose to start a project on a particular topic in order to involve a particular child or group of children in this collaborative work. For example, when a new child who lived on a farm joined her class, Ms. Fessler decided to start a project on farms, thereby increasing the likelihood that the child would actively participate. Similarly, Tyler, who was reluctant to socialize with other children, had a special interest in trains, so Ms. McCormick elected to start a project on trains. Ms. McCormick knew that it was likely that other children in her class might share Tyler's interest in trains. However, a topic that is too narrow or too specific to one child is not likely to be broad enough to interest enough other children in the investigation or rich enough to support long-term investigation. For example, if Tyler had only been interested in the specific train set at his house, Ms. McCormick would wisely have looked for another topic that would be more likely to involve him in collaborative investigation.

Supporting All Learners Through Responsive Teaching

When experts discuss the Project Approach, they often explain that the teacher's role is to follow the child's lead. Some teachers may fear that this means that they must constantly change the direction of what they are doing at the whim of individual children; of course, that is not likely to be an effective approach. Instead, following the child's lead means that once the project is underway, a teacher considers the focus of the children's interests and plans opportunities for them to satisfy their curiosity. For example, in a project on rabbits, Sallee Beneke (the first author of this book) observed that many of the children's questions were related to baby rabbits (kits). She used this insight to arrange to host a pregnant rabbit. The children were then able to observe and help nurture the kits from birth. Responding to the children's interest in this way contributed to their engagement and therefore to their learning.

The teacher's role in project work is to cultivate a culture of curiosity in the classroom. As the children learn that the teacher will respond and try to help them satisfy their curiosity, they become more engaged in their role as young researchers or investigators. Teachers continuously work to strengthen relationships and collaboration in the classroom, as they bring new questions to the group for their input. For example, during a project on the grocery store, Ariel, a 4-year-old child with limited verbal ability, wondered where the adults in the school went shopping. At the next circle time, her teacher, Ms. Jeans, shared Ariel's question with the group and asked them to help Ariel think of a plan to answer her question. After some discussion, the children decided to conduct a survey of the adults in the building. Ms. Jeans paired Ariel with Hannah, a very verbal child, and after recess, the two of them headed down the hall with surveys on their clipboards to interview the school staff.

Throughout this process, teachers strive to stay at least one step ahead of the children so that they are knowledgeable about the topic and can anticipate what their students might discover and what might catch their interest as they move forward with the project. As teachers learn more about the topic they might discover aspects of the project that they predict will catch the interest of one or more of the children in their care, or they may plan a classroom experience intended to provoke children's curiosity.

Modeling for Children and Planning to Build Community

The role of the teacher in project work also shifts from being a distributor of information to a leader and co-learner in the investigation. As the children become apprentices in an investigation, teachers are able to model critical behaviors for them. For example, teachers intentionally model respect for *all* other students' ideas, views, and experiences. As teachers engage in active listening and increased wait time, they model these strategies for their students. In addition to modeling, teachers build community in their early childhood environments by planning activities that require collaboration. They prompt and acknowledge children's efforts to help each other and solve problems together, and they encourage children to ask each other for assistance when needed. Through their own behaviors, teachers actively teach children to listen to each other, respect each other, and work together to solve problems.

Teachers also help children share their own perspectives, so other students learn how they and their families see the world. Teachers strive to assist their students in realizing that their perspective is not the only view. To do this, teachers need to develop cross-cultural competence and use culturally relevant practices (Barrera & Corso, 2003). In this way, teachers and children celebrate the way different cultural and linguistic perspectives are acknowledged during project work.

Deepening Children's Understanding of What They Already Know

During project work, the teacher's role is to help children deepen their understanding of what they already know about a topic and to move toward mastery of content in the early learning standards. Becoming a careful observer and documenter can help with both of these goals. To deepen and broaden children's understanding of a topic, teachers regularly monitor and evaluate children's perceptions based on what they say, what they make, and what they do. Teachers observe children in action and reflect on their observations regularly. Teachers understand that the longer they wait after an observation to reflect on what they saw or heard, the fewer details they will remember and the greater the chance for inaccuracies. Therefore, an important skill for teachers to develop is to plan time to reflect on their observations as part of their daily routine.

Observing children in action is not a passive activity. Teachers can ask children questions and play with them to understand more about what they are thinking. For example, if a child is stringing beads and making a pattern of red, blue, and yellow, and then stops stringing with a yellow bead, the teacher might ask, "Wow, you stopped with yellow. How did you know when to stop?" Questions such as this typically result in a child's effort to explain his or her understanding of patterns. Learning to ask questions that uncover children's thinking is a skill that Project Approach teachers cultivate.

Another way that teachers learn about what children know and can do is to talk with their family members about the child's prior experiences with the topic and their behavior at home and in their neighborhood. This can be especially useful when the family's culture and language differ from those of other members of the class. Family members often have insights to share; they need to know that their perspective about their child and his or her interests and abilities is valued. Multiple viewpoints about the same child offer the teacher a more detailed and accurate understanding of the child and his or her development.

Once teachers have gathered information on children's knowledge about a topic, they need to decide what insights they can gain from this information and what they will do with this information. At the beginning of a project, these observations let teachers gauge children's baseline knowledge about the topic, and over time, they help teachers document changes in the children's knowledge, feelings, and dispositions. This information can help teachers anticipate the direction of an individual child's interest. However, hindsight is better than foresight, and teachers cannot know with any certainty where a child's interest will go or what he or she will learn from project work. For this reason, it is important to save samples of children's work from the very beginning of a project. Teachers may later be able to use these samples to create a visual picture of a child's learning with Time 1 and Time 2 (or even Time 3) samples of work that reflect the child's developing awareness of the diverse elements of the topic that is being investigated. In addition, teachers can review all of their students' work samples to watch for evidence of emerging interests of the larger group.

Documenting children's learning requires a collaborative effort, and it is important for all of the adults who work with children in the room (e.g., teachers, co-teachers, assistant teachers, speech-language pathologists, physical therapist, occupational therapists) to review the children's work and share their own impressions of what the children have accomplished to date and where they might go next with the project. These adults may learn about a particular child from carefully evaluating his or her work, and often they develop insights about the significance of the work to share with others. Teachers and specialists who work with children with identified special needs report that sharing authentic work that has been collected as part of a child's portfolio is a helpful resource at meetings where the child's individualized education program (IEP) is reviewed (Scranton & Doubet, 2003).

As noted earlier in this guide, the Project Approach is never the whole curriculum. Rather, it provides a framework for assessing participants' progress, and it can involve opportunities for teacher-directed instruction to introduce or practice new knowledge and skills. However, observing a child's spontaneous actions during project work helps professionals see to what degree a child understands how and when to apply the knowledge and skills that have been taught to him or her. It also helps the adults document the child's progress toward mastery of early learning standards and plan experiences that support growth and development.

To plan effective instruction, teachers must be aware of the areas of development included within their state's early learning standards, as well as the scope and sequence of each area of development. Teachers should closely observe a child's progress toward meeting a standard, interpret the meaning of the observation, and set goals for the child. It is not enough to observe a child and collect samples of the child's work; teachers must understand the significance of what they see and collect, and they must understand its implications for teaching children in a way that is meaningful to the child. For example, if a teacher notices a child repeatedly spending time organizing the five baby bottles in the dramatic play area into a row, the teacher might realize that the child is working on one-to-one correspondence and should then be able to set a "next step" or goal for the child (National Association for the Education of Young Children, 2002). According to the Illinois Early Learning Standards (Illinois State Board of Education, 2013), the next step in the development of this skill would be to "point to or move objects when counting out loud without effectively tracking the items counted" (p. 45). Therefore, the teacher might encourage the child to use number names to count the baby bottles that he or she has organized.

A significant feature of project work is that it provides teachers with countless opportunities to observe authentic instances of what a child understands and what a child misunderstands about the topic of study and about content across the domains of learning. Recording these observations and systematically collecting samples of children's work that reflect what they know and can do are one form of documentation. These observations and samples can be saved in a portfolio that reflects a child's growth over time. In our experience, children gradually understand that the teacher is looking for samples of their best work and will spontaneously self-evaluate and suggest samples to the teacher. Teachers and their students can engage in valuable conversations about what makes one work sample better than another, thereby providing children with specific ideas about what to work on next. For example, when Oscar signed his name at the bottom of his picture, his teacher noted that his writing was really improving and that she especially liked the tall vertical line and the short horizontal lines in his capital "E." The teacher then suggested that he work on limiting the horizontal lines to one at the top, one at the bottom, and one in the middle.

> A significant feature of project work is that it provides teachers with countless opportunities to observe authentic instances of what a child understands and what a child misunderstands about the topic of study and about content across the domains of learning.

Documenting Children's Learning

Documenting what children say, make, and do through observation is critical to monitoring and planning for further learning. Teachers may use a variety of tools to do this, ranging from low-technology items, such as pen and paper, to high-technology tools, such as iPads and video recorders. This information can contribute to the recording of the progress of the project on the Implementation Checklist introduced in Chapter 1. In addition, teachers can document children's work for display. This type of display may tell the story of one child's experience in the project, or it might include the work of several children or the entire class and tell the story of a shared learning experience. In addition, teachers can include their own reflections on the insights they gained from a project in a display (Helm, Beneke, & Steinheimer, 2007).

In preparation for documentation, children and teachers can talk together about what should be included in a display. This type of discussion leads to metacognition, or thinking about one's own thinking, a higher order thinking skill. As children think about their own thinking, they reflect on what they have accomplished individually and with peers, what they have learned, and what they are able to do that they were not able to do before the project. A sense of community is built as students and teachers reflect on their experiences together, what they have accomplished, and how their plans worked out. The items included in the display are often referred to as documentation (a noun), which differs from the act of documenting children's learning (a verb). As teachers begin to document children's learning, they can include documentation of children's Phase I project work, such as samples of their drawings, dictated stories, and photographs of dramatic play. The children's topic web and the list of questions they posed are important documents to feature in a display that the class will revisit throughout the project.

Typically, this documentation is initially collected on a bulletin board within the classroom as a visual record of the events in the project. It is helpful if this bulletin board is directly adjacent to the area where the teacher meets with the group of children for circle time. The teacher and children can then refer to the documentation as they review their progress, add to their web, and add to their questions (for more on webbing, see Chapter 3). Samples of project-related events can gradually be added to the documentation. The teacher can invite children to select the samples to be added (e.g., "What work did we get done today on our project?"), and children can be encouraged to be sure the work of every child in the class is included on the board (e.g., "What photos should we put up on the Project History Board to show what we as a class did?" "Whose drawing should we display?"). Engaging in reflection on their group and individual accomplishments can help strengthen children's interest in further project work.

The Project History Board is a place for *working* documentation that is dynamic and not static. Labels are typically handwritten sticky notes or informal labels. The visual nature of the documentation board and its presence as a resource during discussions provide a support for all children. For DLLs, samples and images included on the board can provide teachers with opportunities to discuss and reinforce new vocabulary. Nonverbal children can point to images or samples on the board as a means to communicate their ideas about the project. In this book, we refer to this type of classroom display board as a Project History Board.

As a project develops, teachers may find themselves running out of display space. When this occurs, teachers may use the earlier documentation to begin developing a more formal display about the project, to be displayed in the hallway and thus shared with other members of the school community. In this case, teachers take extra care to display the work in a way that is aesthetically pleasing and informative to potential viewers.

Some teachers prefer to use desktop publishing to create a documentation panel or poster on their computer that can be printed on a large-format printer. Formal wall displays or documentation panels present children's work with the respect it deserves. In addition, panels created digitally can be shared in other locations outside of the school. For example, after a project on the local bank, panels documenting the children's work were displayed at the bank that the class had visited. This helped educate the community about the value of emergent learning experiences, such as the essential nature of project work.

Helping Families Get the Most From Documentation

When families are new to documentation, teachers can provide them with an orientation to acquaint them with it. This can help family members understand their children's learning experience and appreciate the teachers' efforts to share it. For more information on this topic, see "Displaying Documentation: Providing Supports for the Viewer of the Display" (Beneke, 2011), "Documentation: The Basics, Part 1" (Katz, 2013a), and "Documentation: The Basics, Part 2" (Katz, 2013b).

Teachers also can share their class's documentation of project work through newsletters or binders of project documentation, by e-mailing or sending home video clips, or through secure web sites. For example, when this book's first author (Dr. Beneke) was a classroom teacher, she regularly sent home newsletters that featured her class's project work, beginning with Phase I.

AN IN-DEPTH LOOK AT THE PROJECT APPROACH

Teachers in three different types of early childhood settings have been generous enough to provide documentation of their projects for use in this book, enabling us to bring to life the strategies we describe and recommend. We are extremely appreciative of the time and effort they took to assist us with this work as they shared the Garden Project, the Dog Project, and the Library Project.

The Garden Project took place at Jefferson Early Childhood Center in East Moline-Coal Valley School District No. 40. Jefferson, a program with strong family involvement, houses 15 classes and can serve up to 250 preschoolers. During the school year when the Garden Project was implemented, the children enrolled at Jefferson spoke 14 different languages, and 74% of the students were considered to be from families who were at the poverty level. Ms. Karissa Utz, a teacher in one of the state-funded, half-day inclusive prekindergarten classrooms, graciously shared her project work with us. Her class included DLLs; children with IEPs for behavior, speech delays, and developmental delays; and children who were receiving extra help with math and early literacy.

In late spring, Jefferson's principal announced that all classes would be taking a trip to the botanical center. Ms. Utz was looking for a topic for a project and hoped that an interest in plants would emerge from this trip. A project did indeed emerge from the trip, and Phases I, II, and III are documented in Chapters 3–5 using photos, samples of children's work, and anecdotes.

The Dog Project took place at the John L. Hensey Elementary School in Washington, Illinois' District 50. This school houses the superintendent's office and students in kindergarten through third grade. Ms. DeLuca and Ms. Burd were the lead teachers in two half-day, self-contained, early childhood special education classes at Hensey; their two classes often collaborated on project work. These classes included children who were on the autism spectrum, children who had developmental delays, children with speech delays, and children with complex health care needs. Ms. Lavin was the second-grade teacher; her students became curious about a visit from a service dog to the early childhood students. Ms. DeLuca's and Ms. Burd's students invited Ms. Lavin's students to their classroom for a presentation about what they had learned in their study of dogs, and the second graders became coinvestigators in the project. A wonderful, rich investigation emerged from this collaboration that benefited all those involved.

The Library Project took place at the St. Ambrose University Children's Campus in Davenport, Iowa. The Children's Campus provides high-quality early childhood education in the context of a full-day child care center. Ms. Andromahi Harrison was the lead teacher of a mixed-age classroom of 3- and 4-year-olds, and Ms. Theresa Berendes was her assistant. The class included children who were DLLs, had speech and language delays, and were engaged in challenging behaviors.

The Library Project will be of special interest to teachers who wonder if they need to wait until children are familiar with their classroom routines and environment before they can begin a project. The project began during the second week of the school year when children discovered key cards in a purse in the dramatic play area and began to pretend that the cards were library cards. Many of the children in the class were very young and had just moved to this prekindergarten classroom from the 2-year-old room. Of the 16 children enrolled, one child was 2 years old (2 years, 11 months), four children were 3 years old, eight children were between 4 and 4.5 years old, and three children were older 4-year-olds. Video clips are used to highlight Phases I, II, and III of these three projects in Chapters 3 through 5 of this book.

CONCLUSION: WAYS TO USE THIS GUIDE AND THE IMPLEMENTATION CHECKLIST

Images, samples of children's work, and anecdotes from the Garden Project, the Dog Project, and the Library Project are used to illustrate strategies listed in the 52-item Implementation Checklist that is included at the end of Chapter 1. Refer to Appendix A to see how the educators from these three projects filled out the Implementation Checklists for their own projects, using it to guide the implementation process. The narrative in Chapters 3, 4, and 5 describes the Project Approach as it is organized in the Implementation Checklist. It is our hope that teachers who are new to the Project Approach will use the Implementation Checklist as a step-by-step support to implement their first projects. In addition, veteran teachers may choose to refer to a section of the checklist to refresh their memory as they simultaneously turn to the narrative that refers to the particular strategy of interest on the checklist for further information. Finally, the Implementation Checklist can be used as a self-reflection measure.

Although we hope that the Implementation Checklist will be helpful to teachers, we caution that it is a *support* that features 52 items that we, and others, have found helpful in implementing project work. Veteran project implementers may have their own ways of implementing project work that may or may not include some of the items on the checklist. For example, with a skillful teacher as their guide, it is possible for young children to engage in an investigation without ever dictating or returning to a web. However, in our experience, the items included on the Implementation Checklist combine to ensure the execution of a high-level project. As teachers become more confident in their ability to lead project work, we encourage them to use these materials as a resource and not as a rigid prescriptive guide.

Implementing With Fidelity

Ms. Carly decided to try starting a project with her students, but she was not sure what the topic should be. Her students were interested in rockets and outer space, and she wondered if that would be a good topic. She decided to discuss the idea with Ms. Tamara, who advised her to come up with a topic that the children could investigate firsthand. Ms. Carly thought about her students' play and remembered that the children often played car wash in the block area. She wondered if this would be a good topic for a project. She also considered what experiences she would need to plan to support firsthand investigation of the car wash and how she might get this project started.

In this chapter, we explore numerous strategies for the effective implementation of Phase I of project work. Components of the Project Approach included in this chapter are as follows: selecting a topic, brainstorming and collecting materials, planning to support language development, launching the project, introducing the Project Approach to families, providing opportunities for expression and representation, identifying initial questions for investigation, and beginning to document the project.

Phase I of a project sets the stage for a successful project investigation, as teachers take preliminary steps to think deeply about the possible subject matter, consider materials that they will need, and prepare for activities related to the project topic. Phase I enables teachers to anticipate, as well as to reflect on, strategies that they may use to support the project. This phase also includes introducing the topic for investigation to the children and initiating activities that engage the children and help them reflect on what they already know about the topic. Teachers usually find that time spent preparing for the introduction of the project in Phase I is time well spent. Through these activities, teachers anticipate possible directions the project might take, along with supports that individual children might need, to ensure the ultimate success of the project.

> Phase I sets the stage for a successful project investigation, as teachers take preliminary steps to think deeply about the possible subject matter, consider materials that they will need, and prepare for activities related to the project topic.

CHOOSING A GOOD TOPIC

Topics for projects emerge in a variety of ways. In some instances, a teacher might wish to start a project related to farms, a requirement of the district's curriculum, or perhaps the teacher's students recently discovered tadpoles living in a pond near their school or center and this experience sets the stage for a project. Whatever the source, the viability of the topic is a key factor in determining whether a rich project can emerge.

Use Appropriate Criteria for Topic Selection

The topic selected for a project influences whether the project becomes a child-initiated inquiry or whether the children wane in their excitement and engagement quickly. Topics that might prove successful for thematic units are often too abstract or are not practical for firsthand investigation. Whether teachers are determining a project topic to propose to the children or picking up on a topic that has emerged from children's play or other events in life, teachers should carefully consider the topic's potential. Using criteria to guide topic selection can help teachers increase the likelihood that the topic selected will be a viable one. Teachers can use the 12 criteria listed in Figure 3.1 to evaluate the potential of a project topic to work. These criteria take into account the prior experiences and cultures of the children within a classroom. For example, children who live in rural Princeton, Illinois, may have many prior experiences with fireflies or lighting bugs, whereas children who live in Bishop, California, may have countless experiences finding interesting rocks. Both topics meet the criteria for firsthand investigation and representation, and they are accessible to the families of the students in their respective communities. Children in Princeton can easily catch and draw sketches of fireflies, whereas children in Bishop can collect and create labeled displays of rocks.

A common mistake made by teachers who are new to project work is to select a topic that seems exotic or fanciful, such as a project on safaris for a group of urban students.

Criteria for Topic Selection

1. The topic is directly observable in the children's own environments (real world).

2. It is within the experiences of most children in the group.

3. Firsthand direct investigation is feasible and not potentially dangerous.

4. Local resources (field sites and experts) are favorable and readily accessible.

5. It has good potential for representation in a variety of media (e.g., role play, construction, writing, multidimensional graphic organizers).

6. Parental participation and contributions are likely, and parents can become involved.

7. It is sensitive to local culture, as well as culturally appropriate in general.

8. It is potentially interesting to many of the children or represents an interest that adults consider worthy of developing in children.

9. It is related to curriculum goals and standards of the school or district.

10. It provides ample opportunity to apply basic skills (depending on the age of the children).

11. It is optimally specific—not too narrow and not too broad (e.g., a study of the teacher's own dog or "buttons" at the narrow end, and the topic of "music" or "the seasons" at the broad end).

12. It is interesting to the teacher.

Figure 3.1.   Criteria for topic selection. (*Source:* Katz & Chard, 1998.)

Although such topics might work as teacher-initiated thematic units, they often lead to short-lived projects. This occurs because the children in the class have no prior experience with the topic, and the resources to sustain firsthand, active investigation are not available. For instance, fireflies do not live in California. If teachers in Bishop, California, were to introduce a project on fireflies, they would not be able to offer the experiences or resources to sustain a long-term, in-depth investigation. The children would most likely not have prior experiences to provoke curiosity, and it is unlikely that families would be able to contribute much to an investigation. Topics that are too far removed from children's firsthand experiences, such as outer space, dinosaurs, or pirate ships, may work as the subject of a thematic unit but are unlikely to succeed as topics for a project.

Ensure Access

When selecting a topic, teachers should consider the age and developmental levels of the children in their class, as well as access to transportation for field site visits. The younger or less developmentally advanced the child, the closer the topic should be to the child's immediate environment. That way, children can return to the subject again and again to observe relevant phenomena firsthand, discuss them, and answer questions that arise. A subject of an investigation that is in the classroom, on the school grounds, or within walking distance from the school is likely to support a higher quality investigation for very young children than one that is remote to them. For example, an infant-toddler class in a center with a thriving garden successfully investigated cooking with spinach. In another class, after a holiday break, a mixed-age group of preschoolers became interested in new additions to the class fish tank, leading to an in-depth investigation of the tank ecosystem. (For more about the Spinach Project, the Fish Project, and the Worm Project, among others, visit the Illinois Early Learning Project web site, at https://illinoisearlylearning.org/resources/pa/projects/.)

Older 4- and 5-year-olds are better able to handle an investigation that revolves around a single field site visit. They are more likely than younger students to remember what they saw when they were there, and they are better able to use secondary sources to conduct their research. For example, children involved in a project on cows made only one field trip to a dairy farm. These 4- and 5-year-old children were in the second semester of the school year. They were able to successfully remember, discuss, and recreate examples of what they had seen. (For more on the Cow Project, visit https://illinoisearlylearning.org/pa/projects/cow-project/.) As you consider which topic to choose for your own project, complete the task sheet in Figure 3.2 to evaluate the viability of topics.

Consider the District or Program Curriculum

Accessible project topics can stem from a variety of sources, including 1) the district, school, or center curriculum; 2) unexpected interesting events; or 3) children's current interests. In some cases, school districts or centers have predetermined topics or themes that teachers are required to cover at particular grade levels. For example, all kindergarten teachers in a district might be required to cover transportation, farms, ecosystems, and weather over the course of the school year. Many of these themes are too broad or abstract to succeed as topics for a project investigation. However, teachers can look for project topics related to an aspect of these themes that meet the 12 criteria for topic selection. They can think about whether there are aspects of the theme that can

Identifying Topics for Projects

Instructions: Think of three topics for projects that children and teachers at your school or center might investigate. Use the criteria for topic selection in the first column to evaluate the potential topics. If the topic meets the criterion, place a checkmark in that box.

Criteria for topic selection	Topic #1: _____	Topic #2: _____	Topic #3: _____
1. Directly observable			
2. Within most children's experiences			
3. Firsthand direct investigation is feasible			
4. Local resources are available			
5. Has potential for representation			
6. Parental participation is likely			
7. Sensitive to local culture			
8. Interesting to many children			
9. Related to curriculum goals			
10. Opportunities to apply basic skills			
11. Not too narrow or broad			
12. Interesting to the teacher			

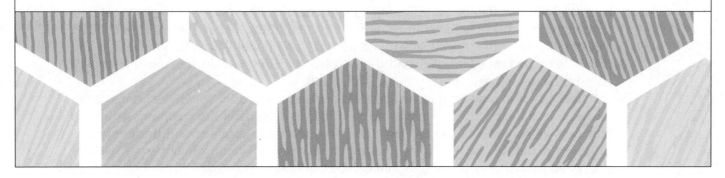

Figure 3.2.   Task Sheet: Identifying Topics for Projects.

be touched, counted, measured, discussed, researched, and represented in a variety of ways (e.g., dramatic play, drawing, construction). For example, if the required theme is farms, the teacher might consider topics such as barns, grain bins, tractors, or cows. Children could feel the roughness of the wooden barn, count the number of doors and windows, measure the width of a stall, discuss the possible purposes of a barn, research how farmers in their region use barns, and construct their own barn.

A project also might begin as a result of a special schoolwide theme or experience that is planned. For example, the Garden Project introduced in Chapter 2 began because the school received funding to plant a school garden and to send each class on a field trip to the Quad Cities Botanical Center. One teacher, Mrs. Utz, decided that a class project on gardening would be a natural fit, given these ongoing school activities.

Consider Children's Interests

> When children are interested in a topic, they are motivated to learn more about it.

When looking for project topics, consider the interests of the children in the class. When children are interested in a topic, they are motivated to learn more about it (Bowman, Donovan, & Burns, 2001). For instance, research has shown that 4-year-old children with autism spectrum disorder stayed on task and engaged in fewer disruptive behaviors when they were motivated and interested in class activities (Koegel, Singh, & Koegel, 2010).

Teachers learn about children's interests as they develop relationships and engage in casual back-and-forth conversations with children about their experiences. In addition, actively observing, listening to, and reflecting on what children talk about with one another, what they engage in during pretend play, and what they draw can offer clues about children's interests. Sometimes teachers can learn a lot about what children know about a particular topic by entering into their play. For example, Ms. Harrison noticed that children in her mixed-age class were using hotel key cards to play library.

She was curious what Brynlee, age 2 years and 11 months, understood about the process of checking out a book, so as Brynlee assumed the role of librarian, Ms. Harrison asked her how to proceed. See Video 3.1 for a clip of this interaction. She learned that Brynlee believed that library patrons needed to present the librarian with both money and a library card and that the librarian selected books for patrons.

Another way to learn about children's interests is to talk with children's family members or conduct an informal survey. Educators can send home copies of Figure 3.3 or Figure 3.4, which are two surveys that families complete to share their child's interests. Teachers may need to devote special attention to determine the interests of dual language learners (DLLs). Families of DLLs can help teachers identify topics of interest that relate to a child's home culture. These topics might focus on games, food choices, clothing, or home life. Effective early educators "intentionally activate knowledge and concepts in the home language and then explicitly help the child transfer this knowledge to the new language" (Espinosa, 2015, p. 80).

Teachers also may need to pay careful attention to children who have limited communication skills in order to determine their interests. By carefully watching children's play behaviors, teachers can ascertain their interests and capitalize on these interests in lesson planning. For example, a young child with a disability may be particularly interested in numbers, a strength that can be capitalized on during project work as he

Date: _____

Dear Family,

We are planning to start an in-depth investigation of something the students in our class find interesting. This survey is to help us understand your child's special interests. Please list people, places, or things that fascinate your child. Please list three or four for each possible topic. I have included some examples to help you get started.

Possible topics	Topic #1:	Topic #2:	Topic #3:
1. People	Firefighter	_____	Horses
	_____	_____	_____
	_____	_____	_____
	_____	_____	_____
2. Places	Fire station	_____	_____
	_____	_____	_____
	_____	_____	_____
3. Things	Fire trucks	_____	_____
	_____	_____	_____
	_____	_____	_____
	_____	_____	_____

Thank you!

Sincerely,

Figure 3.3. Home Survey: Identifying Topics for Projects.

Date: _____

Dear Family,

We would like to start a project investigation in our class! This will be a firsthand investigation of a topic that is interesting to most of the children in the class. We need your help! Please list three things that interest your child:

1. _____

2. _____

3. _____

Hints: Think of local places your child likes to go. Are there animals or jobs your child likes to pretend about? Are there things he or she likes to do?

Watch for an announcement about the final topic for our class project. We will have suggestions for ways that you can get involved!

Sincerely,

Figure 3.4. Home Survey template.

or she helps tally survey data, count materials needed to create a project, or measure the dimensions of construction items. Likewise, a child with a disability who is fascinated by trains might inspire the teacher to propose trains as a topic for a class project.

Families of children with developmental delays and disabilities can help teachers identify topics that are likely to be of special interest to their children. Such partnerships are especially critical if a child has limited communication skills or significant disabilities. For example, families with students who use augmentative and alternative communication (AAC) devices might help program vocabulary before a project begins so that nonverbal students can actively participate in discussions to select a topic. Likewise, once a topic has been identified, parents can program vocabulary so that their child can engage with peers and teachers about the topic. Such parental involvement will enable children to use their AAC device at home and school to share information on project work. Centering a project on a topic with which a particular child has expertise can place that child in the role of in-class expert. The teacher can then support the inclusion of the child in the classroom by encouraging the child to share his or her expertise with others.

An interest that is shared by several children in the class is more likely to set the stage for a successful project investigation than a strong interest in a particular topic that only one child holds. When enough children are interested in a topic, teachers are more likely to be able to engage them in discussion and encourage their questions. In addition, children are better positioned to spark each other's continued interest, as they share discoveries, engage in dramatic play, and construct representations together.

> When many children are interested in a particular topic, the children are better positioned to spark each other's continued interest as they share discoveries, engage in dramatic play, and construct representations together.

Once teachers have identified an interest that is shared by many of their students and that meets the criteria for topic selection, they can help sustain and strengthen continued interest by providing new experiences that will encourage children's deeper thinking around the topic. Teachers also can provide children with opportunities to satisfy their growing curiosity. One of the many benefits of project work is that finding the answer to one question often leads to another question.

Take Advantage of Unexpected Events

Sometimes rich and appropriate topics for projects emerge unexpectedly in the course of unanticipated events. For example, a child might announce to the rest of the class, "My mom is going to have a baby!" or "My grandma got a new wheelchair yesterday." Or, a rainstorm may cause a plethora of worms to appear on the school playground, causing heightened interest by young children. A dedicated teacher committed to the project approach is always on the lookout for opportunities such as these that meet the criteria for topic selection and can be explored firsthand. For example, during the fall semester, Ms. DeLuca and Ms. Burd had observed many of their students engaging in pretend dog play. Early in the spring semester, class members had several unexpected encounters with dogs. For example, a friendly dog approached them when the class walked to a nearby garden. In addition, one classmate was visited by a service dog while in the hospital, and another child in the class reported that she had just been presented with a puppy puppet. Given the interest among their students in pretend dog play and the specific dog-related experiences of individual class members, these two teachers decided to initiate a project on dogs. As an opening event, the teachers invited a service dog to visit their class, and they posted the following announcement about the visit on the class web site that day, inviting families to view photos of the visit.

Exciting Dog Visit

March 13

Our Morning Class had an exciting surprise therapy dog visit today. Eli is a certified therapy dog who was brought to spend time with our morning friends today. He will come on Monday for the PM class. Children had some very nice, real hands-on time and experience with Eli, and he was so gentle and sweet with everyone. ☺ Happy Day for all.

Make a Teacher Planning Web

Teachers can create visual webs to organize and record their ideas about the potential content of a project topic. This section describes the general processes for developing a web and the specific processes for creating a teacher planning web.

Often recorded on chart paper, the teacher begins a web by placing a word representing the main subject of the project in the center of the page. The teacher then records related ideas in such a way that they radiate out from the main subject and are connected to the main subject with lines. Further branches and relationships between subcategories can be indicated by dotted lines; a web on fruit is presented in Figure 3.5.

There are typically two types of webs in project work, teacher planning webs and children's topic webs. A teacher planning web is a tool the teacher creates to organize and record everything *the teacher* knows about the topic. Although the teacher will make topic webs with her students throughout a project, the teacher planning web should not be shared. Instead, teachers use this web as a starting point to think about the various

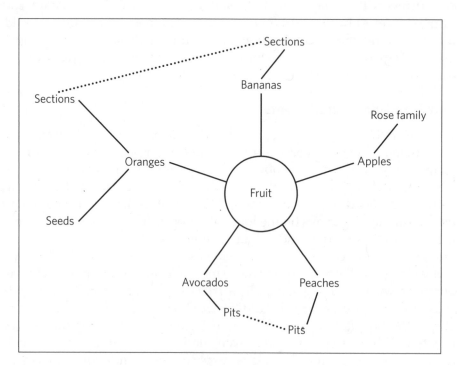

Figure 3.5.   A web can show relationships among elements of a topic.

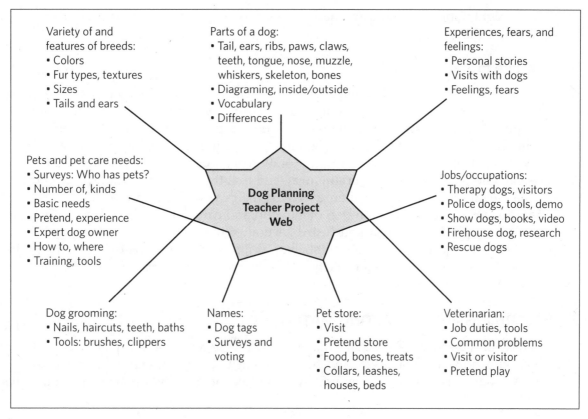

Figure 3.6. Dog project teacher planning web.

directions the project might take, the materials needed, possible field trips, potential experts to contact, and relevant community resources. Creating a teacher planning web helps teachers gain perspective on the depth of a project, and the web can be used to reflect on aspects of a project the teacher plans to introduce to the children first. If a project has developed in response to an unexpected event, teachers can use a web to think about logical next steps. Sylvia Chard (1998) has written instructions for how to support a group of two or more teachers who would like to develop a planning web together. Anyone who will be involved in the project can contribute to the richness of the planning web (e.g., teachers, teaching assistants, student teachers, therapists, family members). Ms. DeLuca and Ms. Burd created a computer-generated planning web as they began their project on dogs (see Figure 3.6).

Plan a Preliminary Investigation

In addition to thinking about what they already know about the project topic, teachers should conduct a preliminary firsthand investigation on their own. For example, if a teacher is planning a project on the construction site across the street, he or she should make one or more advance visits to the site to see what the children might encounter so that the teacher can anticipate what the children might discover when they take a field trip to the site. Preliminary visits are an important idea, even when a topic is familiar to the teacher, because details emerge that might go unnoticed during the teacher's everyday life. For instance, teachers may have taken their own pet to the veterinary clinic many times, but when visiting it with their students, as the subject of a project, they might notice that there are many types of dog grooming tools for sale; they might also note the name of each tool.

Decide Where to Start

There is often a great deal of information on a teacher planning web, so a teacher needs to zoom in on or select an area that he or she thinks will make a good entry point. For example, Mrs. Utz knew that she wanted to do a project on gardening with the pre-schoolers in her inclusive classroom. After reviewing her teacher planning web, she decided to begin the project with an exploration of gardening tools—something the children could get their hands on right away and that they could use in the dramatic play center. In another classroom, after reviewing their co-constructed web, Ms. DeLuca and Ms. Burd decided to focus on dog ownership and care. Finally, in a third early childhood setting, Ms. Harrison had heard several of her students discussing the library shelves, so she decided to focus on shelves as a place to begin the discussion with her students. See Video 3.2 to view a clip of Ms. Harrison and her assistant, Ms. Berendes, developing their teacher planning web.

BRAINSTORMING AND COLLECTING MATERIALS

Hands-on investigations require materials to investigate firsthand and materials that a child can use to create two- and three-dimensional representations about the topic. These materials may be commercially produced or materials that come from other sources.

Collect Open-Ended Materials and Real Objects

Whatever the source, it is important that the materials are open-ended. Open-ended materials can include art media, such as clay and paint, and can also include "reusable resources such as quality, unwanted, manufacturing business by-products, otherwise destined for the landfill . . . cloth remnants, foam, wire, leather, rubber, and wood" (Drew & Rankin, 2004). There is no one right way to use such materials. Commercially produced arts and crafts supplies typically come in primary colors and limited shapes. While useful for some activities, they do not have the flexibility that children desire as they represent their ideas through two- or three-dimensional art. In fact, when teachers embark on their first project, they are often pleasantly surprised at the level of children's engagement when provided with open-ended materials, such as cardboard, cardboard boxes, paper bags, pieces of wood, paper in neutral colors, string, yarn, and fabric (Beneke & Ostrosky, 2009). Materials that lend themselves to the topic of the project also should be included. For example, in a project on cars, the teacher made aluminum foil and metallic paint available so that children could create representations that mimicked authentic car parts (Beneke, 1998). In anticipation of their dog project, Ms. DeLuca and Ms. Burd collected pet care artifacts and supplies, as well as cardboard boxes that children could use in their three-dimensional representations. Likewise, Ms. Harrison began to collect materials such as cardboard that children might use to construct shelves.

Teachers also report that having available real objects related to the topic of the project can support children's engagement (Beneke & Ostrosky, 2009). Although early childhood classrooms are often equipped with cute, cartoon-like versions of real-life items, consider using the real-life items, as long as they are safe. For example, in the Garden Project, Mrs. Utz added small gardening tools and a basket to the housekeeping area (see Figure 3.7). As the children played with them, Mrs. Utz observed and found out what each of the children already understood (or misunderstood) about gardening. Although filling a classroom with too many real objects may be overwhelming for children, incorporating a few real objects to provoke discussion and dramatic play can be beneficial.

Figure 3.7. The addition of gardening props and hand trowels inspired children to represent their knowledge of gardening through their play.

For young children with disabilities, the benefits of real objects include increased engagement, shared joint attention, new vocabulary, decreased problems with generalization, and opportunities for peer interaction around objects of interest (Beneke & Ostrosky, 2009).

Find Child Reference Materials

Because a project investigation is a research effort, teachers should gather reference materials that children can use to conduct their own research. Children's literature that includes fantasy or inaccuracies will not be useful in this case. For example, in *The Very Hungry Caterpillar* by Eric Carle (1969), the caterpillar eats pickles, plums, and cupcakes. Although this classic book is a wonderful example of children's literature, it would not be useful in a project on caterpillars and butterflies because the foods represented are not typically eaten by caterpillars and butterflies. As an alternative, *Caterpillar to Butterfly* by Laura Marsh (2012) provides simple language, topic-related vocabulary, and informative illustrations, and thus would be a better choice for use in project work. *The Very Hungry Caterpillar* would be appropriate to read at the end of the project, when children have become experts on the topic, and they can see the humor in it and critique the accuracy of the book. Teachers can work with their school or community librarians to pull together a collection of topic-related reference books.

Other sources of information also can be gathered to use as reference tools. For example, teachers can collect a set of links to age-appropriate, topic-related web pages that children can explore. Teachers can contact agencies that may provide speakers and materials, such as their state's Department of Natural Resources, university extension offices, professional associations, and local citizens who may have resources to share as a result of a hobby or vocation. In an effort to offer their students reference materials, Ms. DeLuca and Ms. Burd collected books about dogs from the school library and gathered brochures and flyers from a local veterinarian's office. Because family members often have expertise to share, teachers should reach out to them through informal conversations or by sending notes or a newsletter home to request their assistance with project work.

Select Materials Children Can Use to Gather Data

As children conduct an investigation, they need ways to record or otherwise save the data they collect. During Phase I, teachers have the opportunity to review their topic web and imagine all the possible places the children might go to gather data and the types of data they might collect. They can then gather materials that will support the investigation, such as inexpensive clipboards. Clipboards allow children to carry several pieces of paper without dropping them and provide a solid surface for sketching observations. In addition, teachers may want to gather tools the children can use for measuring (e.g., rulers, string), plaster of Paris for making castings, modeling clay for recording impressions, and paper and crayons for making rubbings. To ensure the participation of children with fine or gross motor delays, teachers should provide access to alternative or adaptive materials such as pencils with grips, slanted clipboards, no-slip placemats, cameras instead of writing utensils, and thicker crayons. Having such materials available for all children avoids singling out any children as needing special accommodations and supports a universal design for learning philosophy, enabling any child to use the materials that he or she needs or wants to complete the task. If cameras are available for the children's use, teachers should be sure they have memory cards and are charged and ready to use.

SUPPORTING LANGUAGE DEVELOPMENT

As teachers help young children plan and implement a project, they will have many opportunities to support children's language development. As the children uncover new aspects of the topic, they will have more to discuss and share.

Anticipate Vocabulary That Children Might Learn

When children participate in a project investigation, they have opportunities to learn a great deal of new vocabulary. Teachers and parents (as in the previous example about parents programming vocabulary into a child's AAC device) can take advantage of these opportunities by thinking ahead about new vocabulary and related concepts that may

emerge. Teachers can prepare space on the wall, in or near the classroom writing area, to display cards with project-related words and images; laminated index cards can be used for this purpose (see Figure 3.8), or such cards can be placed on a book ring to create visual supports. In addition, teachers might create Braille labels, develop Picture Exchange Communication System cards (Pyramid Educational Consultants, n.d.), or teach signs to support children with disabilities, depending on their specific needs; these alternate modes of communication are often a source of interest, excitement, and support for typically developing children as well.

Figure 3.8. Word cards were available for the children's use during the Dog Project.

When introducing new vocabulary to DLLs, it can be helpful to pair the novel word with a word in the child's home language that has the same root and sounds similar. Teachers can think ahead about words to include as they work on their teacher planning web. They can take advantage of preliminary planning time to research topic-related words that might have the same root words as that of the home language(s) of DLLs in their class. Teachers can use these similar-sounding or cognate words to help create a bridge between a child's home and school languages. For example, in a project on dogs, a teacher might consider partnering *paw* and *la pata*. In a project on the zoo, the teacher might consider *lion* and *leon*, *elephant* and *elefante*, or *giraffe* and *jirafa*. In a project on food, the teacher might consider pairing *spaghetti* and *espaguetis*.

Develop a Project History Board

One of the most useful strategies for supporting ongoing discussion about the children's investigation is to reserve space for a history board on a wall adjacent to the area where the class gathers for meetings or on a classroom bulletin board. Samples of what children say, things they have made, and images of experiences they had can be displayed on this Project History Board. This board can be used on an ongoing basis to display raw documentation of the project as it develops (i.e., children's work that has not been scanned, handwritten narrative and labels, images of children engaged in project work). In addition, teachers can use this area to help children think about the development of their project by reviewing what has been accomplished so far and making decisions about additions to the Project History Board. This helps children develop a sense of time and make connections between their experiences, a task that can be challenging for young children (Beneke, Ostrosky, & Katz, 2008). Visual supports such as a Project History Board can also be extremely helpful to children with limited communication skills such as DLLs and some children with disabilities.

Reviewing and discussing the evidence of their project work as displayed on the Project History Board is likely to lead to meaningful discussions in which children exchange ideas. Conversations in which adults and children, or peers, take turns initiating and responding to each other are critical for children's language development (Mashburn et al., 2008; Weizman & Snow, 2001).

GETTING STARTED

Teachers are often eager to get the project underway, and they sometimes skip some of the steps in Phase I that help children engage with the topic (see items under Phase I on the Implementation Checklist in Chapter 1). These steps include planning an opening event and finding out what children already know about the topic.

Plan an Opening Event

Introducing a topic for investigation to a group of children can be as simple as reading a book about the topic, sharing a memory related to the topic, or bringing in objects to get the discussion started. Mrs. Utz chose to bring in objects used in gardening (e.g., a hand trowel, gardening gloves, hand rake, and other tools) to gauge her students' interest in the topic. The children's interest in these real objects became apparent, and Mrs. Utz used this introduction as a springboard for a discussion about what the children already knew about the gardening. Meanwhile, the opening event for Ms. DeLuca's

Figure 3.9. Therapy dog visit.

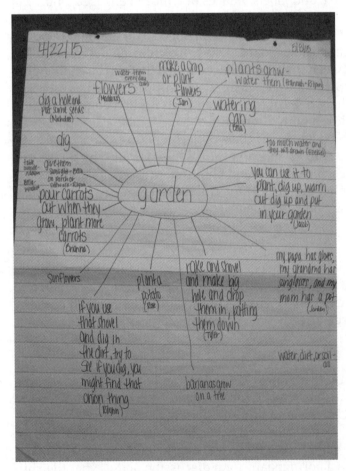

Figure 3.10. Children's topic web on gardening.

and Ms. Burd's classes was a visit by Eli, the therapy dog (see Figure 3.9).

Uncover What Children Already Know

Once the topic has been introduced, teachers can ask the children what they know about it. The teacher might hold up a hand trowel and ask, "Have you ever seen one of these? What can you tell us about it?" The teacher can then record the children's ideas on a web. These recordings are typically in the form of words, but words can be combined with pictures and/or symbols, depending on the needs of the children in a class. Unlike the teacher planning web, the children's topic web is used by the children, and it is prominently displayed in the classroom. In the Garden Project, as Mrs. Utz asked the children what they knew about gardening, she used a large piece of chart paper to record their thoughts (see Figure 3.10). As the Library Project got underway, Ms. Harrison spent time with individual and small groups of children adding to the initial topic web. This strategy gave her the opportunity to listen carefully to the children and to ask them probing questions. She spent time recording Addelyn's memories of what people see when they walk into the library. See Video 3.3 for an example of this process.

Making the initial topic web is just the beginning of the webbing process, as the web can serve as a living document where new knowledge is recorded as it is discovered. A teacher can help young children discover this process by modeling it, as well as suggesting it. For example, during center time, Mrs. Utz overheard one child telling another child, "My mom pours bags of stuff that looks like dirt on the garden to help it grow." Mrs. Utz said, "Oh, that stuff is called soil. We don't have that one on our web about gardening. Should we add it?" She brought this addition to the attention of the other children when they gathered for large group meeting, saying, "Look class, Levi and I added soil to the web. Do you know what soil is?" At large group meeting time, Mrs. Utz also asked the children if they had learned anything new that should be added to the web. Some teachers use a different-colored marker or pen each day that they make additions, as a way to track the children's growing knowledge about the topic.

Similarly, Ms. Harrison periodically took the topic web off the Project History Board and asked children to add to the web. She began by reviewing what was already recorded on the web and then prompted children to offer additions about the library. For example, 4-year-old Graham suggested "no running." He explained that if children run, they might "knock down the old people." See Video 3.4 to watch this process in Ms. Harrison's class.

INVOLVING FAMILIES

There are several ways to introduce family members to the Project Approach. Teachers can send home an informational letter, hold an informational meeting, or help family members learn about the Project Approach by involving them as helpers in the project investigation (see Figure 3.11).

Involving parents and other family members in project work can significantly increase a teacher's ability to support the project investigation. Once family members begin to understand how projects work, they are often eager to become involved in the project (e.g., by suggesting a site for a field trip, vol-

> Involving family members in project work can significantly increase a teacher's ability to support the project investigation.

unteering to be a guest expert, reaching out to someone they know who can serve as a guest expert). Helping out with projects is one of the ways that parents learn how projects work.

Many parents are willing to contribute materials to projects. This can be especially valuable when parents have access to special materials related to a particular topic (e.g., an array of gardening tools or special dog grooming tools). However, when the topic of an investigation is part of the everyday lives of most families, opportunities for parents to contribute materials and resources increase. For example, when Ms. DeLuca's and Ms. Burd's classes investigated dogs, they sent the following note home to each family asking them to send in a photo of their dog or the dog of a friend:

> Do you have a picture of your family pet or favorite dog that you know that you could share with our class? You can send the photo to school and we can copy it or you can email a digital picture to [the teacher's email address]. Help the children with their investigation!

Educators can send home a letter to the parents (see Figure 3.12) to introduce parents to the Project Approach.

PROVIDING OPPORTUNITIES FOR EXPRESSION AND REPRESENTATION

Some children in a class may know little or nothing about a project topic, whereas other children may have a lot of knowledge. These more knowledgeable children can serve as in-class experts. In Phase I, teachers provide children with opportunities to connect

Engaging Families in the Project Approach

1. Send a letter to families before the beginning of the school year to introduce the Project Approach.

2. Hold an informational meeting for families and include examples of project work.

3. Provide families with regular newsletter updates on the progress of your project, and explain how it is helping their child learn.

4. Offer to send the newsletter electronically.

5. Display ongoing documentation of the project as it develops.

6. Talk about the project when you have face-to-face interactions with students' family members.

7. Prompt children to tell their parents about what is happening in their project.

8. Create parent–child homework activities that add to the breadth and depth of the project.

For more detailed information, see http://illinoisearlylearning.org/illinoispip/blogs/beneke/2008sept23.html.

Figure 3.11. Ways to involve families. (*Source:* Illinois Early Learning Project, 2018).

Date: _____

Dear Family,

This year our class will be doing child investigations called projects! Projects are investigations of high-interest topics that typically have three phases. In Phase I, the children represent their individual prior experiences with the topic through drawing, storytelling, and dramatic play. At the end of Phase I, the children and I will make a list of all the things they want to find out about the topic. During the second phase, the children will conduct research to find the answers to their questions. They will likely use many methods to do this research. For example, they might use informational books, interview experts on the topic, and create observational drawings to learn more about the topic under investigation. Finally, in the third phase, the children will summarize their findings with a culminating event.

Some of these project investigations may last a few days, and some of them may last as long as a few months! Either way, be assured that this is an effective way to provide your child with opportunities for using and developing knowledge, skills, and abilities.

I welcome your participation in these projects! You can contribute materials, ideas, expertise, or time. Please watch our newsletter for lists of materials we need to complete a project, and don't hesitate to offer suggestions. On some occasions, your child will have project "homework" and will need your assistance. For example, if we study flashlights, we might ask each child to develop a list of all the things at his or her house that use batteries.

I look forward to doing many interesting project investigations with your children this year. As always, please let me know if you have any questions.

Sincerely,

Figure 3.12. Letter to parents.

Figure 3.13. Toy dogs and accessories in the dramatic play area encouraged children to talk about dogs.

with their prior knowledge about the topic. As the children share these connections, the teacher can use samples of what the children say, make, and do to document where the individual children in the class are on the continuum of knowledge and understanding of the topic. Activities such as these offer opportunities for many children to share their expertise and for teachers to highlight children who might otherwise not emerge as leaders in a class. For example, a child with a disability who has extensive knowledge about insects yet rarely connects with peers may emerge as a leader during a project on gardening.

Uncover Prior Knowledge and Experience

Teachers can plan a variety of activities and enhance the environment to help children express and represent what they know about a topic. For instance, they can read books about the topic to spark children's interest and lead a discussion about it. Props can be added to classroom interest areas so that children can use them in dramatic play, the art center, or the block area. For example, in Phase I of the Dog Project, Ms. DeLuca and Ms. Burd added stuffed animals and dog accessories to the housekeeping and block areas (see Figures 3.13 and 3.14).

As teachers observe children, they can note what the children represent accurately and what they do not know or misunderstand. For example, through her observations, Ms. Harrison learned that children had misperceptions about how patrons select books at a library.

Figure 3.14. Toy dogs in the block area prompted children to build dog houses for them.

At the beginning of a project, teachers often prompt children to draw or paint pictures about something related to the topic. They then talk with each child about his or her picture and record the child's description of the content of the drawing (see Figure 3.15). These pictures can be compiled into a class book that can be shared in the reading area. For example, Ms. Harrison asked a few children at a time to join her at a table to sketch pictures and dictate stories about their experiences at the library. She had a binder sleeve all ready for each child's work, and she took time to review the work of children who were not present with those who were. See Video 3.5 for

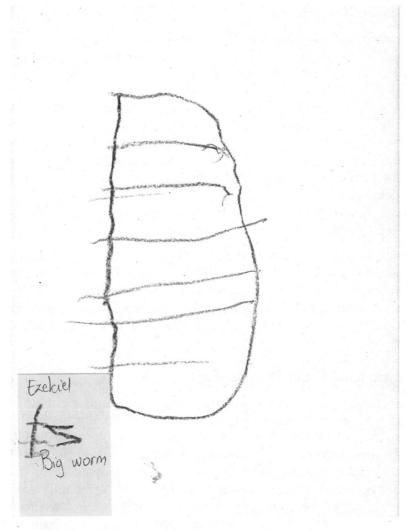

Figure 3.15.   One child represented his prior knowledge about gardens by drawing a worm.

an example of sketching and dictating from memory. Similarly, teachers can provide children with open-ended materials that can be used to create individual three-dimensional representations. For example, children might build doghouses with cardboard boxes and Popsicle sticks, sculpt them with clay, or use loose parts such as sticks, fabric, and stones.

Identify Possible Guest Experts

Although inviting guest experts into the classroom or taking children on field trips typically is part of Phase II, teachers should think about possibilities early on so that they can quickly make arrangements once the focus of children's interest begins to emerge. A guest expert might be a professional whose work revolves around the topic, such as a veterinarian who can discuss dog care or a master gardener. However, teachers should think about other possibilities in case a guest expert is not available. For example, other people who could serve in the role of the veterinarian might include a dog groomer, veterinarian technician, dog trainer, or dog owner.

Identify Locations for Fieldwork

Although teachers may know the general topic of the project, they likely will not really know the primary focus of the investigation until the end of Phase I. The focus of children's fieldwork will depend on what aspect of the project topic they are most curious about (i.e., what they want to find out). However, teachers can think ahead about locations where children are able to investigate, depending on the direction their investigation takes. For example, a teacher might introduce the topic of farming to a group of children in Phase I, realizing that by the end of that phase the focus may have narrowed to one particular aspect of farming, such as tractors or grain bins. Reviewing the teacher planning web can help teachers consider a broad spectrum of possible locations for fieldwork.

IDENTIFYING QUESTIONS

The children's questions that are gathered in Phase I will drive the beginning of the project investigation in Phase II. Teachers use these questions as a guide to plan the initial investigation. These questions can be gathered in a variety of ways. In this section, we discuss gathering questions during small and large group discussions and by using active listening during play. We then discuss using children's questions to guide lesson plans.

Hold Large and Small Group Discussions

Projects are group investigations, and discussions help to bring together group members' shared vision of the investigation. At the beginning of a project, these discussions might be about the children's prior experiences with the topic and ideas for sharing or representing what they already know. Short discussions can be successfully held during large group meetings. However, for many young children, attending in a large group can be challenging, especially early in the school year when children are younger and are just learning the class routines. In these cases, teachers may choose to meet with children in smaller groups. For example, Ms. Harrison, who had a very young class and was starting her project at the beginning of the school year, met informally with small groups of children to begin collecting their questions. A tactic that also works well is for a teacher and the assistant teacher or student teacher to divide the class in half, hold discussions about the topic, and then share the results of the two discussions at the next large group meeting. Alternatively, the teacher might hold discussions with small groups at a designated area during choice time.

As Phase I draws to a close, the topic of group discussions includes generating questions for further investigations. Notably, although young children frequently ask questions, they often are confused at first when asked to intentionally generate them. Teachers might prompt these questions by asking the children, "What else do you want to find out about this topic?" or "What else do we need to know?" In addition, it may be helpful for teachers to model asking questions or making "I wonder" statements (e.g., "I wonder if dogs eat vegetables"). Sometimes children make statements about dogs that can be rephrased as questions (e.g., "Dogs like ice cream" can be rephrased as "Do you think ice cream is all right for dogs to eat?"). As the children's questions emerge, teachers can record them on a chart that is displayed in the group meeting area and can easily be referenced or updated. For example, children in Ms. DeLuca's class and Ms. Burd's class came up with the following questions:

- Are you afraid of dogs?

- Are all dogs the same?

- Do dogs get sad?

- Can dogs be blue?

- Do dogs die?

- Do dogs eat meat?

- Do dogs' teeth fall out?

- What kind of hair do dogs have?

- Can puppies go to school?

- Can dogs go to work?

- How do dogs talk?

- Why do dogs dig?

The more prior knowledge the children have about a topic, the more questions they are likely to have. It is not necessary to have an extensive list of questions to start, but it is important for teachers to sense that there is enough interest among multiple class members to continue the project. There might not be enough buy-in to a topic if only one or two children in the class are really interested in learning more about the subject. If teachers are not certain that there is enough interest to continue, they might extend Phase I, provide another activity to stimulate interest, and then provide children with another opportunity to dictate questions.

As Ms. DeLuca's and Ms. Burd's preschoolers became engaged in their investigation of dogs, Ms. Lavin's second graders became curious about their activities. Ms. Lavin saw this as an opportunity to partner with another class, so she arranged for her students to visit Ms. DeLuca's and Ms. Burd's classes. As the preschoolers shared documentation of what they had accomplished so far, the second graders were eager to join the investigation. They returned to their own classroom and filled three charts with webs of questions (see Figure 3.16).

Capture Questions in the Natural Environment

Although it is important for children to have the experience of discussing their questions during small and large group meetings, it is not the only way

Figure 3.16.   Second graders made their own webs of questions about dogs.

Questions	Predictions	Findings
How does the sauce go from tomato to sauce?	The cook mashes the tomatoes into sauce. The tomatoes get cooked.	The cook cuts up the tomatoes and cooks them. Pizza sauce can come in a can.

Figure 3.17. Sample prediction chart.

to capture their curiosity. Teachers also can take advantage of opportunities to capture children's questions in the natural environment. For example, as they interact with and actively observe children during choice time, teachers can listen for things that the children want to find out about the project topic. Upon hearing such statements, they can ask the children whether their question should be added to the list. In this way, the list of questions provides an ongoing record of the children's interests, rather than their ideas at one particular moment in time. It may be helpful for teachers to carry a note pad and pen with them so that they can record children's questions as they arise, whether they are out on the playground, in the hall, waiting for the bus, or in the classroom. This practice sends children the message that their questions are important and worth saving and sharing with others.

Help Children Make Predictions

Typically, some of the children's questions will have more potential for learning than others. In fact, some of their questions may actually be statements. For example, during a project on pizza, one child's question was, "What is the shovel for? Putting pizza in the ovens?" Essentially, it is a question that requires only a yes or no response, and the child has provided the answer to the question. However, another child asked, "How does the tomato go from tomato to sauce?" Investigation of the latter question has the potential to help young children explore liquids and solids, cooking, and the process food goes through from farm to table. We recommend that teachers select one or two questions with rich potential for learning and ask children to make predictions about possible answers. As children discover answers during the course of an investigation, they can report these to the teacher, and the teacher can record the findings. A prediction chart works very well for this purpose (see Figure 3.17).

Focus on Children's Questions

Once teachers have collected questions, they can use them to guide lesson planning. Teachers then consider what materials and experiences will help the children answer their questions. For example, teachers can begin to think about possible sites for field trips, potential guest experts they can invite to visit the class, and resources they might bring into the classroom. In the Library Project, children wondered where books came from, so Ms. Harrison began to search for a guest expert who could visit the classroom to answer this question.

DOCUMENTING THE PROJECT

Teachers begin the process of documenting the project when they allocate space for a Project History Board. The board can include documentation of children's Phase I project work, such as samples of their drawings, dictated stories, and photographs of

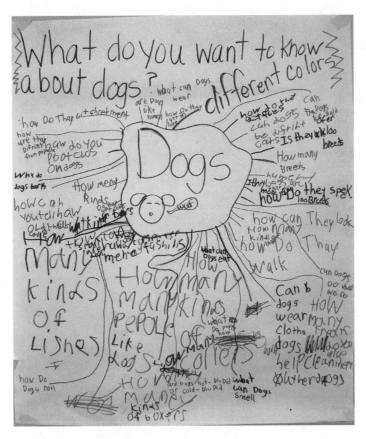

Figure 3.18. Ms. DeLuca met with small groups of children to get their input on the topic web. The complete web became a centerpiece of the class Project History Board.

dramatic play. The children's topic web and the list of their questions are important documents featured in the display that the class will revisit throughout the project.

Children can be encouraged to participate in documenting their individual and group project work; a teacher might ask, "What work did we get done today on our project?" Teachers can encourage this practice by regularly asking children what should be documented and what samples of work should be included (e.g., "What photos should we put up on the Project History Board to show what we did? Whose drawing should we display?"). Engaging in reflection on their group and individual accomplishments can help to strengthen children's interest in further project work. Figure 3.18 presents a web that was a key feature of the Project History Board.

> It is essential to build on children's interests when selecting a topic for project work.

CONCLUSION

In this chapter, we provided an overview of Phase I, including the components and some strategies to help ensure a successful launch of the project. It is essential to build on children's interests when selecting a topic for project work. In the next chapter, we explore components of Phase II, the heart of a project, as children begin conducting their investigation. We share strategies that help teachers support child-initiated, hands-on investigations.

Supporting the Investigation

Once the project on the car wash was underway, Ms. Carly was thrilled! Her students had questions about where the water in the car wash comes from, the type of soap used on the cars, the screen where the customers push buttons to select a wash, and the industrial vacuum cleaner. Ms. Carly and her assistant teacher, Mr. Tom, wondered what to do next. Now that they knew what the children were curious about, they wondered how they should proceed. Ms. Tamara shared her copy of the Implementation Checklist with the team to help plan "next steps." The teaching team began to gather materials that the children could use to find answers to their questions, and the teachers brought to the dramatic play area props that the children could use to play car wash. Ms. Carly contacted the owner of a car wash that was a block away from her school to see if he had any artifacts they might borrow for the length of their project. She also asked him if he would be willing to visit the class as a guest expert and allow them to make a field trip to his car wash. Mr. Delroy was delighted that the children were curious about his business and promised to loan her a vacuum hose, samples of soap, and some other props. They arranged a date for his visit to the classroom and a date for the class visit to the car wash.

Authentic child research, the heart of the Project Approach, is discussed in this chapter. In this phase, Phase II of the project, children engage in active investigation to answer their questions related to the topic of the project, and teachers experience the challenge of providing children with opportunities for firsthand research and the satisfaction that comes from supporting children's curiosity. Children's questions gathered at the end of Phase I serve as a guide for lesson planning in Phase II. In response to those questions, teachers gather artifacts and materials for representation, and they plan experiences that will help the children find answers to their questions. As more questions arise, teachers respond by revising the materials and experiences they provide. Children who are engaged in this kind of hands-on research often become experts on the topic. This chapter includes a description of strategies for supporting children's research efforts and teaching them investigation strategies.

> A key feature of project work is children's engagement in seeking answers to their questions, mainly through firsthand investigations.

SUPPORTING CHILDREN'S RESEARCH

One of the key features of project work is the children's engagement in seeking answers to their questions, mainly through firsthand investigations. Therefore, a good topic for a project is one that supports hands-on research.

Access Authentic Materials and Artifacts

Children's firsthand investigations and the course of their project work are supported by the materials and artifacts that teachers introduce into the classroom. Many of the questions posed by children before a project gets underway will inevitably lead to more questions. We have repeatedly seen that one question frequently leads to another!

At the beginning of Phase II, teachers should bring in authentic materials and artifacts related to children's questions about the project topic. These might include things such as tools, accessories, components, or samples of objects related to the topic being studied. For example, a project on shoes might include a shoe stretcher, a shoehorn, a light-up shoe that has been taken apart, and a collection of different types of shoe laces. Although safety is always a primary concern, teachers must make sure that many real materials and artifacts associated with the topic are included in the classroom environment, such as the materials Mr. Delroy was lending to Ms. Carly's class. We refer to these types of items as authentic materials.

Children can explore authentic materials firsthand, use them to answer their questions, discuss them with teachers and peers, use them as props in dramatic play, experiment with them, and represent them through two-dimensional drawings and paintings or three-dimensional sculptures or constructions. Although simply adding materials or artifacts to the environment may be beneficial, children will benefit more from the availability of materials and artifacts if teachers take time to intentionally introduce them to the group, explain how they relate to the project topic, and show the class where the materials are to be kept. Teachers can place the authentic materials in an area or two of the classroom that they believe is most appropriate to assist children with investigating and representing their findings. For example, Ms. DeLuca and Ms. Burd, as part of their project on dogs, introduced a variety of real dog collars, bowls, leashes, toys, bones, beds, cages, and grooming items into the environment. They placed the dog bowls, collars, leashes, and toys in the housekeeping area for the children to use in pretend play, whereas the dog bones and treats were used in math and science explorations, games, and art. In her class, Mrs. Utz introduced gardening tools, including sprinklers and sprayers, along with soil and peat moss (see Figure 4.1).

Provide Materials to Support Experimentation

Teachers can encourage exploration and experimentation by providing materials associated with the project topic that can be acted on by the children. Consider materials that can be touched, smelled, heard, weighed, measured, mixed, mashed, folded, cooked, cut, assembled, or disassembled. For example, in the Dog Project, Ms. DeLuca and Ms. Burd placed a collection of furs and fur-like fabrics on a table for the children to touch and compare (see Figure 4.2). In the Garden Project, Mrs. Utz planned opportunities for children to repot plants into larger containers. In the process, they explored the structure of each plant and the

Figure 4.1. Mrs. Utz brought in a sprinkler, which sparked her children's curiosity about gardening.

properties of potting soil (see Figure 4.3). In the Library Project, Ms. Harrison borrowed a scanner from the local library. She also borrowed a set of wooden shelves that the children could refer to as they considered building their own set. This allowed Ms. Harrison to bring important aspects of the shelves to the children's attention. Watch Video 4.1 to see how Ms. Harrison's class drew plans for a bookshelf using a real shelf as a reference.

Support Understanding Through Props for Dramatic Play

Dramatic play typically takes place in the housekeeping center of the classroom. Other classroom centers, such as blocks, manipulatives, outdoor play, and art areas, can lend themselves to dramatic play as well. Dramatic play helps children understand the roles of people and materials related to the project topic; pretending to use dog grooming tools might help a child understand the importance of proper equipment for dog care, whereas pretending to use a watering can might help a child understand that water is important for plant growth. Teachers can spark this type of play by providing props such as hats, uniforms, equipment, tools, signs, and images in these centers. As teachers observe children's play, they can provide additional props in response to emerging play themes. For example, Ms. Burd and Ms. DeLuca initially developed pet care areas in

Figure 4.2. In the Dog Project, children used their senses to explore different furry textures.

their housekeeping centers. Over time, this area in Ms. DeLuca's room evolved into a pet store, whereas this area in Ms. Burd's room became a veterinarian's office. As they became increasingly involved in the Dog Project, second graders from Ms. Lavin's class set up a rotation so that several second graders could spend time with their preschool buddies every day. The second graders and their preschool friends spent time exploring the topic in the early childhood dramatic play areas. The second graders modeled and encouraged their partners to engage in more advanced levels of play. Teachers can give children a role in planning additions or making changes to dramatic play. For example, as depicted in Video 4.2., when one of Ms. Harrison's students suggested that they move the class book stand to make it part of their library, Ms. Harrison took her suggestion seriously and encouraged other children to help move the stand.

Gather Open-Ended Materials for Representation

Effective project teachers collect and provide a variety of open-ended materials that children can use to represent their ideas about a topic. They understand that teaching children techniques and strategies for using open-ended materials will support children's ability to represent their ideas more effectively, rather than waiting for the children's abilities to spontaneously emerge (Huntsinger, Jose, Krieg, & Luo, 2011). For example, teachers at the St. Ambrose University Children's Campus have developed a list of art materials that they intentionally teach young children to use (see Table 4.1).

Figure 4.3. In the Garden Project, children repotted plants into larger containers.

Children's representations can range from two-dimensional drawings or paintings to three-dimensional constructions or sculptures. A child may begin with a representation in one media and then, over time, explore making it with various other media. These representations may be the work of individual children or collaborative work developed by two or more children. For example, children in Ms. Harrison's class initially represented their understanding of shelves with individual drawings. However, they then combined their understanding of the bookshelves in a construction that developed over time. The entire

Table 4.1. Art media used in early childhood classrooms at the St. Ambrose University Children's Campus

Drawing	Painting	Three-Dimensional	Tools	Collage
Markers	Easel	Play dough	Scissors (snip)	Wooden pieces
Colored pencils	Tempera paint	Play dough tools	Scissors (blunt)	Googly eyes
Regular pencils	Watercolors (cakes)	Clay	Scissors (pointed)	Fabric scraps (patterned)
Pencil sharpeners	Watercolors (liquid)	Clay tools	Scissors (training)	Fabric scraps (textured)
Crayons	Finger paint	Clay boards	Scissors (left-handed)	Natural materials
Chalk (white)	Paint daubers	Modeling clay	White glue	Felt
Chalk (colored)	Ink pads	Small wood pieces	Glue sticks	Tissue paper
Permanent thin-tip markers	Ink stampers	Craft sticks	Masking tape	Pom-poms
Oil pastels	Paintbrushes (watercolor)	Craft wire	Scotch tape	Magazines
Charcoal pencils	Paintbrushes (tempera)	Sponges	Stapler	Newspaper
Chalkboards	Paint palettes	Bowls for water	Hole punchers	Contact paper
Wipe-off boards	Small paint containers	Pipe cleaners	Straws	String
Dry erase markers	Small water pitchers		Paper bags	Ribbon
Papers in varying sizes	Paint smocks		Egg cartons	Yarn
Card stock	Miscellaneous painters (e.g., sponges, rollers, string)			
Tracing paper				

class participated at some point in the planning and construction of the shelves, and Ms. Harrison supported and prompted their work by asking them questions. See Video 4.3 and Video 4.4 to watch how her class used the real shelves as reference for their construction and how they discovered a possible support for the top of the shelf. Although some children might need teacher prompting or support throughout Phase II, in the Dog Project, several children spontaneously created collars they could wear as they pretended to be dogs, collars for stuffed dogs in the dramatic play area, doghouses, dog toys, and dog models (see Figures 4.4 and 4.5). Ms. Lavin's students borrowed some of the materials from Ms. Burd's and Ms. DeLuca's classrooms, and they regularly spent time in the early childhood classrooms experimenting alongside the early childhood students. Once they became aware of the topics under study, staff members from other classrooms began to donate relevant materials for the Dog Project, such as yarn in the colors of dog fur.

TEACHING CHILDREN STRATEGIES FOR INVESTIGATION

The more strategies children have to use during their investigations, the more likely they are to find answers to their questions and the better prepared they are to help one another. Useful strategies include teaching children how to 1) use new vocabulary, 2) use drawing as a way to record information, 3) find information in reference books, 4) represent their ideas and share their plans, 5) view peers as resources, 6) use clipboards and markers to record information, and 7) think creatively in response to open-ended questions. Teaching children strategies for investigation can sustain the life of a project because finding the answer to one question often leads to another question and discovering something new as part of an investigation

> Teaching children strategies for investigation can sustain the life of a project because finding the answer to one question often leads to another question and discovering something new as part of an investigation is likely to reinforce a child's image of him- or herself as a capable investigator.

Figure 4.4. A girl in Ms. DeLuca's class pretends to be a dog. She wears a dog-collar that she made.

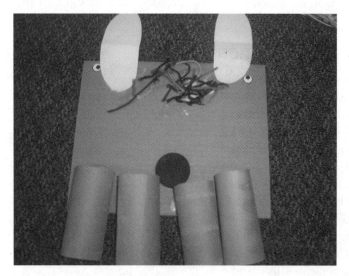

Figure 4.5. A selection of open-ended materials made it possible for a child in Ms. DeLuca's room to create this unique representation of a dog.

is likely to reinforce a child's image of him- or herself as a capable investigator. For example, as the children in Ms. Harrison's room began to talk about building a library, Ms. Harrison demonstrated how looking at a map of a library in a nonfiction book might help the children find information about what they might want to include (see Video 4.5). Around this same time, the children in the class began to notice bar codes on books and other items. They became very curious about bar codes and wondered what they were for and why they were on books. They also questioned whether bar codes were on other items. Instead of telling them the answers to these questions, Ms. Harrison and Ms. Berendes looked for opportunities to engage the children in dialogue and asked them questions to see if the children could come up with their own hypotheses. See Video 4.6 and Video 4.7 for examples of these engaging conversations on bar codes.

The younger the children, the more support they are likely to need to use these strategies independently. Of course, because development is uneven, some children will use the strategies independently at a younger age compared with their peers. In addition, some children with disabilities are likely to need additional support to draw, use clipboards, use reference books, share their plans, and so on. The type of support or accommodation needed depends on the particular child and the project activity in which he or she wants to participate. For example, three children might need very different supports to enable them to work on a construction project, such as the library shelves created by the children in the Library Project. A child with fine motor delays might need a special handle on his saw so that he can saw cardboard to make shelves. A child with a short attention span might need to be placed in close proximity to the teacher so that the teacher can help her stay on task. Finally, the teacher might need to assist a child with limited social skills learn how to share materials and take turns so that the child can work successfully alongside peers.

Introduce New Vocabulary

The more vocabulary children know related to the topic, the better prepared they are to talk about the topic and join in the investigation. Teachers can plan a variety of ways to introduce new topic-related vocabulary. For example, several of the children in Ms. DeLuca's class and Ms. Burd's class had speech and language delays. Ms. DeLuca and Ms. Burd supported their students' ability to actively participate in the investigation of dogs by agreeing on common dog-related vocabulary words they would use in their discussions with the children, such as grooming, leash, collar, fur, and vet. They wanted to be sure that children with speech and language delays had many opportunities to hear them model the words so that the children could join in conversations. They further supported the children's ability to communicate by providing visual supports such as pictures, word cards, picture labels, videos, and real objects. A visual checklist was created that helped children follow the steps in grooming their toy dog while playing in the class pet store they had created in their classroom. Artifacts such as leashes, dog food, and medicine were labeled, and a picture checklist was created for children to use when shopping at the store. Speech-language pathologists (SLPs) were able to capitalize on the children's engagement in the Dog Project to work effectively on individualized education program (IEP) goals with children with disabilities. For example, one of the SLPs helped a child dictate some words to describe a picture of a dog and labeled the picture with the child's words (e.g., "collar it blue," "down ears," "paw big," "1, 2 eyes").

> Therapists can capitalize on children's engagement in a project to work effectively on IEP goals.

In the Library Project, Ms. Harrison printed out pictures of the library, and children helped her decide which ones to place in clear plastic sleeves in a binder. Both while they compiled the book and after it was complete, Ms. Harrison and the children used the binder to name and discuss various aspects of the library, as depicted in Video 4.8. In fact, the discussion that followed sparked the idea to make bookshelves for the class library.

Use Drawing to Record Information

Drawing in the context of the Project Approach is not typically about aesthetics or art. Instead, the teacher intentionally teaches and encourages children to use drawing as a tool for recording and communicating information. This is different from asking a child to draw something from memory (e.g., "Can you draw a flower for me?"). Instead, within project work, children should draw while observing, looking closely at, or focusing on an object. Consequently, children are likely to notice more features and details about the subject, and their interest in the subject is likely to increase. For example, when Ms. Burd and Ms. DeLuca took a walk to visit a Scottish Terrier in the school neighborhood named Izzy, the children took along clipboards to record their observations. Children intently studied the dog and his surroundings and drew what they observed (see Figures 4.6, 4.7, and 4.8). When a police officer and his dog, Thor, visited the class,

Figure 4.6. A preschooler shows his field sketch of Scottish Terrier, Izzy.

the dog demonstrated how he used his sense of smell to identify and retrieve a special suitcase. One child then shared his understanding of the event through a drawing (see Figure 4.9). Teachers can help children learn to use drawing as a way of recording information by regularly modeling it themselves. As captured in Video 4.9, Ms. Harrison modeled observational drawing of a bar code scanner. Explaining her strategy helped the children who were drawing alongside her to decide where and how to begin their own drawings.

Some children's observational drawings may be easy to interpret and include a great deal of detail that helps the teacher understand what the child notices and/or understands about the subject of his or her drawing. However, even if the drawing appears to be nothing more than random scribbles and lines, teachers can learn something about what children notice by talking with them about their drawings. A teacher might ask, "Is that the dog's bowl and brush?" "I drew the dog's leash. What did you decide to draw?" "Can you point to the things you drew pictures of?" Or, a teacher might engage children by talking out loud about what she is drawing in hopes that her students also will talk about the subject of their work as they draw.

Gather Useful Children's Books

Gathering books that provide factual information and images about a topic is an important way in which teachers support children's ability to do research. As recommended in Chapter 3, teachers should begin collecting reference books and materials as soon as they become aware of the topic for project work. The focus of a project typically narrows or shifts over time, so gathering reference books is an ongoing process. Developmentally appropriate books with clear images that convey accurate information are especially helpful. Teachers should ensure that books are accessible around the classroom for independent reading, as well as for teacher-read story time (see Figure 4.10). For example, during the Dog Project, Ms. Burd and Ms. DeLuca provided a variety of literature, including books, magazines, and pamphlets. Nonfiction

Figure 4.7. Izzy, the Scottish Terrier, was the subject of children's field sketches.

books about dog breeds were very popular with the children during independent reading time. Ms. Burd and Ms. DeLuca also continued to capitalize on children's interest in therapy dogs that began with the visit from Eli by sharing real stories about dogs that needed special equipment to assist children.

Adults can help children learn to use reference materials by modeling their use, talking out loud about what they are doing as they search for relevant information and pointing out and describing attributes, and by asking children questions

Figure 4.8. Some children chose to include details about Izzy's surroundings in their drawing. This child included the fence that kept Izzy in his yard.

that prompt them to search for information in the reference materials and to notice details. For example, if a child asks about the height and weight of the biggest breed of dog, the teacher might say, "Why don't we look in our book about dog breeds?" She can then get the reference book, turn the pages with the child, and discover information on the height and weight of the biggest breed of dog. They can then use a tape measure to compare the height of the tallest dog to the child's own height. Teachers also

can encourage children to make their own topic-related books. The children in Ms. Harrison's class made books, and as they were completed, they were added to the class library.

In addition to books, other print materials can be gathered to use as reference materials. For example, pamphlets and magazines from a local pet store and the veterinarian's office were gathered for the Dog Project, and a variety of seed packets were collected for the Garden Project. In addition, technology can be used to gather information, as was observed when Ms. Lavin's second graders accessed books and print materials online to use as references.

Although the Dog Project began with a visit from a service

Figure 4.9. Child's representation of police dog Thor retrieving the correct suitcase.

dog whose job was to assist people with special needs, Ms. DeLuca, Ms. Burd, and Ms. Lavin used books to introduce their students to ways in which people can assist dogs with special needs. For example, they read *Frankie the Walk 'n Roll Dog* (Techel, 2008), a book about a dog that cannot use his back legs and moves from place to place using a wheelchair.

Teach Children to Use Clipboards

The combination of a clipboard, paper, and writing implement enables children to record their observations, whether out on a field trip or in the classroom. Not only does a clipboard keep papers from slipping away and provide preschoolers with a firm surface for writing, but it also sends a powerful signal to them that they have purposeful work to do. It helps keep them focused on the task of recording data. Children at a variety of developmental levels can use a clipboard. If a child can make marks on paper, he or she can begin to engage in the process of recording observations.

Figure 4.10. Mrs. Utz located books about gardening in all the major interest areas in the classroom. Here a girl reads to her friends about gardening as they play with gardening tools in the dramatic play area.

Clipboards are affordable, adaptable low-tech tools that are easy to use. Clipboards and writing implements are light and easy for most children to carry. Writing implements can be attached to a clipboard with Velcro dots, self-adhesive holders, or string, thereby providing children with immediate access to the tools they need to record their observations. However, teachers may also choose to allow children to carry their clipboards and distribute writing implements when they reach the fieldwork site. Children with physical disabilities, such as cerebral palsy, may not have the strength or coordination to carry their own clipboards. They may have difficulty grasping some writing implements or finding a comfortable position to write on the clipboard. Adaptations, such as providing a backpack to carry the clipboard, a pencil grip to help with grasping the writing implement, and a transportable slope board to position the clipboard appropriately, can support children's participation and use of these resources. In addition, tools such as digital cameras or iPads can be provided for children who are not able to use a clipboard.

There are a variety of types of writing implements that teachers can provide to children for recording their observations. Although an adult artist might sketch with pencils, such tools can be difficult for young children to grasp and use. If the child presses down too hard, the sharp lead of the pencil may tear the paper or the lead might break. Also, the faintness of the pencil lines makes it difficult for children to keep track of the lines drawn on the paper so that they can elaborate on their own observational drawings. Pens or thin, nontoxic, felt-tip markers can help young children have a more successful drawing experience. Pens and markers also eliminate the option of erasing, as preschoolers are rarely successful at using an eraser with accuracy.

Children often use more than one piece of paper during a field site visit. Teachers can save themselves a great deal of time by prelabeling the paper. The name of each child and the date of the field trip can be recorded in the corner of a corresponding piece of paper. The teacher can then photocopy a set of these papers for every child and insert them into their clipboards.

Most preschoolers begin project work without prior experience with clipboards. Therefore, it can be helpful to provide children with an opportunity to practice the process of holding, carrying, and positioning their clipboard to use for representational drawing. For example, a teacher might plan an activity in which the teacher and the assistant teacher divide the class and each of the two groups visits a predetermined site in their building to do field sketching. One group might travel to a neighboring classroom to sketch the class guinea pig, and the other group might sketch the fish tank near the school entrance. Before setting out, the teacher can explain to the children that they are to draw the fish tank (or guinea pig) and that when they return to the classroom they will see if the other group can guess where they have been by looking at their drawings. The teacher may then instruct the children in his or her group on how to hold and carry their clipboards before they set out.

In these initial experiences with observational drawing, teachers can support children's under-standing of its purpose by treating them as apprentices. For example, teachers can observe the subject of the field sketch along with the children and make their own drawing. Modeling their enthusiasm and making efforts to point out important features of the subject may affect how much children record in their own field sketches. In a sense, through this process, teachers educate children in how to focus their attention. For example, when they arrive at the fish tank, teachers might demonstrate their interest in the tank and its contents by changing their tone of voice and using their body language to create anticipation. They can ask the children questions to focus their attention, such as "Look at this. Do you know what this is?" Some children will know more than others and can share their relevant knowledge and experience. Teachers can expand on the details that children report initially noticing. For example, in response to one child's statement that there is a "little house in there" (in the fish tank), they could respond, "Yes, and see, it has little windows and a doorway." As teachers acknowledge and elaborate on children's statements in this way, the children often slow down, focus, and look more intently at the subject of their drawing. By continuing to acknowledge and expand on the children's observations and asking questions that prompt the children to notice additional details, teachers can extend the time that students spend scanning and noting the details of the subject of their field sketch.

> During initial experiences with observational drawing, teachers can support children's understanding of its purpose by treating them as apprentices.

It is also important to encourage children to find a comfortable position for field sketching. Sitting "crisscross applesauce" does not provide enough stability for many children to do their best drawing. After a few minutes of careful shared observations, teachers can encourage children to find a place to settle down on the floor or ground, to find a comfortable position for sketching (e.g., kneeling, squatting, lying on their

Figure 4.11.   A child positioned her body so that she could comfortably create her field sketch.

belly), and to proceed to record their observations on their paper and clipboards (see Figure 4.11). As the children sketch, the teacher can periodically focus their attention on features of the subject that they have not yet noticed or represented. For example, in the case of the fish tank environment, the teacher might ask, "Look, is there something up at the top of the water?" One of the children might then excitedly note, "There's fish food!" Many children benefit from teachers modeling behaviors and find it helpful when teachers point out and describe physical features of the environment. These comments help children organize their drawing. During a field trip to the local library, Ms. Harrison invited the children to find something they wanted to remember from the library, to get comfortable, and then to draw it. Ms. Harrison and Ms. Berendes were then able to move among the children, answering questions and supporting the children's observations. See Video 4.10 for an example of how Ms. Harrison supported a child sketching at the library.

Handling a variety of new materials can be distracting or overwhelming for young children, especially children with attention-deficit/hyperactivity disorder (ADHD) or children on the autism spectrum. If children are going to use other materials in addition to the clipboard on their field trip, it is a good idea to practice using them in advance. For example, one teacher planned to have children observe in a meadow, and she planned to provide each child with a large carpet square to sit on as they sketched using their clipboards. The day before the trip to the meadow, she explained to the children that they were going to practice using their clipboards to record information. She provided each child with a carpet square, and she asked each child to find a comfortable place in the room to work. She invited them to find something in the room that they found interesting and to take it to their carpet square to sketch. The following day when they went to the meadow, the children knew exactly what to do with the carpet squares and clipboards, and they were better able to focus on the plants they found growing there. Teaching children how to use tools and providing them with time to get used to using the tools can help children understand the expectations and also result in more successful experiences.

Teach Children How to Survey Others

Preschool children love to conduct surveys. Teaching them how to independently survey others helps children feel confident in their ability to investigate and discover. Teachers can begin by modeling with a survey on a large piece of chart paper where they record the children's answers to a question. Creating a two-column format with the optional responses at the top of the two columns works well. Teachers can subsequently create a two-column form that children can use to invent their own surveys. Some teachers place these forms in the class writing center, along with clipboards. Teachers can help children to think of survey questions (see Video 4.11). As they become more familiar with the process, children will gradually begin using the forms independently. Tallying the responses is a strategy that young children can use to record their findings. In the Library Project, Ms. Harrison accompanied children to other classrooms to conduct their surveys (see Video 4.12).

Ask Children to Draw a Plan

As children learn more about the topic of their project, teachers should ask them what they would like to make to show what they have discovered so far. Children are often enthusiastic about using open-ended art materials to make individual or group constructions that represent objects they have investigated during project work. One way to help children think about how they will create their construction is to ask them to draw a plan. Children with special needs may need additional support through physical and/or verbal prompts to complete their plans.

Reminding children to use reference materials can help them create more accurate plans, especially if the topic of the project is not a very familiar one. Simply providing reference materials, nonfiction children's books, nonfiction adult books, and artifacts may not be enough direction to ensure that children will use them, especially if the children have had little experience with this type of research or have difficulty focusing their attention. For example, after researching many types of doghouses, children in Ms. DeLuca's class and Ms. Burd's class created plans for the doghouses they wanted to build (see Figure 4.12). Collecting and sharing children's plans with the group is a practice that helps children appreciate each other's ideas and helps them develop a shared understanding of the topic. A teacher might gather the children together and say, "I want to share all the ideas you have had for constructing doghouses!" Then the teacher could go through the children's drawings and point out features that are depicted in each one (e.g., "Look, Peter's doghouse has a dog bed and a window!"). The teacher can point out their common interests and variations on the features and can ask individual children to describe the features portrayed in their drawing. Children can be invited to comment on each other's ideas and ask each other questions about their plans (e.g., "Does the window open?"). Children can then refer to their plans and to those of their peers as they make their constructions (see Figure 4.13). Such conversations can support peer interaction between children with and without special needs.

In situations where children are planning a large group construction, this planning process can help individual children begin to anticipate what will

Figure 4.12. Ms. Burd gathered references for the children to use in constructing their doghouses, including plans developed by children.

Figure 4.13. Preschoolers' plans can be quite detailed, but it is the process of planning and thinking through what they want to do that is most valuable.

One of the biggest benefits of the Project Approach is the opportunity it provides for children to use their strengths or expertise to contribute to the project.

need to be done. In addition, it can help the class as a whole develop a shared vision of the work they need to complete together. Once the plans have been shared, teachers and children can refer to the plans as children work on their construction (e.g., "Remember the window we saw on Peter's plan? How could we make one?"). Although children can work individually on their own plans, several children may want to work together on one plan. For example, the children in Mrs. Utz's class decided that they wanted to build a big planter for flowers. The children first voted on what they wanted to plant in the planter (see Figure 4.14), and then they drew a diagram for the planter they wanted to build. Four children collaborated to design this plan. With Mrs. Utz's assistance, they measured and recorded the measurements. A parent of one of the children then brought tools to class and constructed the planter with the assistance of some children. Once the planter was completed, a small group of children went through a collection of packets of seeds and selected marigolds and vegetables to plant.

Encourage Children to Use Peers as Resources

One of the biggest benefits of the Project Approach is the oppovrtunity it provides for children to use their strengths or expertise to contribute to the project. Many of these opportunities arise naturally as children become engaged in a group construction. Teachers can capitalize on these experiences to further enhance children's abilities to make contributions and to appreciate the strengths of their peers.

Group constructions provide hands-on experiences and typically evolve over a period of days or even weeks. Thus, there are many possibilities for a variety of partners to work together on simple and complex tasks. Teachers can intentionally encourage partner work that will take advantage of a child's strengths in one domain to support his or her development in another. Intentionally partnering children whose strengths are complementary can help support children's growth. For instance, by pairing an outgoing child with a peer who has limited social skills, both children can benefit. As the children in Mrs. Utz's class began the construction of the planter, many tasks arose that required a range of skills. These tasks provided Mrs. Utz with opportunities to involve children who might otherwise avoid social situations. For example, she invited a socially withdrawn child to work on a simple task with a boy who was outgoing and friendly.

One way that teachers can help children recognize and take advantage of one another's strengths is to intentionally create opportunities for children to acknowledge those strengths. For example, at circle time, Mrs. Utz pointed out that there are images and words on the sides of many planters, and she showed the children several examples. She then asked for volunteers to create a design and paint each of the four sides of the classroom planter. The other children were then able to acknowledge and praise the work of the painters.

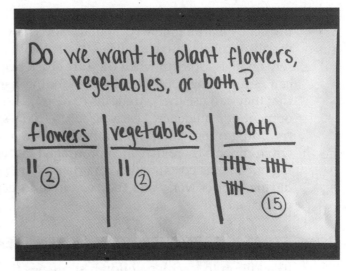

Figure 4.14.   Mrs. Utz created a chart to record the children's votes.

Encouraging cooperative work with partners can help children support one another's learning and build a strong classroom community. Ms. Lavin's second graders worked with the preschoolers on a daily basis as models, co-researchers, and peer investigators. They read books about dogs to their preschool friends and shared information about dogs that they had discovered through their own research. As the second graders played in the pet store or veterinarian office in the dramatic play areas, they naturally modeled more advanced language and play skills for the preschoolers.

Ms. Burd's and Ms. DeLuca's preschoolers also provided models that inspired the second graders. The range of abilities of the preschoolers in their rooms was broad, and the class included several students who were very skilled at creating three-dimensional representations with boxes, tools, and tape. When Ms. Burd and Ms. DeLuca provided cardboard and cardboard boxes, several preschoolers designed and constructed rather elaborate doghouses. These artifacts inspired Ms. Lavin's second graders, and they began to research doghouses in books and online to create their own designs.

When teachers see the potential for learning during group construction, they spend time supporting the learning opportunities that often arise. For example, group construction provides many opportunities for children to practice problem solving and conflict resolution. It took Ms. Harrison's students more than a week to complete their bookshelf construction. Over that period, it underwent many revisions, and there were numerous opportunities for children to collaborate and to successfully encounter and resolve conflicts. For example, as Addelyn and Stella worked on the shelves, Addelyn wanted to use the piece of cardboard that Stella was working with. Addelyn tried explaining why it was important, but when Stella said she was using it, Addelyn adjusted and found another piece that would work. Ms. Harrison provided a safety net by staying in close proximity to the children as they negotiated. See Video 4.13 for an example of how the teacher supported both children as they figured out materials.

Teaching children strategies that can help them be successful investigators enables them to become more independent, confident, and engaged researchers. Teacher-implemented supports and accommodations can help all children realize these benefits. Helping children to understand that they can communicate their ideas about a project by learning new vocabulary and drawing their plans motivates them to engage in future collaborative inquiries. Learning that their peers are a resource that they can rely on to assist them when they are stuck helps children develop confidence that they can figure things out. This understanding happens in concert with children learning that they can use their strengths to help their peers too, which also supports the development of confidence. Learning to use tools such as clipboards and pens as a way of recording information can motivate children to collect and share data. Learning in an environment where they are encouraged to think creatively engages children in thinking outside the box and in taking risks. Young children gradually learn these strategies during project work, and they continue to develop with every project in which they participate.

USING STRATEGIES TO SUPPORT CHILDREN'S LEARNING

In addition to teaching children strategies that will help them become capable investigators, there are strategies that teachers themselves can use to provide a context in which children have optimal opportunities to develop their knowledge, skills, dispositions, and feelings within a project. Teachers can support children's learning when they 1) hone children's ability to ask thought-provoking questions, 2) encourage children to use a word wall, 3) promote participation in a Project History Board, 4) periodically revisit children's knowledge of the topic, and 5) periodically help children review and revise their questions about a topic.

Ask Thought-Provoking Questions

Strategically posed questions can help children develop a deeper understanding of a topic and provoke them to deepen their understanding and think more creatively. In general, open-ended questions are more useful than closed-ended questions. Here are some examples of starters for open-ended questions:

- Why do you think that happened?
- Why is the . . . ?
- What makes you think so?
- What do you think might happen?
- What would happen if . . . ?
- What is happening?
- How could we find out more?
- How could we . . . ?
- I wonder how we could . . . ?
- What else could we try?
- Where else could we go?

Closed-ended questions have only one right answer and require a child to retrieve information. In essence, once the child answers the question, the conversation is over.

Conversely, open-ended questions encourage children to use their imagination, to collaborate, and to engage in further conversation with others. Engaging in meaningful conversations supports the development of oral language, and research has shown that

preschool teachers do not provide adequate opportunities for this type activity (Whorrall & Cabell, 2016). Project work provides a child-centered environment in which teachers are curious about what each child thinks, what each child wonders, and how each child thinks the group should proceed. This way of teaching sends a message to children that their ideas are important and can contribute to the work of the group. Interactions are most beneficial when teachers pose open-ended questions to prompt children

> Project work provides a child-centered environment in which teachers are curious about what each child thinks, what each child wonders, and how each child thinks the group should proceed.

to respond and when teachers allow adequate wait time so that children can process the information before responding. During the Library Project, Ms. Harrison asked questions to prompt children to make predictions about how things work at the library. For example, she referenced a conversation she had been having with a child about a torn page in a book, as she wondered out loud about how they fix books that are damaged at the library. See Video 4.14 in which Ms. Harrison prompts children to makes predictions.

Note that many children respond to questions or prompts quickly, but some children need extra time to process what they heard. This is especially true for children with certain disabilities such as deafblindness or multiple disabilities (Johnson & Parker, 2013). Waiting a few extra seconds for a child to respond before prompting a response can result in important benefits. Experts recommend that teachers wait 3–5 seconds before repeating or rephrasing a question. This can be challenging for teachers who are used to moving conversations along quickly. It requires that adults become active listeners who intentionally monitor their own wait time.

When teachers model asking thought-provoking questions, children learn to enjoy the stimulating discussions that follow, and they begin to ask their own questions. At the beginning of the Dog Project, Ms. Lavin introduced her second graders to the idea of recording their thoughts and questions on a web. She started each web on chart paper and made it accessible to her students, who recorded their questions on these webs throughout the project. This was a new teaching strategy for Ms. Lavin that she grew to value because it engaged the children with research questions that they could work to answer. For example, a discussion about animal shelters began as a result of questions that the children had recorded on the web, and a class project to raise money for a local no-kill animal shelter grew out of these initial questions. The second graders conducted a school-wide fundraiser and collected $618.00 in donations in 1 week for the shelter (see Figure 4.15).

Use a Word Wall

A word wall is a space on the classroom wall where vocabulary words are displayed, along with pictures that symbolize each word. These words also can be displayed on the Project History Board. Sometimes the words on the word wall are arranged alphabetically in columns; for example, the wall might display a column for words that begin with the letter *A*, a column of words that begin with the letter *B*, and so on. Words related

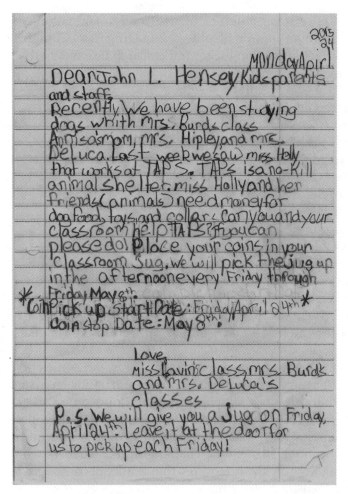

Figure 4.15. The second graders wrote this fund-raising letter to the other children and staff members at their school.

to the project topic are great additions to the class word wall. Many teachers also like to print a version of these words as word cards and provide them on a book ring for children to use in the writing center. By using the word wall or the book ring, children can copy words when they want to make project-related labels or signs.

Teachers can make the identification of project-related words for the word wall a part of their regular classroom routine. For example, after reading a topic-related book to the large group, teachers can ask their students if there are any new words they learned that they would like to add to the word wall. These words can be written on index cards, and corresponding images can be added by drawing pictures or pasting images from magazines or the Internet onto the cards. In some situations, children might be interested in writing the words or drawing the images themselves. This can provide teachers with opportunities to encourage children to become writers, and it provides teachers with opportunities to scaffold children's emerging writing skills.

Ms. Burd and Ms. DeLuca made a word wall that was specifically about dogs. They drew an image of a dog on a large piece of butcher paper and posted it on the wall. Over the course of the project, they labeled parts of the dog and dog accessories (see Figure 4.16). The diagram could be removed from the wall and placed on a table so that children could comfortably draw and label pictures on it.

During the Library Project, Ms. Harrison posted library-related words in two places. She used a portable word wall that incorporated child-made word cards and provided a written model of the word for children to copy. She then coached them through writing the word, as depicted in Video 4.15. Ms. Harrison also posted labeled photographs of elements of the library on the Project History Board. She labeled some of the photographs, whereas others were labeled by children.

Build Participation in the Project History Board

Teachers should update the Project History Board throughout Phase II. Samples of daily project-related events that tell the story of the evolution of the children's investigation and their most current findings and questions serve as the documentation used on the Project History Board. Decisions regarding what to include on the Project History Board do not need to be the teacher's alone. Consulting the children about what samples should be added to the board can help teachers gain insight into children's thinking about a project. This practice also increases children's reflection on their own thinking, or metacognition. In addition to selecting samples for the Project History Board, children can dictate narratives that describe the samples they select and what these samples reveal about the progress of the project. The Project History Board created by Ms. DeLuca and Ms. Burd included a variety of

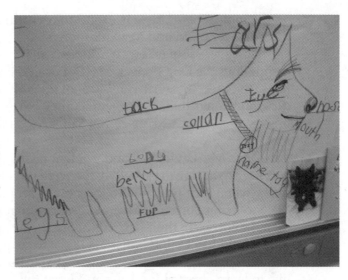

Figure 4.16. In this alternate type of word wall, children and teachers labeled parts of dogs and dog accessories.

types of documentation, such as photos, sketches, sculptures, and charts. Ms. Harrison regularly consulted with her students about what should be posted on the Project History Board, and she encouraged them to make individual contributions. For example, when a child used emergent writing to record her question, Ms. Harrison assisted her in posting it on the board.

Revisit Knowledge of the Topic

The topic web is a living document that exists throughout the course of a project. At the beginning of Phase II, there may be only a few entries on the topic web, especially if the topic is unfamiliar to many children. However, as teachers revisit the web over time, they can discuss ideas for what should be added with the children. Teachers can track the development of children's understanding about the topic by using a color-coding system. For example, they might add ideas from the children on February 6 with a green marker and record the date in green in a key in the margins of the web. A few days later, on February 9, they might revisit the web with their students and record their additions with a purple marker. They would then use the purple marker to add February 9 to the key in the margin.

Because projects are long-term investigations and are not the whole curriculum, it is not unusual for there to be days when project work does not occur. Teachers sometimes wonder if children have lost interest in a topic and if they should bring the project to an end. Interest can often be reignited by revisiting the topic web or by introducing a new experience or object. When Ms. DeLuca and Ms. Burd felt that interest was waning in the Dog Project, they revisited the topic web with their students to identify new areas to research.

Review and Revise Questions About the Topic

As the project progresses, uncovering the answer to one question may lead to another question. As children learn new information during visits from experts, firsthand investigation, research in books and online, and fieldwork, they gradually become experts on the topic. Therefore, it is useful to revisit the children's questions with them, record their answers, and add new questions.

However, some "big questions" may last throughout a project. For example, throughout the Dog Project, Ms. DeLuca, Ms. Burd, and Ms. Lavin continued to revisit the questions, "In what ways are all dogs the same, and in what ways are some dogs different from others?" Over time, they researched similarities and differences in dog breeds, dog color, texture of fur, tail sizes, and ear position (e.g., up or down, short or long).

Once Ms. Lavin's second graders heard the preschoolers talk about their experiences with the dog project, they too were full of questions, which they recorded on chart paper when they returned to their own classroom after the preschoolers' presentation. Ms. Lavin supported her second graders in generating more questions by asking them to make entries in their journals about their research findings and to describe what else they would like to find out about dogs. New questions that emerged were more specific and reflected the children's growing expertise. For example, one child wrote, "I would like to learn about a dog's jaw and what the jaws do." Other examples follow:

- Why do dogs hate cats?

- How many breeds are there?

- How are dogs different from people?

- Do dogs talk in different languages?

- Do dogs have their own language?

- How do you tell how old a dog is?

- What kinds of leashes and collars are there?

- What do you use to groom a dog?

- Can dogs do what we do?

- What is dog food made of?

Ms. Harrison selected a few of the questions from the children's initial list and asked them to make predictions about the answers. As they began to learn more about the library, she revisited the questions with her students, recording their answers, so that they could see if their predictions were accurate (see Video 4.16). For this purpose, teachers use their judgment to select questions that the children will likely be able to answer and that have potential to result in new, useful information.

Teachers can use strategies to provide a context in which children have ample opportunities to develop their knowledge, skills, dispositions, and feelings within a project. Asking thought-provoking questions can help children think more deeply and creatively about a topic. Encouraging children to use a word wall not only helps children learn to read and write, but also builds project-related vocabulary and supports communication about the project. Encouraging children to participate in the documentation of a project on the Project History Board helps children feel a sense of ownership in the project, and when the teacher periodically revisits what children have learned about the topic, their new knowledge can be recorded there. Similarly, periodically revisiting and revising the children's list of questions is a way to document their growing knowledge about the project topic and the direction of the inquiry.

Invite Guest Experts to Visit

Inviting guest experts to visit the class can add significantly to the children's interest in learning more about the project. Teachers can use several strategies to help children obtain optimal benefit from the visit.

Teachers can tell the children a little bit about the person who will be visiting, so they can begin to anticipate the visit. For example, in the Library Project, Ms. Harrison arranged to have Ms. Malavika Shrikhande, a librarian from the St. Ambrose University library, visit. Ms. Harrison shared that Ms. Shrikhande was the parent of a child who had been in Ms. Harrison's room previously and that she was coming to answer their questions.

Teachers can ask the children if they have any questions that they would like to ask that are specific to the guest expert and their job. Ms. Harrison provided several opportunities for children to think of questions in both small and large group settings. One morning shortly before Ms. Shrikhande's visit, Ms. Harrison asked each child to think of a question he or she especially wanted to ask Ms. Shrikhande, and she recorded the questions on a paper with the child's name on it. That helped her to have individual conversations with the children about the visit; it also allowed her to individualize the amount of scaffolding that she provided for children who were learning to form questions. In Video 4.17, Ms. Harrison records a question, while promoting a child's emergent writing.

When teachers contact guest experts and invite them to the classroom, it is helpful to the guest experts if teachers provide them with some background information about the project, such as how it developed, what the children's current questions are, and what they hope the children will get out of the visit. It is also helpful if teachers explain the level of detail that should be included and the ideal length of the visit. This is especially important when the guest expert does not have experience communicating with preschoolers. When Ms. Harrison invited Ms. Shrikhande, they spent 45 minutes chatting about the project, the children's questions, and the goals of the visit.

On the day of the visit, children may be very excited, so it is helpful if teachers set clear expectations about the children's role in hosting a guest expert. Ms. Harrison helped the children practice saying Ms. Shrikhande's first name, Malavicka, and they discussed how to treat a visitor. On the day of the visit, the children greeted Ms. Shrikhande very graciously, as captured in Video 4.18. On the day Ms. Shrikhande visited, Ms. Harrison passed out the question each child had dictated to help the children remember what to ask. One child was curious about whether there were toys at the library, which led to a conversation about the difference between buying something and checking out a book from the library.

Children will get more benefit from the guest expert's visit if the teacher helps them reflect on what they learned and records the answers they received to their questions. Ms. Harrison worked with small groups to record the answers to their questions (see Video 4.19).

SUPPORTING FIELDWORK

Fieldwork (also referred to as a field trip) is an important component of the Project Approach. In addition to books, web sites, and other written reference materials, children need opportunities to do hands-on research.

Identify Opportunities for On-Site Fieldwork

Teachers often do not have access to transportation or permission to take their students on field trips. Even when teachers can take a field trip with their students, they may only be able to go on one field trip. Bringing authentic materials into the classroom can allow for on-site fieldwork and therefore serve as a way to overcome these barriers. For example, in the case of the Garden Project, Mrs. Utz provided children with hands-on experiences with a variety of plants and planting in a variety of containers. The class explored a variety of gardening tools and experimented with composting. Children in Ms. DeLuca's class and Ms. Burd's class initially took a field trip to PetSmart. To supplement that experience, the teachers brought many dog accessories and grooming tools into the classroom, and the class had multiple visits from the therapy dog. On one of these occasions, the class was able to observe the therapy dog having his fur trimmed. In addition, the class invited a staff member from the animal shelter to visit their room, which led to a fund-raiser organized by the second graders. Finally, toward the end of the Dog Project, a police officer and his dog visited the students at school.

Prepare Children to Ask Questions During Fieldwork

Fieldwork allows children to venture outside of their school environment and explore new or unfamiliar places. The location of the fieldwork might be easy to access, such as a walk down the hall to the school's library, or it might require transportation by automobile or bus. In either case, teachers should arrange for an expert to meet the children at the field site; the expert should be someone who is willing and prepared to answer their questions. Prior to a field trip, teachers can prepare children by recording a list of the questions they hope to have answered during their visit. Teachers can help the children successfully interview an expert by providing them with opportunities to practice posing the questions. For example, teachers can ask children to volunteer to ask specific questions from the list. Teachers can write each child's question on an index card and encourage the children to draw an illustration to accompany their question. Children can carry their cards with them when they interview a guest expert, as the cards provide a visual reminder of the question. Ms. Burd and Ms. DeLuca found that this process helped the children to understand the interview process. In addition, the teachers noticed that by the time the police officer visited their class toward the end of Phase II, the children spontaneously asked their own questions.

Prior to taking a field trip, teachers can make a preliminary visit to the field site so that they can anticipate opportunities for the children to make discoveries about the topic during their trip. This is particularly important when the site of the field trip is unfamiliar to teachers. Teachers also can share the list of child-developed questions with the experts before the trip and talk with the experts about the level of detail that is appropriate for the group of children, given their age. Teachers also can inform the expert about any special seating or other accommodations that may be needed due to students' disabilities. Ms. Harrison took her students to a local library for their field trip. She prepared for this trip by visiting with the children's librarian who would lead their tour and by providing the librarian with the children's questions. Consequently, when the children visited, the tour included information about repairing books and bar codes, two aspects of the library that children had been curious about throughout the project. In Video 4.20, the children pretend to check out a book at the library by scanning the bar code.

Fieldwork is a major element of project work as it provides children with firsthand experience and knowledge of the topic, and they are able to engage with the topic with all their senses. When transportation is limited, it is important for teachers to bring authentic, firsthand experiences into their classrooms. Fieldwork will be more successful when children are prepared in advance to ask questions and collect data and when the representatives at the site are aware of the children's interests and questions.

> Fieldwork is a major element of project work and provides children with firsthand experience and knowledge of the topic.

CONCLUSION

In this chapter, we covered ways in which teachers can support and deepen young children's active investigations. Children develop a sense of confidence in their own abilities as they uncover the answers to their questions through firsthand investigations and through conducting research using nonfiction books and informative web sites. They delight in representing their knowledge of a topic through individual and group representations. Children also find it satisfying to summarize what they have learned on Project History Boards. In the next chapter, we look at ways in which teachers can help young children summarize and represent their learning in Phase II and how they plan and hold a culminating event in Phase III.

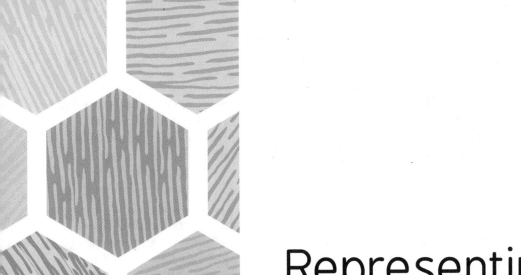

Representing and Sharing Project Work

The field trip to the car wash was a wonderful success. Ms. Carly was amazed at how attentive the children were, how much they understood, and how engaged they were during the question and answer part of the visit. After the field trip, even Ms. Carly had a new appreciation for the way car washes work. As the class returned to their school, Ms. Carly found herself wondering where to go next with the project. She noticed that Item #41 on the Implementation Checklist suggests that teachers ask children what they would like to make to show what they have learned about the topic they are investigating. She decided to give this a try at group meeting, and she was not at all surprised when all of her students expressed a strong desire to build a car wash. The children dictated a list of what would be involved in completing this construction, and soon the building of a classroom car wash was underway. Ms. Carly was so pleased to see all of her students involved in the project in some way.

Once children have completed their fieldwork, interviewed relevant experts, and conducted sufficient in-class research to answer their questions, the teacher should guide them to summarize what they have learned. As children reflect on their experiences and findings and organize the information, they typically create something together that represents an important aspect of the topic they have come to understand over the course of the project. The class might create a convertible in a project on cars, a cow in a project on farm animals, or a check-out lane in a project on the grocery store. When the children are satisfied that they have learned all they want to about the topic and have adequately represented it, the teacher should help them plan one or more culminating activities or events. Culminating events bring closure to the project and take place during the final phase of a project. For example, children may give a presentation to parents or to other classes in which they describe the project and share their findings and possibly some documentation, or they may share a group representation from Phase II (Illinois Early Learning Project, 2018). Planning and presenting a culminating event compose Phase III of a project. This chapter discusses the various ways that children can represent their new knowledge and understanding, as well as the ways that adults can help children to plan, celebrate, and summarize their learning.

PHASE II: EXPRESSING NEW KNOWLEDGE AND UNDERSTANDING

After interviewing guest experts and conducting in-class research and fieldwork in the beginning of Phase II, children typically have acquired a great deal of new information. Next, teachers can guide them in organizing and expressing this information in a variety of ways with the goal of helping them to reflect on and integrate or consolidate it. They may do this by helping children develop group visual organizers and representations.

Involve Children in Creating Visual Organizers

As children collect data through their research in the classroom and on field trips, the teacher can help them organize and display the information in a variety of ways. Visual organizers help children show the ways in which the experiences they have had and the knowledge they have gathered are related. As the teacher critically considers the nature of the information that children have acquired, he or she can then determine the format for the display.

Children will have experience with concept maps or webs throughout Phases I and II of the project, as discussed in Chapter 3. As Phase II draws to a close, the teacher can invite the children to revisit some of these webs to see if there are other details they would like to add, or the children may decide to combine information from different webs. As the teacher revises the webs on behalf of the children, children get to see the processes of revising and editing in action.

In addition to webs, the children may choose to use other types of graphic organizers to summarize their new understandings. They can organize their findings using a Venn diagram, flow chart, timeline, cycle, or graph. For example, as they began their project, Ms. DeLuca and Ms. Burd sent home a survey to ask about dogs that were a part of each child's family. Once the completed surveys were collected, children assisted in transferring their individual survey data to a chart that showed classwide results (see Figure 5.1). The chart was displayed on the class Project History Board. The children also created graphs that showed who did or did not own a dog, and they made charts about what types of food dogs eat and the many ways to care for dogs. They also made charts depicting the various colors and fur types they observed in dogs.

Children also surveyed other classes about whether they preferred dogs or cats and created a graph that summarized that data. In addition, the children made flow charts that explained how to care for dogs and the steps for giving a dog a bath. After their trip to observe a dog that lived in the school neighborhood (Izzy, the Scottish Terrier), Ms. Burd and Ms. DeLuca recorded the children's observations on a chart; they included children's names on the display because this helps children recall their thoughts. Following is the list of children's observations that Ms. Burd and Ms. DeLuca posted:

Figure 5.1. A center was set up so that children could participate in the class chart that summarized family survey data.

Izzy can run. – Liam

The dog licks us. – Aiden

Izzy barks. – Christian

Izzy can go super fast. – Liam

Izzy barks when she sees a squirrel. – Zane

Her can play. – David

Izzy can go potty. – Liam

She peed and pood. – Christian

Her can run super fast. – Draven

Izzy is black. – Everybody

She can run, run, run. – Liam

Her can sit. That's her trick. – Draven

Her ears pop up when she hears stuff. – Zane

Izzy flips, spins around, and runs in circles. – Christian

When we say Izzy her ears pop up. – Draven and Arden

Izzy is a girl. – Amelia

Izzy is a Scottie. – Ms. Burd

She tried to run to it. – Zach

Izzy can run from squirrels. She doesn't like them. – Zach

Izzy has a big nose. – Luke

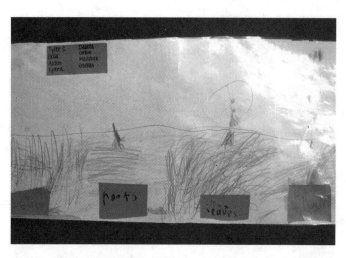

Figure 5.2. A team of eight children developed a mural that showed the stages of development of plants. Each stage was labeled (i.e., seed, roots, stem and leaves, flower).

In her class, Mrs. Utz's students created a mural depicting the stages of growth of plants (see Figure 5.2).

Teachers often collect data from project-related experiences and insert them in binders. For example, Ms. Burd and Ms. Deluca organized a binder with images and artifacts from the preschoolers' class trip to the pet store. They also created notebooks titled, *Eli Therapy Dog and Friend*, *Book About Dogs We Know*, and *Classroom Dog Research*. Ms. Lavin's second graders created their own individual notebooks titled *My Dog Project*. Their notebooks included written descriptions and pictorial plans of the doghouse they planned to build, individual webs about things they learned from guest experts, a description of their favorite dog breed, and a list of their favorite dog names.

Help Children Decide How to Show What They Now Know

After children have completed their fieldwork or interviewed a guest expert, they are typically ready to create a group representation about what they have learned. Working together to represent what they have learned provides a sense of community, helps solidify what children have learned, and often leads to additional questions. The children might collaborate to construct a large model, paint a mural, or develop a playscape, such as a grocery store, bike shop, or veterinarian's office, by transforming the dramatic play area. Teachers may accommodate both needs—the need for a traditional dramatic play area and the need for a project-related playscape—by reducing the size of the housekeeping area and encouraging children to construct an adjacent playscape. (See the Illinois Early Learning Project web site, https://illinoisearlylearning.org/resources/pa/projects, for information about the Tractor Project, Combine Project, Cow Project, Fish Project, and House Project and more details on how this can be accomplished.)

> Working together to represent what they have learned provides a sense of community, helps solidify what children have learned, and often leads to additional questions.

The children in Ms. Harrison's class decided to create a model. While on their field trip to the library, the children were fascinated by the book-sorting machine. Library patrons would drive up to the side of the library and drop their book or other media through a slot. The item would land on a conveyor belt, and the conveyor belt would carry the item to the correct bin for the media type and drop it in. Each child had a chance to send a library item down the conveyor belt (see Video 5.1). After their field trip to the library, Ms. Harrison printed out pictures of the various things they had seen and had conversations with the class about what they would like to make to show what they learned. See Video 5.2, in which one child, Stella, reflects on the book-sorting machine in a conversation with Ms. Harrison. Many of the children were very enthusiastic about constructing a book sorter. Over the course of the next week, the children worked to create the computer terminal, conveyor belt, and bins; Quinn constructed a screen for the sorting machine, as depicted in Video 5.3. Ms. Harrison supported this work by prompting children to examine the construction and by asking them what else was needed. As the book sorter took shape, the children began to pretend with it (see Video 5.4). They continued to add to it until they were satisfied with its accuracy, including the drive-up window. See Video 5.5 and Video 5.6, in which the children revise the book sorter and create a drive-up window.

Teachers might begin the discussion about what kind of group construction children would like to make by reviewing some of the major events in the project up to that point. The teacher can ask, "What are some of the things we've done so far in our project? That's right, we've been to the pet store, we've spent time with a therapy dog, and we've visited dogs in our neighborhood." The teacher might then say, "Wow! We have found out a lot about dogs. What do you think we could create to show what we have learned?" If children are new to project work, they may not have enough experience with group representation to offer suggestions. In that case, to get the discussion started, the teacher can provide some examples of things that the children might make. She might offer, "We could make a giant dog, or a pet store, or a mural about dogs." As children begin to make their own suggestions, the teacher can record them on a chart; disagreements can be resolved by voting.

Help Children Plan for Group Representation

Many benefits are realized by children as they undertake a group representation with their peers. This process requires discussion, compromise, hypothesizing, resolving differences of views, experimenting, problem solving, and collaboration. Children benefit from one another as they use their personal strengths and abilities for the benefit of the group. Imagine a child who has strong numeracy skills or one who has an incredible amount of knowledge related to animals and how these children can serve as resources or experts for their peers. As children engage in group representation, they often come to realize that they need to conduct further research on the topic, which can lead to them sharing their ideas and discoveries with one another.

Once the class has agreed on what they want to make, teachers can engage the children in planning. This can be done during small or large group discussions in which teachers ask children to suggest materials that will be needed, sources for the materials, their suggestions concerning the location for their work, aspects of the topic that they want to include in their representation, and various strategies for completing their work. If these discussions take place in small groups, ideas from the small group discussions can be shared with the larger group when they meet. Teachers may realize that some of the children's suggestions for materials or construction strategies are not going to work, but they should see this as an opportunity for children to problem-solve together. For example, imagine that the children involved in the Dog Project wanted to construct a check-out counter for the pet store, and they suggested that they could make it out of paper, tape, and blocks. The teacher could provide her students with paper, tape, and blocks, but anticipating the potential problems with their plan, she could have other materials on hand, such as boards, large pieces of heavy cardboard, or packing tubes that could serve as counter legs, that the children could experiment with to solve their problem. Teachers can subtly encourage the children to use these materials as a resource by calmly saying something such as, "If you run into any trouble and want my help, I'll be over there, so just let me know."

Teachers who are new to project work are sometimes hesitant to help children begin a group representation. For example, if a class is doing a project on the airport, and students tell the teacher that they would like to build an airplane, the teacher might become anxious if he or she has never built an airplane and cannot envision the materials that will be needed or the steps children will have to take to complete it. However, it is important to keep in mind that the goal of engaging children in group representation is not just the end product; rather, it is providing involvement in the complex processes of working together and solving problems collaboratively as they arise.

Revisit Plans for Group Representation   It is helpful to create opportunities for revisiting the children's plans for their group representations as a part of the daily routine. Teachers can ask the children to review what has been accomplished, discuss revisions in their plans, and make suggestions about additional features to add. As they review the Dog Project, the teacher might ask, "What do you think about making one of those special hair vacuums that the dog groomer used?" Ideas for additions to the representation typically become more detailed as the product takes shape over time. For example, a group construction of a car began with seats and a steering wheel, but by the time it was completed, it included a tinted windshield, windshield wipers, a gas tank, a CD player, a battery, pedals, and an elaborate dashboard (Beneke, 1998).

It is not unusual for project work to slow down or even pause at times due to school or center holidays or special school events. In this case, the teacher may have to reignite interest in the group representation by revisiting plans with the children, bringing in new objects or materials, or demonstrating a new strategy that can be used in representation. For example, in a project on trees, the teacher might demonstrate how to make a leaf print by placing a leaf under a piece of muslin cloth and pounding it with a hammer (Williams, Rockwell, & Sherwood, 1987). This experience would serve to reignite the children's interest in trees and could even lead them to decide to create a group representation of a tree.

Provide Time and Space for Group Representation   Teachers who are new to project work often wonder how working on a group representation will fit into their daily schedule. Preschool teachers typically incorporate project work into their choice time activities, whereby working on the group representation becomes one of the choices available to children. In some cases, there might be more than one center set up to work on the representation. For example, if young children are constructing a large airplane, children at one table might construct propellers, while children at another table design a logo to go on the side of the airplane. Teachers often establish a special time for project work in classrooms with older children, such as first or second graders. This can be helpful when schedules for visits to the library, gym, art, and music rooms can make extended center time a challenge. Because older children can work more independently, several work centers can be arranged.

Although finding a place to work on group representations can at first appear problematic for teachers with limited space, this problem can be resolved in a variety of ways. Some teachers eliminate an existing center, such as the block or art area, for the duration of the project and use that area for the group representation center. Alternatively, the size of one center might be reduced to make space for the group representation.

Other teachers have negotiated the size of the group representation with their students. For example, after staff from the animal shelter visited Ms. Burd and Ms. DeLuca's classroom, the children said they wanted to make an animal shelter. Ms. Burd and Ms. DeLuca suggested that, because they had already made the dramatic play areas into a pet store and a veterinarian clinic, they did not have space for a large animal shelter. Instead, these teachers suggested that the children create a miniature animal shelter on the class train table.

Supply Materials for Group Representation   As teachers listen to children's ideas and plans, they can anticipate materials that will lend themselves to representation. For example, if children plan to create an airplane, the teacher might bring in heavy-duty aluminum foil or silver paint. Likewise, if children want to paint a mural about dogs, the teacher can help them mix paints that reflect the natural colors of dog fur.

Materials that can be used in a variety of ways are useful in representations, especially large-scale group constructions. Recyclables, such as cardboard boxes and tubes can be wonderful resources in this regard. Parents are often eager to assist with project work and willing to provide recyclable materials. One teacher made a display by the door to her class with samples of the types of recyclables the class needed for their construction. She put a box next to the display, and soon parents filled it with exactly the types of materials that she and her students needed.

Teach Children Skills to Use in Group Representation   When children work on large three-dimensional constructions, they are often challenged to use skills or strategies that are not typically taught in school or not typically taught to children of their age or developmental level. For example, children might need to engage in writing, tracing, measuring, drilling, nailing, sewing, gluing, or folding tasks to complete their construction. These skills are not typically taught to young children. The teacher can assist children in developing such skills by providing tools and materials and teaching them how to do these challenging tasks safely.

Scaffold When Tasks Are Too Difficult

We often underestimate what children are able to do with a little assistance. It is the teacher's role to provide each child with the type and level of assistance that the child needs to achieve his or her goal. Instructional scaffolding is a process that requires teachers to evaluate children's current experiences and knowledge in order to effectively build on them as they are learning new skills. To scaffold, teachers offer the amount of support needed to allow a child to accomplish the task that requires the skills. The supports, or scaffolding, are temporary and adjustable, so teachers gradually reduce the amount of support provided as students master the skills and accomplish the task independently (IRIS Center, 2018b). Teachers who have reported success in engaging their pupils with project work indicate that they scaffold for their students so that the students are able to accomplish their goals, while maximizing opportunities for independence and creativity. Individual strengths and needs must be considered. For example, Addelyn wanted to make a fish tank for the class library shelf construction. Ms. Harrison scaffolded for her by holding the tape so that

> We often underestimate what children are able to do with a little assistance. It is the teacher's role to provide each child with the type and level of assistance that the child needs to achieve his or her goal.

Addelyn could cut it herself and by helping her to insert the "fish tank" into the holder Addelyn created (see Video 5.7).

PHASE III: CELEBRATING AND SUMMARIZING ACCOMPLISHMENTS

In Phase III, the project comes to a close. This phase allows children to reflect on their experiences during the project work, share their accomplishments, and show what they have learned. With the teacher's assistance, children are able to look back on the history of their work together, organize their ideas, and communicate their achievements with others through a culminating event. The culminating event may be as simple as inviting another class in to listen to a presentation about the project, or as was done in the case of the Dog Project, it may be as complicated as a reception that includes members of the school, community, and media. In either case, it is a celebration.

Summarize and Celebrate Children's Accomplishments

As in the first two phases of the Project Approach, children continue to make plans and decisions in Phase III. The first step for teachers in Phase III is to ask the children how they would like to celebrate the completion of their project. Children who have been involved in previous projects may make suggestions based on past project celebrations (e.g., "Let's invite Mrs. Smith's class to come over for a party," "Let's invite all our moms and dads and grannies and grandpas and aunts and uncles"). When children are new to project work, it is helpful for the teacher to offer some choices, such as holding an open house, creating a public display, or staging a presentation. The options for a celebration are as limitless as the creativity and energy of the teacher and children. However, as in all stages of the Project Approach, plans and decisions are made in collaboration with the teacher. It is important for teachers to help their students come up with a plan that is realistic and likely to succeed.

> The options for a celebration are as limitless as the creativity and energy of the teacher and children.

In the case of the Dog Project, Ms. DeLuca and Ms. Burd asked the children how they thought they could share all that they had learned about dogs with others in the school and their families. The teachers suggested that the class might create a showcase in the school entry. The children liked this idea and began to plan it.

If several ideas for the culminating event are proposed, the teacher can take advantage of this opportunity for children to vote. Because preschool children are quite egocentric (Trawick-Smith, 2014), they need practice and scaffolding to understand that they may have to set their own ideas aside and adopt those of their peers. Activities such as this provide teachers with opportunities to explain the voting process, and they provide children with opportunities to see how disagreements can be resolved peacefully and how compromise can benefit everybody.

Help Children Plan a Culminating Event

Once the type of culminating event is decided upon, planning can begin. Planning the culminating event is a wonderful opportunity for teachers to engage children in recalling and organizing the events of the project and thinking about how to communicate what they have learned with others. For example, teachers can ask children what they would like their guests to see, where and how the artifacts and documentation of the project should be displayed, and what role the teachers and students should assume in the culminating event. The class can discuss whether refreshments should be served and how much will be needed. They also can discuss how the guests will be invited, such as via phone call, written invitation, verbal invitation, or e-mail. These conversations provide many opportunities for developing language and personal-social skills. For children with individualized education programs, these can be ideal activities in which to work on individual goals.

Teachers assist children in planning for the culminating event by asking them guiding questions and by recording and displaying their plans. Mrs. Utz and her students decided to hold a party in their classroom and invite their families to join them. She began the planning process by recording the children's thoughts as a web (see Figure 5.3). Meanwhile Ms. Burd, Ms. DeLuca, and Ms. Lavin's students decided to host two culminating events over the course of 2 days. The first day was designed for students

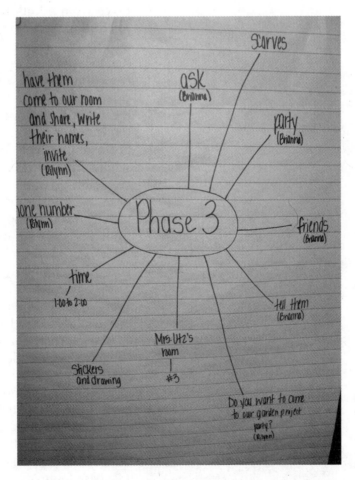

Figure 5.3. Mrs. Utz recorded the children's initial plans for their culminating event as a web.

Figure 5.4. A team of children worked to create the invitation to the culminating event for the Garden Project.

Figure 5.5. The invitation to the Garden Project culminating event read, "Do you want to come to our garden project party? Wed. June 3, 1:00 to 2:00. Mrs. Utz's Room, #3."

and staff at their school, whereas the second day focused on families. The students decided that they would dress up on both days, and they decided to call their culminating events "show-cases." They created a list of four stations that they wanted to develop for the Dog Project Showcase: Dog Research, Eli the Therapy Dog, Izzy, and Thor the Police Dog. As they revisited the plans for the showcase over time, the children and teachers gradually agreed on incorporating additional stations.

Support Children's Efforts to Hold the Culminating Event

Preschoolers typically require assistance from adults to bring their plans to fruition. Teachers support children's efforts by incorporating opportunities for them to create the materials for the culminating event into their lesson plans and by scaffolding children when the tasks they hope to accomplish are too difficult to complete on their own. For example, Mrs. Utz set up a station where children could collaborate to create an invitation to the culminating event of the Garden Project. Children took turns copying print to create the invitations (see Figure 5.4). Mrs. Utz then photocopied the invitations and made sure each child had enough invitations to take home for family members and friends (see Figure 5.5). In addition, her students told Mrs. Utz that they wanted to display their gardening tools during the party, so she planned opportunities for them to create labels for the tools (see Figures 5.6 and 5.7). The children also wanted to give their guests a party favor, so Mrs. Utz helped them create seed packets with a card that read, "Garden Project" (see Figure 5.8).

Ms. Lavin's second graders practiced their communication skills daily as they prepared for the showcases.

They rehearsed how to talk with people, how to stand at their station, what to point out to visitors at their station, and how to ask and answer questions. They decided to record important points on note cards that they could hold at their station, and Ms. Lavin planned a lesson on how to create interesting information for the note cards. Each preschooler was assigned a second-grade partner to present with, and the second graders practiced how to include their early childhood partners in the presentations (see Figure 5.9). As they practiced, the second graders decided it would be nice to

Figure 5.6. Mrs. Utz planned a center where children could work on making labels for tools to use in the tool display at the party celebrating the children's accomplishments in the Garden Project.

have something to give to their guests, so they created dog tags to give away. One side of the dog tag featured a greeting, and the other side had a fact about dogs that they discovered through their research. The second graders also created posters that advertised the Dog Project Showcase (see Figure 5.10).

Ms. Lavin's second graders encountered an unexpected challenge during their first showcase. Students reported that they were having difficulty talking with other students, especially because some of the students in the audience were staring at them. According to Ms. Lavin, the situation created a great opportunity to learn "about how to communicate with other students and plan how to react to someone who responds in a different way, and to understand that it takes a while for some people to process

Figure 5.7. The children who created the labels for the garden tools prepare to display the labeled tools at their party.

Figure 5.8. Children presented guests at their culminating event with a meaningful party favor: packages containing seeds. The packets were labeled, "Garden Project, 2015."

information, and how to respect others' reactions." This lesson helped the children engage in successful social interactions.

Ms. Harrison's students held a discussion about how they could share what they had learned. There were so many items on their list that they decided to create a book about the library. In Video 5.8, Ms. Harrison explains this planning process. With Ms. Harrison's support, the children worked hard to illustrate and narrate the book. This process is captured in Video 5.9 and Video 5.10, where the children review and write about others' drawings.

Figure 5.9. Second-grade and preschool partners practiced presenting information about the Dog Project that was displayed at their station.

Figure 5.10.   Second graders created this poster advertising the Dog Project Showcase. Posters like this were displayed around the school.

Prepare the Final Documentation Display

Although children can help teachers select the documentation for the final display, most of the responsibility for preparing the final display falls on the teacher. However, to the extent possible, it benefits children to be involved in the process. Ms. DeLuca, Ms. Burd, and Ms. Lavin shared their experience:

> The showcase was created over a period of two weeks with children working in groups to select and move items from classroom creations to create displays. Kids worked on backdrops signs, and labels. Second graders wrote and distributed invitations for the showcase event. Children hand-delivered some invitations to administrators. In the last few days prior to the culminating event, children carried their doghouses and other project work to the display area and helped set up their work for viewing. Children knew this was important work and were eager for people to see it.

Displaying documentation of a project provides an opportunity for the teacher to "open a window" (Beneke, Helm, & Steinheimer, 2007, p. 13) on the learning that took place and how project work supported that learning. It also enables the teacher to reflect on his or her own teaching and how it supported children's learning. Ms. DeLuca, Ms. Burd,

> Displaying documentation of a project provides an opportunity for the teacher to "open a window" on the learning that took place and how project work supported that learning.

Figure 5.11. Ms. DeLuca, Ms. Burd, and Ms. Lavin collaborated to create meaningful displays of documentation about the Dog Project.

and Ms. Lavin spent an evening together arranging the final documentation displays (see Figure 5.11), in which key events in the life of the project were showcased; they chose to feature the dog jobs, police dogs, therapy dogs, same/different ears, doghouse construction, parts of a dog, the field trip to the pet store, Izzy, and the animal shelter. The documentation display also included a list of the early learning standards that were met during the project, webs the children dictated, and the children's questions that arose across the life of the project.

Mrs. Utz created documentation panels about the children's composting project, the creation of the large planter, their experiences planting outdoors in the school garden, and the class trip to the botanical garden. She created a book about the children's study of vegetables that included individual children's drawings and quotes for families and children to browse through (see Figure 5.12). Mrs. Utz also displayed lists of children who served on different teams over the course of the project.

Communicate With Families About Children's Accomplishments

No matter how big or small the culminating event turns out to be, teachers should communicate with families and administrators about the impact of the project on children's learning.

No matter how big or small the culminating event turns out to be, teachers should communicate with families and administrators about the impact of the project on children's learning. This communication can take place through documentation displays, newsletters that are sent home, or social media. Such communication provides the teacher with opportunities to highlight the contributions of individual children to the group. Small and large accomplishments can be celebrated through such venues.

Ms. DeLuca, Ms. Burd, and Ms. Lavin held two showcase events to celebrate the Dog Project, one for members of their school and one for family members and the local press. A television crew covered the presentation of the donations the children had collected to the animal shelter, and the shelter announced that they planned to name the next homeless dog after the school.

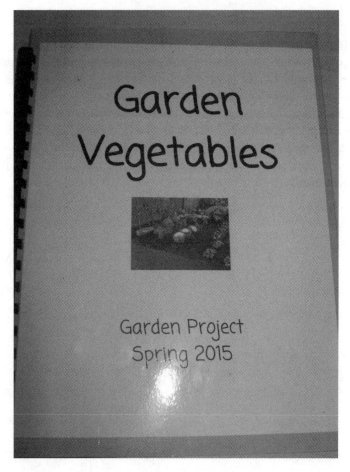

Figure 5.12.   A teacher-made book that documented the children's investigation of gardening. It included children's drawings and thoughts.

To celebrate their project work, Mrs. Utz's class held a party for the children's families and school staff. The children were able to show their family members their work, especially the giant planter they had designed, decorated, and planted. Mrs. Utz shared the documentation with her students' families and further explained the significance of the project for individual children. School staff members who attend such celebrations can see for themselves how capable young children can be and how engaging project work can be for them.

Providing children with opportunities to summarize and reflect on their learning is a valuable component of Phase II. When they are satisfied with their efforts, the class can then plan a culminating event (Phase III). A teacher's efforts to support children's plans for the culminating event and to provide families and decision makers, such as administrators, with attractive evidence of children's learning can contribute to bringing a project to a successful closure.

Teachers who have not previously implemented a project or who attempt to implement a project with inadequate training or support may encounter barriers that prevent them from getting a project started and sustaining it to conclusion.

CONCLUSION

In this chapter, we provided many authentic examples and described ways that teachers can help children organize and share the knowledge they have gained during the investigation through visual organizers or group representations during Phase II of a project. We then described strategies teachers can use for a successful ending, or Phase III, of a project. Although Phase III may be brief, it is important to bring closure to the project and celebrate children's learning. The next chapter examines some of the barriers teachers may experience as they implement project work, and we discuss ways that teachers can find support for growth in their ability to implement the Project Approach successfully.

Sustaining the Project Approach

For their culminating event, the children in Ms. Carly's class invited three other classes to come and hear a presentation about their car wash project. The teachers in the classes, Ms. Alice, Ms. Abby, and Mr. Cam, were amazed at the details children remembered about their field trip and their interest in telling about it. The teachers marveled at the detail reflected in the car wash that the students had constructed. The next day as the teachers were eating lunch, they shared these reflections with Ms. Carly, and she asked them if they would like to form a Project Approach study group. The teachers enthusiastically agreed, so Ms. Carly asked them to share topics they would like to discuss at their first lunchtime meeting. The teachers wondered if the Project Approach would add more work to their already-full plates and how they could combine project work with the early childhood curriculum they were required to use. They wondered if doing project work would be expensive and how they would locate guest experts and field sites. A child in Ms. Alice's class was nonverbal, and she worried that he would not be able to participate in project work. Mr. Cam worried that implementing a project would take away from the time he needed to get his students ready for kindergarten. Ms. Carly shared that she originally had many of the same questions and concerns, and she was still working through some of them. She suggested that they find a book on the Project Approach that they could use as a basis for their discussions and that they invite Ms. Tamara to their first study group meeting to respond to these initial questions.

The Project Approach is not a cookie-cutter approach to teaching; it takes effort, deter-mination, and practice to implement it well. Although this book intends to guide teach-ers smoothly through the process of implementing their first project or reflecting on how existing project work is going, our extensive experience with the Project Approach indicates that a variety of barriers to implementation may arise. In this chapter, we dis-cuss barriers that we and other teachers have confronted. We then share proven solu-tions that educators can apply to their own practice.

BARRIERS AND STRATEGIES FOR IMPLEMENTING THE PROJECT APPROACH

Although the Project Approach has proven benefits for children and educators alike, educators may struggle to change their existing approach, to secure the necessary resources, or to gain the support of important stakeholders. We and teachers whom we have worked with have confronted barriers, including doubts about the ability of children to make real decisions, worry that it will not be possible to teach children with a range of abilities in project work, and insecurity due to a lack of peer support for this way of teaching.

Trust Children to Make Real Decisions

Sharing the control of planning can be difficult for teachers who are new to project work. Teachers may struggle with achieving a good balance between child-led and teacher-directed activities. Teachers may be accustomed to planning in advance for everything that they intend to have happen in the classroom the next day, the next week, or even the next month. They may be accustomed to planning art experiences that produce beautiful or cute products or to running large group time in a fairly organized and consistent manner. Giving some of the control of forthcoming events over to children by asking them what they want to find out or what they would like to make to demon-strate what they know can be challenging. Teachers may not trust children's ability to make good decisions. They may be afraid of embarking on a long-term project in which children continually make decisions about the topic of study and the types of activities that will take place. Giving up this control can be difficult.

To ease into this shared planning and decision making, teachers can preview the experience by providing children with opportunities to make decisions about things where the impact or results are limited or seem manageable to the teacher. For example, teachers might ask children to vote about whether the class should adopt a fish or a hamster, or teachers might identify two thematic units with which they are comfort-able and ask the children to vote for the one they would like to start next. As teachers become more comfortable with offering children choices, they can then open up pos-sibilities for decisions that are elements of project work and are more likely to sup-port inquiry. For example, teachers can list children's questions about the topic of study and create a prediction table, develop their own survey questions and conduct surveys, and ask children to suggest what the class could construct to represent what they have learned. As they give more choice or control to children, teachers may find that chil-dren are more motivated and engaged. For example, during work on a project about butterflies, Sallee Beneke (the first author of this book) asked the preschoolers in her class what they would like to make to show what they had learned. Four children said they would like to make a giant chrysalis. When asked what they would like to use to build the chrysalis, they replied that they wanted a "bunch of plastic soda bottles, some pieces of wood, tape, and some big pieces of paper." In this case, the teacher gave the children total control of planning, and the materials they suggested were provided for them the next day. The four children spent 45 minutes manipulating the materials and discussing how they would put them together to form a chrysalis. In the end, they created a big bundle made up of bottles and small pieces of wood that were taped together. To an outsider's eye, this might not have resembled a chrysalis, but the children were satisfied with their work. If their teacher had been preoccupied with controlling the quality of the end product and had instructed them about what to make it from and how to construct it, the children likely would not have experienced the same level of interest, persistence, teamwork, problem solving, and sense of accomplishment.

Teachers may have many questions: Did children learn as much as they would have if the adults had made the decisions or choices for them? Did the children's control of planning have an impact on their interest and motivation? Were they eager to find out more? Experimenting with elements of the Project Approach can help to build teachers' confidence and trust in the children's eagerness to learn.

Similarly, teachers may want to support children in their self-initiated, independent investigation, but then notice that the children are frustrated and struggling with a problem that they need help to solve. Teachers may wonder when it would be best to step in. A rule of thumb is to only provide as much assistance as children need to be able to continue on their own. Some children need more assistance than others, so the type and amount of support will vary depending on the child and the activity. For example, during the Library Project, Martin wanted to repair a book that had lost a page. After he decided that the pages needed to be taped into the book, Martin struggled with the tape and the tape dispenser, so

> A rule of thumb is to only provide as much assistance as children need to be able to continue on their own. Some children need more assistance than others, so the type and amount of support will vary depending on the child and the activity.

Ms. Harrison assisted him by teaching him how to use the tape dispenser to cut the tape. Martin could then continue to independently repair the book (see Video 6.1).

In other circumstances, children may want to make something, but they might not be sure of how to do so. If that is the case, then it is appropriate for teachers to scaffold for them. For example, teachers might offer children possible choices, like this book's first author did when the preschoolers voted that they wanted to make a giant butterfly. When asked what they would make it from, the children responded with blank stares, so the teacher offered, "Well, you could make it out of large sheets of cloth that you color, or you could make a giant mural, or maybe you could make it out of paper mâché." The children did not know what paper mâché was, but they were intrigued with the idea, and that is what they spent the next week learning about as they constructed a giant butterfly.

Support Children With a Range of Abilities

Teachers with mixed-age preschool classes must address a wide range of abilities. Many teachers work in inclusive settings and therefore teach students with disabilities or developmental delays. Some teachers labor under the misconception that they cannot do project work with struggling learners. But, in fact, teachers experienced with project work are always adjusting the work to the abilities of individual children in their

The degree or type of adjustment or differentiation depends on the child, regardless of whether the child has disabilities, the child is a nonnative speaker, or the child is developmentally advanced. Teachers need to observe carefully and provide opportunities for each child to move forward, and a wonderful characteristic of project work is that there is almost always something for everyone to do at his or her own level of ability.

classes to provide the most satisfying experience for each one. The degree or type of adjustment or differentiation depends on the child, regardless of whether the child has disabilities, the child is a nonnative speaker, or the child is developmentally advanced. Teachers need to observe carefully and provide opportunities for each child to move forward, and a wonderful characteristic of project work is that there is almost always something for everyone to do at his or her own level of ability.

The democratic nature of the Project Approach contributes to the inclusion of all children. For example, children frequently vote during project work on issues big and small (e.g., "Which topic should we study?" "What color should we paint our car?"). Each child has an equal vote, including children with disabilities.

Teachers are sometimes apprehensive about implementing project work in their inclusive settings if they are unsure of how best to support a child who is nonverbal or who has significant language delays. Teachers might be uncertain about the "right way" to involve these children in discussions about what they know or what they want to find out. Teachers may wonder about how to prompt children to ask questions. Veteran teachers who are project implementers and have creatively supported children with a range of abilities have shared useful strategies for supporting the participation of children with language delays in project work. For example, one teacher shared her insights that in such situations she typically includes visual images on the project web so that she can have a child point to something on the web when asked what he or she wants to know more about. If that is too difficult, the teacher might put visuals on a choice board for the child to use or on small cards attached to a ring.

Watching children's play and body language also often provides insight into their knowledge and questions. For example, Shalan Knapke, Gail Lawrence, and Mindy Moses were teachers of young children in the Honeybee room at the St. Ambrose University Children's Campus, where they conducted a Spinach Project. Children in the Honeybee room attend 8 hours a day, 5 days per week. The Spinach Project took place from March through May of 2012. Eight children between the ages of 8 months and 23 months participated in the project, which involved cooking, growing, and eating spinach. The teachers' description of their project is instructive because the children had limited expressive vocabulary, and the teachers took their cues for next steps in the project by introducing materials and watching the children play:

> One day, when Eli (23 months), Conlan (22 months), and Reese (16 months) awoke from their afternoon naps, Gail placed the blender on the floor (after removing the blade) along with a basket of pretend food. The toddlers took turns taking off the lid and placing food inside the blender. Gail watched their investigations and their play using the appliance and decided it would be a good opportunity to bring out a bag of fresh spinach from the classroom refrigerator. She presented it to the children and asked them if they knew what it was. "Milk!" Eli said. "No. What else can it be?" she asked. "Meat!" Eli responded. "Juice!" Eli was making inferences based on his knowledge of food, but it appeared that bags of leafy green vegetables were new to him! "Open!" Eli exclaimed. "We will open the spinach for snack. Would you like to put some in the blender to make smoothies?" Gail asked. "Yes!" Eli responded. (Knapke, Lawrence, & Moses, 2018)

In their reflection on the Spinach Project, the teachers noted that it was very helpful to teach the children to sign words that were useful in the project, such as spinach and carrot, given their emerging verbal abilities.

Lynn Lubben, another veteran teacher of very young children, advised that when "children are learning language, we are giving them the language about the topic as we talk about what we see, what they feel, what they are doing. We can model questioning by putting their actions into a question" (personal communication, March 22, 2017). Ms. Lubben often records each child's question on a separate piece of paper. For example, Sallee Beneke witnessed the arrival of a guest expert, a farmer who brought his sheep, onto the playground. Without prompting, Ms. Lubben's 2-year-old students ran to the classroom to get their questions, which were on sheets of paper taped to the wall, and returned to the playground to eagerly present them to the guest expert.

Ms. Burd, one of the teachers from the Dog Project, shared another strategy, using communication cards:

> I set out books, items of possible interest, new items and then watch . . . adjust . . . watch . . . to see if they start using the "I want" comments with their communication cards/books. This shows me their real interest and more. Many of our children need the introduction more organized for them, and so I give limited choices to begin focusing their attention on the topic. This helps them begin to think and hopefully wonder more about it. I believe that even if they cannot demonstrate to us their full abilities at this time, if we continue to teach and present them with project work, they will benefit. Nonverbal students who have moved on to kindergarten and beyond are now more able to attend to new learning. This is huge.

Teachers have found many creative ways to include nonverbal children or children with limited language in project work, including children who are nonnative speakers. And, as Ms. Burd indicated, these efforts may have a big impact on children's future school success. In addition, the strategies used with one child may prove beneficial for other children as well.

Find Peer Support for the Project Approach in Your School

Ideally the whole teaching staff of a school will decide to learn the Project Approach as a team; this is a wonderful way to get started on including project work in the curriculum. More often, an individual teacher has received training in the Project Approach, but no one else in his or her school is using it. In this case, a teacher may feel isolated and give up trying to implement the approach because of lack of peer or mentor support. When co-teachers and assistant teachers have not had training in the Project Approach, it may be especially difficult to implement it effectively within a classroom. Several strategies and resources are available to help in these situations.

A number of online resources are available that can support teachers in integrating the Project Approach in their classroom and school. For example, since 2007, the Illinois Early Learning Project has sponsored a Project Approach section of their web site that has provided support, resources, and information to teachers, specialists, administrators, and trainers interested in implementing the Project Approach (https://illinoisearlylearning.org/pa/). This site features many resources that can be helpful to teachers who are beginning to implement the Project Approach, including detailed, illustrated reports on projects that teachers have submitted to share. These reports include descriptions of Phases I–III as well as teachers' reflections on the projects. The site also includes blogs by the authors of this book on topics that help teachers successfully implement projects, a Director's Corner where administrators share their insights about supporting teachers who are implementing project work, resources for lesson planning, and links to related resources on the web. In addition, a private Project Approach Facebook group provides opportunities for teachers to interact with one another directly, as a community of practice. Teachers on this site ask each other for advice and share accomplishments and project-related news. A link to join the group is available on the Illinois Early Learning Project web site.

Another useful strategy to garner support is for teachers to form a regional study group to enable them to build their own community of practice. For example, Dawn Johnson formed the Southeast Iowa Project Approach group. She manages a private Facebook page for the group, and teachers from her area post examples of the project work they have done in their classrooms:

> In 2013, I formed the Southeast Iowa Project Group as one of the recipients of the Iowa Association for the Education of Young Children's Leadership Fellowship. This group was established to enable preschool teachers and administrators to exchange experiences and thoughts related to project work, and as a venue to provide professional development, encouragement, and support to teachers implementing the Project Approach.

The Southeast Iowa Project Group also hosts an annual project group meeting to share projects.

Co-teachers or assistant teachers who have not had training in the Project Approach may be nervous at the beginning of a project if they are not sure what to expect. Many of the resources in this book can be a helpful introduction, but face-to-face professional development experiences focused on the approach are encouraged. Professional development might take the form of an in-service provided by a teacher who has attended Project Approach training or by individuals who provide statewide or regional technical assistance to teachers in the district.

> Displaying documentation of students' project work in shared spaces of a school can increase communication about project work with others.

Never underestimate the power of documentation to build support for emergent learning. Displaying documentation of students' project work in shared spaces of a school can increase communication about project work with others. As colleagues become curious about project work exhibited, they might approach the teacher whose classroom is doing project work to find out more about it. Although they may not yet be doing project work themselves, increased awareness of project work may result in more support for this approach.

Another way to garner support for project work is to invite another class to join the project. For example, in the Dog Project, as discussed in Chapter 3, Ms. Lavin's students were curious about the visit from the service dog to Ms. DeLuca's class and Ms. Burd's class. When Ms. Lavin mentioned this to Ms. DeLuca and Ms. Burd, they invited Ms. Lavin's students to a presentation to learn more about their project. Soon, Ms. Lavin's students were included in the investigation.

Implement Projects in Part-Time or Variable-Attendance Classes

Teachers often wonder if it is possible to do project work when they teach classes that only meet for half-day sessions or they have children who do not attend every day. The answer is a resounding yes! Teachers who do project work in these settings have found project work to be beneficial. For example, if a teacher has a morning and an afternoon class, the two classes can write each other messages (e.g., "I like the check-out counter you made for our grocery store. We are going to make a scanner!"). One can imagine each class looking forward to discovering what the other class has been up to when they arrive at school each day. Teachers from a variety of part-time settings have found that there were very few conflicts over materials between the two classes and that the long-term nature of the Project Approach provides continuity so that children have an expectation about what will happen at school the next time they attend it (Beneke, 2000).

Link Project Work With the Required Curricula

Another challenge to implementation of project work may be coordinating it with curricula that is already in place and required by a center or school. With the push-down of curriculum that has occurred in response to requirements for annual school progress, the advent of the Common Core, and an emphasis on evidence-based practices, preschool teachers often find themselves with multiple commercially produced curricula packages that they are required teach. For older children, school days become even more packed with these types of packaged curricula. Many of these curricula have pacing guides that require teachers to move through the material on a set schedule. This requirement can decrease some of the flexibility that teachers might use to accommodate peak periods in project work; however, it should not deter teachers from doing project work in their classrooms.

Classes for children who are kindergarten age or older also may have more rigid daily schedules for special learning opportunities on curriculum elements such as art, music, and library. These requirements may partition teachers' schedules into short time periods and make it difficult to provide longer blocks of time in which children have opportunities to immerse themselves in developing rich project investigations. Conversely, many preschool teachers are still able to embed the Project Approach in their schedule so that it flows throughout most of the day and their projects can develop steadily. However, teachers with scheduling challenges may need to limit project work to certain blocks of time. For example, teachers might schedule project work for 1 hour a day, 3 days per week. It is likely that it will take their class longer to do their investigation, but it can work, and children will look forward to having this time to conduct project work.

Develop Administrative Support

Teachers typically welcome support from their administrators for implementing the Project Approach. When administrators understand the value of the Project Approach for young children, they can assist teachers in accessing materials and resources and can encourage other members of the school faculty to seek training in the Project Approach, thereby creating a community of learners and a natural support system.

> When administrators understand the value of the Project Approach for young children, they can assist teachers in accessing materials and resources and can encourage other members of the school faculty to seek training in the Project Approach, thereby creating a community of learners and a natural support system.

One way that teachers can build administrative support is to document the impact of project work on children's learning. Some teachers post a list of early learning standards that were met through project work in their displays of children's work (see Table 6.1). Other teachers have included mention of the standards that were met in the narrative they use to describe various elements of the display. Teachers also

Table 6.1. Mathematics standards met during the Dog Project

Content area	Math knowledge and skills from *Iowa Early Learning Standards* (2012)	Children's activities related to standards in the Dog Project
Comparison and Number	Counts to five.	• Survey of children and adults: "Do you have a dog?"
	Counts objects, pointing to each one correctly while counting.	• Counting number of parts on toy dogs (i.e., eyes, ears, legs, tail) • Counting number of toy dogs in block area • Counting dog bones
	Uses language such as *more* or *less* to compare quantities.	• Charting and comparing: "What is your favorite kind of dog?" • Comparing dog types by features (e.g., ears up versus ears down) • Sorting and charting: "Which is a dog? Which is not a dog?"
	Begins to recognize small quantities without counting them.	• Subitizing dog bones • Subitizing small toy dogs
	Starts recognizing and naming numbers.	• Discussing results of surveys • Playing game: Count out the number of dogs indicated on the numeral card
Patterns	Recognizes and creates patterns moving from simple to complex.	• Making dog collars decorated with a variety of patterns
	Predicts what comes next in a pattern.	• Finishing patterns started with colored dog bones
Shapes and Spatial Reasoning	Demonstrates understanding of spatial words such as *up, down, over, under, top, bottom, inside, outside, in front,* and *behind.*	• Building doghouse enclosures with roofs and playing with dogs in the block area
	Identifies two- and three-dimensional shapes.	
	Notices characteristics, similarities, and differences among shapes, such as corners, points, edges, and sides.	• Drawing individual plans for three-dimensional doghouses • Constructing three-dimensional doghouses • Comparing three-dimensional doghouses
	Notices how shapes fit together and can be taken apart to form other shapes.	• Building doghouses with unit blocks • Building doghouses with magnetic tiles at table toy area

can make their administrators aware of the ways that using the Project Approach reflects the recommendations of professional standards for early childhood and early childhood special education teachers. For example, Standard 4, Using Developmentally Effective Approaches, is one of the National Association for the Education of Young Children's (NAEYC) Professional Preparation Standards (NAEYC, 2011). It emphasizes the importance of responsive teaching, using integrative approaches to planning curriculum, and teaching through social interaction. In addition, Standard 5, Using Content Knowledge to Build Meaningful Curriculum, emphasizes that "implementing meaningful, challenging, curriculum will also support young children's ability—and motivation—to solve problems and think well" (NAEYC, 2011, p. 38). The Division for Early Childhood's Recommended Practices (Division for Early Childhood, 2014) advised that teachers "with the family, identify each child's strengths, preferences, and interests to engage the child in active learning" (p. 12). Standards and recommended practices such as these are examples of ways that the Project Approach matches current practices in the field.

Providing administrator training on the Project Approach can also help administrators see the potential value of project work. Teachers can invite their administrators to attend Project Approach training events with the classroom team. Or, teachers might work with state professional development providers to initiate a webinar or face-to-face training tailored for administrators. Administrators who have experience with teachers doing project work might be invited to share their views on the benefits of this approach. Finally, in the spirit that seeing is believing, teachers might invite their administrators to visit their classrooms when special project-related events are taking place (e.g., creating a list of questions, interviewing a guest expert, constructing a shared representation, holding a culminating event).

Access Financial Support for Materials and Field Trips

In our experience, a key characteristic of the Project Approach is that the materials typically do not cost a great deal of money. Objects related to topics of interest to children are typically things that families or teachers have in their homes and can lend to the group, or they can be borrowed from a nearby relevant field site. For example, in a project on pizza, Sallee Beneke contacted a local pizza parlor to arrange a field trip. The owners were honored that the children wanted to study their pizza parlor and offered to loan the class uniforms and special tools that are used to bake pizza. In our experience, this willingness to share materials is a fairly common reaction when teachers approach others for assistance.

Cardboard boxes and other recyclables make great open-ended materials that children can use to construct models and other representations in a project. For example, in the Pizza Project, preschool students constructed their own pizzeria in the dramatic play area, which included a meat grinder, a pizza warmer, and an oven. To solicit certain types of recyclables, the teacher attached samples to a display board that she placed by the entry to her classroom. She placed an empty cardboard box next to the display, and a sign on the display board asking families and other staff to collect and drop off similar items. The class soon had more materials than they could use. However, there are times when money is needed to purchase special materials or a piece of equipment, such as an incubator, special paper, or plants. At these times, teachers might work with their administrators to submit a request to the parent–teacher organization or to a local service organization, such as the Rotary Club or Junior League.

Accessing funds for field trips also can be a challenge in many communities. If funding is not available, one option might be to ask families to take their child to visit a specific field site during nonschool hours. However, there is a chance that some children might not have a chance to make such a trip. A better option is for teachers to consider project topics that are in the school or within a short walk (5–10 minutes). Topics related to nature, such as the ants on the playground or fish in the school fish tank, or topics related to social studies, such as a bike shop or a tire store, might be considered. A teacher also can bring the subject of a potential project investigation into the classroom to see if it sparks children's curiosity. For example, one teacher brought her parakeet to visit the class, and the children were so interested in him that he remained a classroom guest for several weeks while the students studied him. It is important to remember that the younger the child, the more critical it is that the topic is something the child can visit and revisit to find answers through firsthand exploration.

Find Guest Experts, Volunteers, and Locations for Fieldwork

As a teacher listens to children's suggestions, carefully observes their play, and considers possible topics for projects, it is important to keep the availability of guest experts in mind. Requests for experts can be made to community members or local service organizations, although this is not always feasible or successful. If no guest expert on the topic is available to visit the class, consider someone else who might know enough about the topic that he or she could take on the expert role. For example, in a project on rabbits, a teacher invited a veterinarian to speak to her kindergartners and answer their questions; however, the veterinarian was not available. After brainstorming with the principal, she invited the second-grade teacher, who had experience raising rabbits, to take on the role. She provided the second-grade teacher with the children's questions in advance, and on the day of the visit, the second-grade teacher arrived wearing a lab coat and fully prepared to answer the children's questions. The children were very satisfied with this experience. In project work, someone is needed to fill the role of guest expert so that children can have the experience of asking questions and having them answered by someone knowledgeable about the topic. If no one is available to serve in this role, the teacher may want to consider a different topic for the class project.

One way to develop a list of potential guest experts and potential fieldwork sites is to develop a speaker's catalog. Family members can be asked if they are willing to share their knowledge and experience about their occupation or hobbies and if they are willing to host a class field trip. This information can be entered into a database so that when a teacher is unsure about whether a guest speaker or location for fieldwork is available for a particular topic, he or she can contact a potential speaker from the school database.

Respond to Pressure to Get Children Ready for Kindergarten

Preschool teachers frequently complain about feeling pressured to ask children to do the kinds of activities and tasks that formerly were taught in first or second grade. Standardized tests have made their way to the preschool level, and kindergarten teachers share concerns that preschoolers are not well prepared when they enter elementary school (e.g., knowing all of their letters and how to read some sight words). Play, which was once a key component of the preschool curriculum, is disappearing in some programs, despite the fact that neuroscience has demonstrated that "children's brains need to be immersed in real life, hands-on, and meaningful learning experiences that are intertwined with a commonality and require some form of problem-solving" (Rushton, 2011, p. 92).

It can be challenging for educators to counter this pressure and teach young children in ways that are known to be successful. One strategy is to document the effectiveness of the Project Approach to help children move toward mastery of early childhood standards. As discussed earlier, teachers may use the narrative they write for their display to emphasize the early learning standards that were met in project work, or they might prepare a separate display to highlight the standards that were present in the project. For example, consider the Library Project. Were standards met? How could Ms. Harrison and Ms. Beherendes demonstrate children's outcomes to families and other decision makers who are unfamiliar with identifying learning in young children's work? Those who are not early childhood professionals do not recognize the learning represented in the children's work. One way to share this knowledge with others is to post a narrative with the documentation that is displayed. A sample narrative for the Library Project might read as follows:

> The children have accomplished so much during their investigation of the library! They have been so engaged and motivated to learn about the library that they have met many early learning standards across the curriculum. For example, consider the important social studies learning that took place. The children learned a great deal about how the library works and the rules that visitors to a library must follow. They participated in voting as they made decisions about what to make to demonstrate their learning. Different children took on leadership roles as they made group constructions, such as building shelves and a book sorter. They participated in a variety of roles as they pretended and played library, and they learned about the job the librarian does

and some of the special tools librarians use. As they constructed the bookshelves and the book sorter, children had to share materials and compromise. They found out that you do not need to use money to check out a book; you just need a library card! They periodically reflected on their investigation and summarized what they had learned and ultimately made a class book about the library. The children became familiar with geography as they made maps or floor plans of libraries, and they discussed the reasons for rules about book care and behavior in the library. To take a closer look at how these discoveries and activities represent mastery of social studies standards for young children, see Table 6.1. You will find that 10 out of 15 Illinois early childhood social studies benchmarks were met! Happily, the class celebrated this same kind of success for the areas of language arts, math, science, physical development, the arts, and social-emotional development.

Not only can this type of narrative and table be displayed with the children's work, but it can also be incorporated into a class newsletter or sent home as a stand-alone document.

Sometimes the number of benchmarks covered in a project can be overwhelming. One way to keep track of the benchmarks is to record them in the notes column of the Implementation Checklist. Teachers can record benchmarks they anticipate children meeting, and they can use checkmarks to document that they were met.

Another strategy teachers can use to highlight benchmarks that were met during project work is to add benchmark labels to documentation displays. Consider the learning represented in the documentation display of the Dog Project, discussed in Chapter 5. The depth and breadth of topics covered are quite impressive. Alternatively, a list of the benchmarks met could be added to each panel displayed. Some teachers have printed a list of the benchmarks and highlighted those that were met. Perhaps more than at any other age or grade level, preschool teachers must be advocates for their students and families. Informing other teachers and administrators about the power of project work to interest and motivate all young children to learn in a meaningful way is an important role of the preschool teacher.

Continue to Grow: Consider Ways to Use the Implementation Checklist

Learning to use the Project Approach is not simple. We hope that the Implementation Checklist will serve as a useful tool for novice and veteran teachers of the Project Approach continuing on their journey toward mastery.

Remember that the Implementation Checklist can be used in a variety of ways. Novice or veteran teachers can use it to record and date the events that take place during class projects. The checklist can be completed by a single teacher or a classroom team.

A novice Project Approach teacher might read this entire book and study the checklist as he or she prepares lesson plans for the next day or week. If the teacher finds an item on the checklist that he or she is unsure about, the teacher can revisit the section of Chapters 3, 4, or 5 that describes the item in more detail. If a novice teacher has the support of a mentor, the two of them can use the checklist as a basis for discussing the progress of the project. They can use it as a starting point to brainstorm materials or strategies for next steps in the project. For example, Sallee Beneke served as a mentor to a teacher as she learned to implement the Project Approach. They used the Implementation Checklist as a tool in a variety of ways. For example, they reviewed the items in the relevant phase as they considered possible activities and experiences to incorporate into lesson plans.

Sallee Beneke observed in the teacher's classroom on a weekly basis, and she and the teacher each took notes on their own copy of the Implementation Checklist. When they met, they compared notes and used the checklist as a basis for discussion. At times, the teacher had questions about how to implement items on the checklist and she would consult with Sallee to elaborate on the item. If novice teachers do not have a mentor, they might share the checklist with another teacher who is also beginning to implement the Project Approach. The partners can support each other by providing a sounding board and helping one another brainstorm strategies. Sometimes two teachers who have decided to do this will start a project on the same topic and then share the direction the topic takes due to the unique interests and abilities of the children in each class.

Veteran project implementers might use the Implementation Checklist as a resource or as a way to self-evaluate. They might review the checklist periodically to reassure themselves that they are providing children with optimal opportunities to engage with the project topic and to decide what areas they want to strengthen. They also can refer to Chapters 3, 4, and 5 to refresh their memory on these specifics.

A group of teachers who want to learn to implement the Project Approach together might form a study group around this book and the Implementation Checklist. They might read about a phase and try implementing it simultaneously, then get together to reflect on their experiences and support one another before planning the next step.

CONCLUSION

We hope that readers will continue to grow in their ability to implement the three phases of the Project Approach and that the Implementation Checklist will serve as a tool to both guide novice teachers and support experienced teachers as they reflect on their implementation of project work. Teachers who use this approach report that it is as interesting and motivating for them as it is for their students. They head to school in the morning curious about what developments will emerge in the project that day. Teachers have found that project work puts them in touch with the art of teaching and creates a stimulating component of the curriculum for *all* children, due to its flexibility and responsiveness to the individuals in a class. In addition, the Project Approach provides teachers with many opportunities to connect with and involve families.

At a time when preschoolers are suspended or expelled from school for behavior problems at three times the rate of students in kindergarten through grade 12 (Gilliam, 2005), it is important for early childhood leaders to identify curriculum approaches that are engaging and motivating and have the flexibility to serve young children from diverse cultural backgrounds and children with diverse abilities. Early childhood curricula that are heavily focused on academics tend to stress acquisition and mastery of discrete skills through instructional activities that often discount how young children learn best. Yet we know that young children are capable of doing deep intellectual work when they have experiences that ignite their curiosity; provide them with opportunities to learn with their hands, bodies, and senses; and help them better understand their everyday world. Whereas some overly academic programs deny young children's need to play, other early childhood environments where young children spend their time can be filled with meaningless activities, low expectations, and opportunities for children to entertain themselves by misbehaving.

The Project Approach provides children with opportunities to exercise their intellectual dispositions, self-regulation skills, and academic skills in a play-based context. During project work, children have opportunities to take risks, problem solve, fail, and try again. The Project Approach provides the kinds of experiences that can support children in becoming the types of leaders we will need in the not-so-distant future—people who are confident, persistent, and thoughtful. The Project Approach supports the development of individuals who take the initiative and are collaborative, curious and eager to use their skills to better understand the world they inhabit.

Most important, the Project Approach 1) builds a sense of community among culturally diverse children, as well as individuals with a broad range of abilities, 2) helps them value one another's strengths, and 3) provides support in areas where students struggle. It is our hope that teachers who are new to the Project Approach and teachers who have experience implementing the Project Approach will find that the suggestions and examples we have provided in this book can assist them with current as well as new aspects implementation. We wish you the best as you embark on this endeavor to use the Implementation Checklist, and we look forward to hearing about your projects and your successes with bringing Phases I–III to fruition.

References

August, D., Carlo, M., Dressler, C., & Snow, C. (2005). The critical role of vocabulary development for English language learners. *Learning Disabilities Research and Practice, 2*, 50–57.

Baldwin, J. L., Adams, S. M., & Kelly, M. K. (2009). Science at the center: An emergent, standards-based, child-centered framework for early learners. *Early Childhood Education Journal, 37*, 71–77.

Barazzoni, R. (2000). *Brick by brick: The history of the "XXV Aprile" People's Nursery School of Villa Cella.* Reggio Emilia, Italy: Reggio Children.

Barrera, I., & Corso, R. M. (2003). *Skilled Dialogue: Strategies for responding to cultural diversity in early childhood.* Baltimore, MD: Paul H. Brookes Publishing Co.

Beineke, J. A. (1998). *And there were giants in the land: The life of William Heard Kilpatrick.* New York, NY: Peter Lang Publishing.

Beneke, S. (1998). *Rearview mirror: Reflections on a preschool car project.* Champaign, IL: ERIC Clearinghouse on Elementary and Early Childhood Education.

Beneke, S. (2000). Implementing the Project Approach in part-time early childhood education programs. *Early Childhood Research and Practice, 2*(1). Retrieved from http://ecrp.uiuc.edu/v2n1/beneke.html

Beneke, S. (2011). *Displaying documentation: Providing supports for the viewer of the display* [Blog post]. Retrieved from http://illinoisearlylearning.org/illinoispip/blogs/beneke/2011oct05.html

Beneke, S., Helm, J. H., & Steinheimer, K. (2007). *Windows on learning: Documenting young children's work.* New York, NY: Teachers College Press.

Beneke, S. J., & Ostrosky, M. M. (2009). Teachers' views of the efficacy of incorporating the Project Approach into classroom practice with diverse learners. *Early Childhood Research & Practice, 11*(1). Retrieved from http://ecrp.uiuc.edu/v11n1/ostrosky.html

Beneke, S. J., & Ostrosky, M. M. (2015). Effects of the Project Approach on preschoolers with diverse abilities. *Infants & Young Children, 28*, 355–369.

Beneke, S. J., & Ostrosky, M. M. (2016). Universal design for learning. In D. Couchenoour & J. K. Chrisman (Eds.), *The Sage encyclopedia of contemporary early childhood education* (pp. 1403–1406). Thousand Oaks, CA: Sage.

Beneke, S. J., Ostrosky, M. M., & Katz, L. J. (2008). Calendar time for young children: Good intentions gone awry. *Young Children, 63*, 12–16.

Blank, J., Damjanovic, V., Peixoto da Silva, A. P., & Weber, S. (2014). Authenticity and "standing out": Situating the Project Approach in contemporary early schooling. *Early Childhood Education Journal, 42*, 19–27.

Bowman, B. T., Donovan, S., & Burns, M. S. (2001). *Eager to learn: Educating our preschoolers.* Washington, DC: National Academy Press.

Burns, M., & Lewis, A. L. (2016). How the Project Approach challenges young children. *Gifted Child Today, 39*, 140–144.

Carle, E. (1969). *The very hungry caterpillar.* London, United Kingdom: Penguin.

Chard, S. C. (1998). *The Project Approach: Making curriculum come alive (Book 1).* New York, NY: Scholastic.

Chun, E. J., Hertzog, N. B., Gaffney, J. S., & Dymond, S. K. (2011). When service learning meets the Project Approach: Incorporating service learning in an early childhood program. *Journal of Early Childhood Research, 10*, 232–245.

Clark, A. M. (2006). Changing classroom practice to include the Project Approach. *Early Childhood Research & Practice, 8*, 1–10. Retrieved from http://ecrp.uiuc.edu/v8n2/clark.html

Cremin, L. A. (1964). *The transformation of the school: Progressivism in American education 1876–1957.* New York, NY: Random House.

Curtis, D., Lebo, D., Cividanes, W. C. M., & Carter, M. (2013). *Reflecting in communities of practice: A workbook for early childhood educators.* St. Paul, MN: Redleaf Press.

Dewey, J. (1899). *The school and society.* Chicago, IL: The University of Chicago Press.

Dewey, J. (1910). *How we think.* Boston, MA: D. C. Heath.

Dewey, J. (1916). *Democracy and education.* New York, NY: Macmillan.

Dickinson, D. K., & Porche, M. V. (2011). Relation between language experiences in preschool classrooms and children's kindergarten and fourth-grade language and reading abilities. *Child Development, 82,* 870–886.

Division for Early Childhood. (2014). *DEC recommended practices in early intervention/early childhood special education 2014.* Retrieved from http://www.dec-sped.org/recommendedpractices

Division for Early Childhood & National Association for the Education of Young Children. (2009). *Early childhood inclusion: A joint position statement of the Division for Early Childhood (DEC) and the National Association for the Education of Young Children (NAEYC).* Chapel Hill: The University of North Carolina, FPG Child Development Institute.

Drew, W. F., & Rankin, B. (2004). Promoting creativity for life using open-ended materials. *Young Children, 59*(4), 38–45.

Dweck, C. S. (2006). *Mindset.* New York, NY: Random House.

Dweck, C. S., Walton, G. M., & Cohen, G. L. (2014). *Academic tenacity: Mindsets and skills that promote long-term learning.* Retrieved from https://ed.stanford.edu/sites/default/files/manual/dweck-walton-cohen-2014.pdf

Edwards, C., Gandini, L., & Forman, G. (Eds.). (2012). *The hundred languages of children: The Reggio Emilia experience in transformation* (3rd ed.). Santa Barbara, CA: Praeger.

Espinosa, L. M. (2013). *PreK-3rd: Challenging myths about dual language learners, An update to the seminal 2008 report.* Retrieved from https://www.fcd-us.org/prek-3rd-challenging-common-myths-about-dual-language-learners-an-update-to-the-seminal-2008-report/

Espinosa, L. M. (2015). *Getting it right for young children from diverse backgrounds: Applying research to improve practice with a focus on dual language learners* (2nd ed.). Boston, MA: Pearson.

Figueras-Daniel, A., & Barnett, S. W. (2013). Preparing young Hispanic dual language learners for a knowledge economy. *Preschool Policy Brief, 25.* Retrieved from http://nieer.org/policy-issue/policy-brief-preparing-young-hispanic-dual-language-learners-for-a-knowledge-economy

Gandini, L. (2008). Introduction to the schools of Reggio Emilia. In L. Gandini, S. Etheredge, & L. Hill (Eds.), *Insights and inspirations from Reggio Emilia: Stories of teachers and children from North America.* Worchester, MA: Davis Publications.

Gandini, L. (2012). History, ideas, and basic principles: An interview with Loris Malaguzzi. In C. Edwards, L. Gandini, & G. Forman (Eds.), *The hundred languages of children: The Reggio Emilia experience in transformation* (3rd ed., pp. 27–72). Santa Barbara, CA: Praeger.

Gilliam, W. (2005). *Prekindergarteners left behind: Expulsion rates in state prekindergarten programs. FDC Policy Brief Series, No. 3.* New York, NY: Foundation for Child Development.

Griebling, S., Elgas, P., & Konerman, R. (2015). "Trees and things that live in trees": Three children with special needs experience the Project Approach. *Early Childhood Research & Practice, 17*(1). Retrieved from http://ecrp.uiuc.edu/v17n1/griebling.html

Harn, B. A., Damico, D. P., & Stoolmiller, M. (2017). Examining the variation of fidelity across an intervention: Implications for measuring and evaluating student learning. *Preventing School Failure: Alternative Education for Children and Youth, 61,* 289–302.

Harte, H. A. (2010). The Project Approach: A strategy for inclusive classrooms. *Young Exceptional Children, 13,* 15–27.

Helm, J. H., Beneke, S., & Steinheimer, K. (2007). *Windows on learning* (2nd ed.). New York, NY: Teacher's College Press.

Higher Education Opportunity Act of 2008, PL 89–329 (2008).

Hill, J. B. (2016). Questioning techniques: A study of instructional practice. *Peabody Journal of Education, 91,* 660–671.

Hord, S. M. (2009). Professional learning communities: Educators work together toward a shared purpose—improved student learning. *The Learning Professional, 30,* 40–43.

Huntsinger, C. S., Jose, P. E., Krieg, D. B., & Luo, Z. (2011). Cultural differences in Chinese American and European American children's drawing skills over time. *Early Childhood Research Quarterly, 26*(1), 134–145.

Illinois Early Learning Project. (2018). *Project approach definitions.* Retrieved from https://illinoisearlylearning.org/pa/project-definitions/

Illinois State Board of Education. (2013). *Illinois early learning and development standards—preschool.* Springfield, IL: Author.

Iowa Department of Education. (2012). *Iowa Early Learning Standards.* Retrieved from http://www.state.ia.us/earlychildhood/files/early_learning_standarda/IELS_2013.pdf

IRIS Center. (2018a). *Evidence-based practices (Part 2): Implementing a practice or program with fidelity.* Retrieved from https://iris.peabody.vanderbilt.edu/module/ebp_02/cwrap/#content

IRIS Center. (2018b). *What is instructional scaffolding?* Retrieved from https://iris.peabody.vanderbilt.edu/module/sca/cresource/q1/p01/

Johnson, N., & Parker, A. (2013). Effects of wait time when communicating with children who have sensory and additional disabilities. *Journal of Visual Impairment & Blindness, 107,* 363–374.

Katz, L. G. (1993). *Dispositions as educational goals. ERIC Digest.* Retrieved from http://files.eric.ed.gov /fulltext/ED363454.pdf

Katz, L. G. (2012). *Perspectives on the Project Approach: Standards of experience* [Blog post]. Retrieved from https://illinoisearlylearning.org/blogs/perspectives/standards-experience/

Katz, L. G. (2013a). *Documentation: The basics, part 1* [Blog post]. Retrieved from https://illinoisearlylearning .org/blogs/perspectives/documentation-basics1/

Katz, L. G. (2013b). *Documentation: The basics, part 2* [Blog post]. Retrieved from https://illinoisearlylearning .org/blogs/perspectives/documentation-basics2/

Katz, L. G., & Chard, S. C. (1989). *Engaging children's minds: The Project Approach.* Stamford, CT: Ablex.

Katz, L. G., & Chard, S. C. (1998). *Issues in selecting topics for projects.* Champaign, IL: ERIC Clearinghouse on Elementary and Early Childhood Education.

Kilpatrick, W. H. (1909). *Kilpatrick's diaries* (Vol. 5). New York, NY: Teachers College, Columbia University.

Kilpatrick, W. H. (1918). *The project method: The use of the purposeful act in the educative process.* New York, NY: Teachers College Press.

Klassen, J. (2012). *I want my hat back.* Somerville, MA: Candlewick Press.

Knapke, S., Lawrence, G., & Moses, M. (2018). *Cooking with spinach.* Retrieved from https:// illinoisearlylearning.org/pa/projects/spinach-project/

Koegel, L. K., Singh, A., & Koegel, R. (2010). Improving motivation for academics in children with autism. *Journal of Autism & Developmental Disorders, 40,* 1057–1066.

Lascarides, V. C., & Hinitz, B. F. (2011). *History of early childhood education.* New York, NY: Routledge.

Lickey, D. C., & Powers, D. J. (2011). *Starting with their strengths: Using the Project Approach in early childhood special education.* New York, NY: Teachers College Press.

Lindsay, G. (2015). Reflections in the mirror of Reggio Emilia's soul: John Dewey's foundational influence on pedagogy in the Italian educational project. *Early Childhood Education Journal, 43,* 447–457.

Maple, T. L. (2005). Beyond community helpers: The Project Approach in the early childhood social studies curriculum. *Childhood Education, 81,* 133–138.

Marcon, R. A. (2002). Moving up the grades: Relationship between preschool model and later school success. *Early Childhood Research and Practice, 4*(1). Retrieved from http://ecrp.uiuc.edu/v4n1/marcon.html

Marsh, L. (2012). *Caterpillar to butterfly.* Washington, DC: National Geographic Society.

Mashburn, A. J., Pianta, R. C., Hamre, B. K., Downer, J. T., Barbarin, O. A., Bryant, D., . . . Howes, C. (2008). Measures of classroom quality in prekindergarten and children's development of academic, language, and social skills. *Child Development, 79,* 732–749.

McClelland, M. M., Acock, A. C., & Morrison, F. J. (2006). The impact of kindergarten learning-related skills on academic trajectories at the end of elementary school. *Early Childhood Research Quarterly, 21,* 471–490.

McCormick, K. K., & Twitchell, G. (2017). A preschool investigation: The skyscraper project. *Teaching Children Mathematics, 23,* 340–348.

Mitchell, S., Foulger, T. S., Wetzel, K., & Rathkey, C. (2009). The negotiated Project Approach: Project-based learning without leaving the standards behind. *Early Childhood Education Journal, 36,* 339–346.

National Association for the Education of Young Children (2002). *Early childhood mathematics: Promoting good beginnings.* Washington, DC: Author.

National Association for the Education of Young Children. (2011). *2010 NAEYC standards for initial & advanced early childhood professional preparation programs.* Washington, DC: Author.

National Center on Universal Design for Learning. (2014). *About UDL.* Retrieved from http://www.udlcenter .org/aboutudl/whatisudl

National Center on Universal Design for Learning. (2017). *UDL guidelines: Theory & practice version.* Retrieved from http://www.udlcenter.org/aboutudl/udlguidelines_theorypractice

New, R. (2007). Reggio Emilia as cultural activity: Theory in practice. *Theory into Practice, 46,* 5–13.

Office of Head Start. (2008). *Dual language learning: What does it take? Head Start dual language report.* Retrieved from https://eclkc.ohs.acf.hhs.gov/hslc/tta-system/ehsnrc/docs/DLANA_final_2009%5B1%5D.pdf

Prieto, H. V. (2009). *One language, two languages, three languages . . . more?* Retrieved from http://www .smartbeginningsse.org/wp-content/uploads/2016/03/esl_infant-toddlers.pdf

Pyramid Educational Consultants. (n.d.). *Picture Exchange Communication System (PECS).* Retrieved from https://pecsusa.com/pecs/

Rothenberg, D. (Ed.). (2000). *Issues in early childhood education: Curriculum, teacher education, and dissemination—Proceedings of the Lilian Katz symposium, November 5–7, 2000.* Urbana-Champaign, IL: Early Childhood and Parenting Collaborative, University of Illinois at Urbana-Champaign.

Rushton, S. (2011). Neuroscience, early childhood education and play: We're getting it right! *Early Childhood Education Journal, 30,* 89–94.

Scranton, P., & Doubet, S. (2003). Practical strategies. In J. H. Helm & S. Beneke (Eds.), *The power of projects: Meeting contemporary challenges in early childhood classrooms—Strategies and solutions.* New York, NY: Teachers College Press.

Slobodkina, E. (1968). *Caps for sale*. New York, NY: Harper & Rowe.

Souto-Manning, M., & Lee, K. (2005). "In the beginning I thought it was all play": Parents' perceptions of the Project Approach in a second grade classroom. *The School Community Journal, 15*, 7–20.

Spodek, B., & Saracho, O. N. (2003). "On the shoulders of giants": Exploring the traditions of early childhood education. *Early Childhood Education Journal, 31*, 3–10.

Techel, B. G. (2008). *Frankie, the walk 'n roll dog*. Elkhart Lake, WI: Joyful Paw Prints.

Tennenbaum, S. (1951). *William Heard Kilpatrick: Trailblazer in education*. New York, NY: Harper & Brothers.

Trawick-Smith, J. (2014). *Early childhood development: A multicultural perspective* (6th ed.). Upper Saddle River, NJ: Pearson.

Warash, B., Curtis, R., Hursh, D., & Tucci, V. (2008). Skinner meets Piaget on the Reggio playground: Practical synthesis of applied behavior analysis and developmentally appropriate practice orientations. *Journal of Research in Childhood Education, 22*, 441–453.

Weizman, Z. O., & Snow, C. E. (2001). Lexical input as related to children's vocabulary acquisition: Effects of sophisticated exposure and support for meaning. *Developmental Psychology, 37*, 265–279.

Whorrall, J., & Cabell, S. Q. (2016). Supporting children's oral language development in the preschool classroom. *Early Childhood Education Journal, 44*, 335–341.

Williams, R. A., Rockwell R. E., & Sherwood, E. A. (1987). *Mudpies to magnets: A preschool science curriculum*. Lewisville, NC: Gryphon House.

Yuen, L. H. F. (2009). From foot to shoes: Kindergarteners', families', and teachers' perceptions of the Project Approach. *Early Childhood Education Journal, 37*, 23–33.

Completed Project Approach Implementation Checklists

APPENDIX A.1

Ms. DeLuca and Ms. Burd completed the Project Approach Implementation Checklist to demonstrate how the Dog Project developed. In their study of dogs, children in these two classes conducted surveys, made observational drawings of dogs in their neighborhoods, and received visits from service and police dogs. They visited a pet store, and one class constructed a pet store in their dramatic play area, while the other class constructed a veterinary clinic in theirs. In addition, each child planned and constructed an individual doghouse. Ms. DeLuca and Ms. Burd used the Project Approach Implementation Checklist to help monitor what they had completed and to think about and plan additional activities. Teachers can use the blank version of this checklist (included as an appendix with Chapter 1) to document and guide the development of their projects.

Project Approach Implementation Checklist

Phase I		
	Record Yes, No, or N/A	**Record notes about the activities and dates that you implemented these items**
1. Select a topic based on children's interests, district curriculum, or an unexpected event (e.g., topics of conversations among children, unexpected event such as a new baby, or a neighborhood construction project).	Yes	*Early February (after back into school routine):* We observed children during first semester in all classes and noticed some pretend dog play. We recalled interest in dogs from a neighborhood walk, and one child had shared an experience with a therapy dog during a hospital stay.
2. Select a topic that meets the criteria for a topic.	Yes	*Our team was looking for a common interest—one in which many would have experience and one for which we could generate common experiences.*
3. Generate a teacher topic web with co-teacher(s).	Yes	*2/12* Kim, Laura, and our assistants met after school to draw a topic web and brainstorm all the ways we could guide learning. To help clarify for all team members, we also made a checklist/chart for "phases" and what could possibly happen during that time.
4. Select an aspect of the topic to use as a starting point (e.g., an aspect of the topic that is most likely to interest the children and lend itself to firsthand investigation).	Yes	*Late February* Our first "zoom in" was simply on pet/dog care and ownership. Who has dogs? How many? What kind? Names? What do they do with their dogs at home? Pretend play, artifact exploration, and the real dog visits occurred during this time. Toy dogs and supplies were added to the home living area.
5. Brainstorm a list of open-ended materials to begin collecting (e.g., papers, boxes, cardboard tubes, lids).	Yes	*Late February* We began to collect pet care artifacts and supplies and asked for donations from families. We also collected cardboard boxes of all kinds for the children to use in construction.
6. Brainstorm a list of child reference materials to begin collecting (e.g., children's reference books and nonfiction; adult manuals with diagrams and photos; and magazines or brochures).	Yes	*Late February* Books were collected from the school library about dogs. Parents sent in books as well. We had several breed-specific research/fact books that were a huge hit with the children during independent book time. A vet office donated brochures and flyers.
7. Begin to collect materials and tools that children may use to gather information.	Yes	*Early March* We used a home survey in which families recorded info about the dogs in their child's life (grandma's dog, neighbor's dog, etc.). We charted this info as a class and also collected surveys/pictures in a book we called "Dogs We Know."
8. Brainstorm a list of vocabulary words and/or terms children might learn as a result of participating in the project (e.g., words for topic-related tools, processes, objects, or jobs).	Yes	*We did this within our teacher topic webbing. Both classrooms began developing a wordlist chart of common words. Vocabulary cards were added to writing centers.*

Phase I		
	Record Yes, No, or N/A	Record notes about the activities and dates that you implemented these items
9. Identify an area of wall space at the large group meeting area where ongoing documentation of the project will be displayed on a Project History Board (e.g., low bulletin board or wall area that children can view and reference during class meetings).	Yes	Bulletin board space, trifold boards, and shelf space were used to display work throughout the room during the duration of the project.
10. Plan and implement an opening event to provoke discussion of the topic (e.g., simple story, topic-related book, presentation of topic-related object, or photograph or poster).	Yes	Simple play, books, stuffed animals, etc., were provided prior to the opening event, and the pet store visit also happened early on, but our first planned "opening event" was the first visit by the therapy dog, Eli.
11. Begin recording children's knowledge of the topic in web format on large paper that is then posted on the Project History Board.	Yes	Each class did this in their own way. Younger groups had simple statement webs. Older, more experienced groups had evolving webs that were added to over time.
12. Explain the Project Approach to families (e.g., send home a written explanation, hold an informational meeting, and/or send e-mail informational links).	Yes	We included a brief explanation in our "Beginning of the Year" note about program curriculum, including the Project Approach. We shared project updates with parents in weekly newsletters.
13. Notify families that the project is beginning and suggest ways they can be helpful (e.g., contribute materials, props, or expertise).	Yes	We did this in newsletters. Early on, we asked parents to donate books, dog care supplies, and pictures of family pet dogs.
14. Provide opportunities for children to reflect on and represent their prior knowledge or experience with the topic (e.g., drawing, painting, sculpting, pretending, or dictating).	Yes	Early March Each class created a book called "Dogs We Know" in which the children dictated stories about the dogs in their lives. Photos and drawings were added to this book. There was lots of pretend play during this time (acting out dog play, dog care, etc.). Many art/creation supplies were available for representation and sparked ideas for children to create or act out what they knew.
15. Begin to generate a list of possible guest experts and locations for fieldwork.	Yes	Early March This was part of our initial teacher brainstorming day. We also did this again after Danielle's second-grade class joined the project.
16. Hold large- and/or small-group discussions to identify and record children's questions about the topic (e.g., "What do you want to find out?").	Yes	3/12 Classes had daily experiences and discussion time. We also brought our classes together to share information and questions. We wondered alongside the children and modeled making or phrasing questions. Sometimes as children shared ideas or comments about dogs, other children would disagree and start a discussion. This is when teachers restated the idea as a question and wrote it on the chart. For example, I know this happened with "Dogs die." One child had experienced the death of his dog. Others had not and argued with him.

Phase I		
	Record Yes, No, or N/A	Record notes about the activities and dates that you implemented these items
17. Select one or two questions and ask children to make predictions about the answers.	Yes	*Late March* *This is something we also had to model and provoke in our students. Some questions we spent time pondering and making predictions about were: Are all dogs the same? What is the same? And what things are different? These questions and predictions fueled much of our Phase II research as children spent time researching types of dogs, breeds, furs, sizes, etc.*
18. Select one or two questions and ask children how they can find out the answers to their questions.	Yes	*Late March* *This is something we also had to model and provoke in our students. We selected "Are all dogs the same?" and "Can dogs go to work?"*
19. Continue to capture children's questions on an ongoing basis (e.g., large- and/or small-group discussions, opportunities in the natural course of everyday activities).	Yes	*Early April* *As we had new experiences, we revisited our list of questions and added to it. We usually did this during large group time.*
20. Display children's web, questions, and samples of Phase I work on the Project History Board (e.g., artwork, photographs, emergent writing).	Yes	*Ongoing.* *Webs, a question list, photos, art, etc., were displayed in the front of the room and around the room and grew over time in both classrooms.*

Phase II		
	Record Yes, No, or N/A	Record notes about the activities and dates that you implemented these items
21. Continue to inform families about the progress of the project on a regular basis (e.g., newsletter stories, notes home, phone calls).	Yes	*Early April* *We continued to send home announcements about what was happening in the project. We also sent home requests for additional materials as we discovered we needed them.*
22. Provide materials that could help children better understand the topic through firsthand exploration (e.g., authentic objects related to the topic such as tools, accessories, components, and/or samples).	Yes	*Early April* *Dog care tools were added to the classroom (collars, bowls, leashes, toys, treats, bones, beds, cages, etc.). Other items were added as questions emerged, such as grooming items, vet/doctor tools, pet store props, etc.*
23. Provide topic-related materials that could help children better understand the topic through experimentation (e.g., mixing, touching, cutting, connecting, mashing, cooking, combining, taking apart).	Yes	*Early April* *Many types of collars and harnesses sparked children's interest in pretend play. Real dog bones and treats were used in exploration, play, games, and art.* *4/13* *A sensory table was put together for children to touch and explore a variety of furs.*

	Phase II	
	Record Yes, No, or N/A	Record notes about the activities and dates that you implemented these items
24. Provide topic-related props that could help children better understand the topic through dramatic play in the housekeeping and block areas (e.g., hats, uniforms, equipment, tools, accessories, signs, components, photographs).	Yes	*March* *Both classrooms had access to pet care props in the early days of the project.* *April* *Later on, DeLuca's room became a pet store and grooming station and Burd's room created a vet's office.*
25. Provide open-ended art materials that children could use to represent their growing understanding of the topic (e.g., a variety of papers, cardboard, tape/glue, staplers, cardboard tubes, cardboard boxes, clay, paint).	Yes	*April* *Children were familiar with the art supplies and free to create things as they wished. Some of the items they created included collars for children to wear when pretending to be dogs, collars for stuffed dogs, doghouses, dog toys, dog models, etc.*
26. Prepare teacher- and/or child-made word cards that include illustrations for the class word wall and for the writing area (e.g., children can suggest new topic-related words, child or teacher copies the word onto the card, and child illustrates it).	Yes	*April* *There were both teacher-created and child-created vocab cards on word wall–type displays near writing centers and group areas. During the second semester, older classes had a journaling time. The words from the display were often used during this time, and children often created new vocab cards during this time.*
27. Teach the children to use drawing as a way to record information.	Yes	*April* *Children drew pictures of our dog visitors and experiences, some at art center during choice time and some during planned "journaling" time.*
28. Read children's books that provide factual information and introduce new vocabulary (e.g., children's reference books, nonfiction books, stories based on factual information).	Yes	*Ongoing* *All types of literature were enjoyed throughout the project. Nonfiction information books about different dog breeds were very popular during independent book choice time. Children liked fun story series like Clifford, Biscuit, etc. We also shared real stories about dogs that needed special equipment for special needs.*
29. Teach the children to use clipboards and pens to record their observations.	Yes	*Mid-April* *Children were familiar with "clipboard work" in our classrooms. Children used clipboards during expert visits when asking questions and recording answers.*
30. Teach children how to conduct surveys.	Yes	*Children surveyed adults and students in our school about who had dogs and their favorite breeds.*
31. Ask children to draw a plan for three-dimensional constructions they intend to build individually or as part of a small group.	Yes	*Late April* *After researching many types of doghouses, children designed/ created plans for doghouses they would like to build.*

Phase II		
	Record Yes, No, or N/A	**Record notes about the activities and dates that you implemented these items**
32. Encourage children to take advantage of their peers' help or expertise (e.g., ask a friend who is good at hammering to help you connect the boards, find someone to hold the tape so you can cut it).	Yes	April We had mixed abilities in our rooms and several "experts" in creations and masters with tools and tape. This was a big role for our second-grade buddies as well when they came to our rooms to work with the preschoolers.
33. Ask open-ended questions to provoke deeper thinking about the topic (e.g., What makes you think so? How could you do that? What else could we try? What do you think will happen if . . . ?).	Yes	Ongoing. This is our method of approaching most teachable moments in our classroom; it is especially effective during creation times, such as creating the doghouses, the pet store, etc. This also often happened after stories were shared and during snack table talk.
34. Regularly invite children to suggest additions to the Project History Board (e.g., new words, graphs, samples, anecdotal notes, quotes, photos, artifacts, drawings).	Yes	April After each event, such as the police dog visit, the walk to visit Izzy, watching Eli get groomed, etc., we continued to add to our research environments with photos, sketches, clay creations, and charts.
35. Provide regular opportunities for children to review and add new knowledge of the topic to the class topic web.	Yes	April Our older 4- and 5-year-old class did this periodically. We often revisited the webs when we found interest waning because it was a way to spark interest in subtopics to research.
36. Provide regular opportunities to review the list of questions, record any findings, and add additional questions.	Yes	Mid-April We continued to revisit the question "Are all dogs the same?" to fuel ongoing research about the variety of similarities and differences in dogs (colors, textures of fur, tail sizes, ears up/down, etc.). The children created a trifold display to document the findings to the question. For example, they sorted and displayed pictures of dogs with ears up and ears down. With each new expert visit or experience, the children worked at creating more questions. For example, they prepared questions for the dog shelter representative, the police officers, and Eli's owner.
37. Invite a guest expert or experts to visit the class. Provide them with background on the project and the children's questions.	Yes	Late March and April Many experts visited the class, including Mrs. Day, a dog owner expert; Eli, a therapy dog; police dogs; and a TAPS animal shelter worker.
38. Provide opportunities for fieldwork (e.g., focused observations of the topic, whether on or off site).	Yes	Late March and April Many experiences were provided including: <u>On site:</u> Mrs. Day, a dog owner expert Eli, a therapy dog visit and later grooming Police dog demonstration and visit TAPS animal shelter worker <u>Off site:</u> Neighborhood walk to visit neighbor dog, Izzy Pet store, field visit to see store and groomer
39. Prepare children to ask questions during fieldwork (e.g., take dictation of each child's question and record it on an index card, provide children with opportunities to practice asking questions).	Yes	March through May In our first kickoff visit to the pet store, the children predicted what they would see, observed and sketched at the store, and returned to chart/recall what they saw. Later fieldwork with our visitors involved more preparation of questions, recording ideas, and practicing asking questions in interview style. By the time the police officers came in early May, we were pleased to see our children were spontaneously asking their own questions during the demonstration.

Phase II		
	Record Yes, No, or N/A	Record notes about the activities and dates that you implemented these items
40. Involve children in a variety of methods to summarize and view their findings (e.g., charting, diagramming, graphing).	Yes	*April and May* *Children participated in all of these and more. Some examples include: Children charted colors of dogs, fur types, etc.; classes graphed who owned dogs; children surveyed other classes about liking dogs or cats; classes charted items seen at the pet store; and charts were made about what dogs eat, how to care for dogs, and steps for giving a bath. Group diagrams were made and labeled for the parts of a dog, and some children created their own skeleton diagrams with toothpicks.*
41. Ask children what the group would like to make to show what they have learned about the topic (e.g., large group construction, playscape, mural, other).	Yes	*February through May* *Several events gave children opportunities to demonstrate and act out their learning in various ways. After the pet store visit, children worked together to create a classroom pet store, a grooming station, and a vet clinic. Later in the project, discussions about doghouses led to individual planning and designing of doghouses by the children. Some doghouses were group projects, some were designed in teams with second-grade buddies, and some were individual masterpieces. A pet shelter playscape was created on the train table after the local pet shelter expert visit.*
42. Ask children to dictate plans for their group representation (e.g., What exactly do they plan to make? How will they make it? What materials do they think they will need? Who will make what?).	Yes	*April and May* *This occurred when the children were working to construct their own doghouses. Plans were drawn, parts charted, materials collected, and lists made. Second-grade peers joined in the project at this point and became involved in partner work almost daily. Second graders assisted preschoolers in planning and constructing as well as taking dictated stories about the doghouse plans.*
43. Revisit and invite the children to update their plans for the group representation regularly (e.g., two or three times per week).	Yes	*April and May* *The groups had to revisit daily work that needed to be done, helping children recall and complete their work in progress. Small teams of second graders came daily to partner with preschoolers, and teachers helped facilitate and assign work tasks for work time, including partners in a playscape like the pet store and vet clinic, doghouse construction, and reading/research buddies.* *Several times throughout the project, the activity was paused for one reason or another (holiday fun, breaks, team meetings, etc.). Topics or work projects then needed to be revisited to figure out to what to do next.*
44. Provide time and space for production of the group representation (e.g., at least an hour of uninterrupted choice time, a designated project production area, and/or learning centers set up for small group work on components of the representation).	Yes	*April and May* *Both preschool classrooms ran on the same schedule with a long project/choice time to allow for play and investigation. Children could choose areas to work/play in either room during project time, allowing them independence and choice of interest area—vet, grooming, construction, shopping, research, art, etc.*
45. Provide a variety of open-ended materials that lend themselves to the construction being produced.	Yes	*February through May* *All classrooms collected recyclables for any and all creations used during the project. Doghouses were made from these materials as well as props created for playscapes. Real artifacts for pet care were provided for props in playscapes, including large dog crate, bowls, leashes, tubs, collars, tags, kennels, brushes, grooming tools, brochures, literature, posters, etc.*
46. Teach children new skills or strategies that will help them accomplish project-related tasks (e.g., writing, tracing, taping, measuring, drilling, nailing, sewing, gluing, and/or folding).	Yes	*April and May* *In our early childhood special education classes, we first needed to teach basic wondering and inquiry skills. We worked with children on asking questions, observation skills, and researching in books and on the computer. As the project progressed, other skills that we needed to support included observational drawing, survey skills, interviewing, data collection, and writing skills. Many opportunities were provided to draw dogs, including Eli, Izzy, police dogs, dogs we knew from home, or dogs we knew from books.*
47. Scaffold when an aspect of producing the representation is beyond children's ability (e.g., sawing thick wood, cutting wire, sewing fabric).	Yes	*Task lists were created as a visual support to help some children be successful in their play and participate in certain playscapes:* *· A list of steps for grooming a dog was placed in the pet store center.* *· A picture shopping list for the pet was placed in the pet store center.* *· Pictures of veterinarians doing their jobs as prompts for representation were visible in the vet clinic.* *Presentation and sharing of information between classes (such as showing doghouse creations) gave children an opportunity to work on communication skills. Teachers used visuals, prompting, and cuing to support children's efforts to share what they were learning.*

Phase III		
	Record Yes, No, or N/A	**Record notes about the activities and dates that you implemented these items**
48. Ask children how they would like to celebrate their accomplishments (e.g., open house for families, inviting another class over, displaying their group representation in a public place).	Yes	*Early May* *Near the end of the project, teachers explained to children that we wanted to share their huge learning project with the school and their families. We enthusiastically discussed with the class how and where we could do this. We modeled excitement about putting artifacts from the project in the hallway to "show" what we learned, thus creating the "showcase" concept.*
49. Invite children to help make specific plans for the culminating event (e.g., deciding who will be invited, deciding what will happen at the event, making displays, designing invitations, and/or creating posters).	Yes	*Early May* *The children were excited by the idea of a showcase and wanted to take everything into the hall. We decided to sort our items by area of research and display artifacts and findings by those areas.*
50. Support the children's efforts to implement the culminating event (e.g., mail invitations, prepare refreshments, and/or communicate with administration).	Yes	*Late May* *The showcase was created over 2 weeks with children working in groups to select and move creations from the classroom and create displays. Children worked on backdrops, signs, and labels. Second graders wrote and distributed invitations for the showcase event. Children hand-delivered invitations to administrators. In the last few days before the event, children carried their doghouses and other project work to the display area and helped set up their work for viewing. Children knew this was important work and were eager for people to see it.*
51. Prepare a final documentation display summarizing important events in the project (e.g., How did the project start? What were the children's questions? What were the salient events? What were the challenges? Which children especially benefited from participation in the project? How did the class benefit from participation in the project? What standards were met?).	Yes	*Late May* *Documentation panels were created in the school entry atrium as part of the showcase event. One board described the project story from beginning to end, including children's webs and questions. Multiple panels were used to display the research and documentation for each interest area of the project, including how dogs are the same or different; dog jobs; police and therapy dogs; doghouse construction; parts of a dog; pet store; Izzy, the neighbor dog; TAPS Animal Shelter; and more.* *We did not highlight challenges in our display; however, challenges of the showcase event included timing of the culminating event during end-of-the-year activities; communicating its value to parents, staff, and administrators; organizing artifacts from five classes; and scheduling the showcase event for five classes to participate.* *Individual children were not highlighted in our showcase documentation at school. This individual project documentation was shared with teachers in a presentation at the Illinois statewide Sharing a Vision Conference later in the year. The presentation caused us to reflect and include more specifics on how project work met individual child needs.* *· Documentation photo stories showed classes working together and partner work and children using academics for practical use during project work.* *· A list of early learning standards was highlighted and posted in our display, showing all the standards that were met through the project.*
52. Summarize and communicate information about the project with families and administrators (e.g., hallway documentation display and/or newsletters or notes to families).	Yes	*Late May* *We held a 2-day showcase event at our school. One day was for classes and staff from the school to view the project work. The other day was for families and press. The panels and displays communicated the hard work and in-depth learning that took place for all involved.* *Children were paired (older and younger) to give information and answer questions about their given station to visitors who attended the showcase. Children also acted as guides for some of their families that came to visit the showcase during class time.*

APPENDIX A.2

Mrs. Utz completed the Project Approach Implementation Checklist to demonstrate how the Garden Project developed. Teachers can use the blank version of this checklist (included as an appendix with Chapter 1) to document and guide the development of their projects.

Project Approach Implementation Checklist

Phase I		
	Record Yes, No, or N/A	Record notes about the activities and dates that you implemented these items
1. Select a topic based on children's interests, district curriculum, or an unexpected event (e.g., topics of conversations among children, unexpected event such as a new baby, or a neighborhood construction project).	Yes	*Early April* *We decided a garden project would be good because we found out that all classes were going to take a field trip to the botanical center.*
2. Select a topic that meets the criteria for a topic.	Yes	*We felt that plants and gardens meet all of the criteria. We know that some of the children have previous experience with gardening.*
3. Generate a teacher topic web with co-teacher(s).	Yes	*Brainstormed and completed the web on the topic of planting and gardening with another teacher and the principal.*
4. Select an aspect of the topic to use as a starting point (e.g., an aspect of the topic that is most likely to interest the children and lend itself to firsthand investigation).	Yes	*We decided to start with an investigation of gardening tools.*
5. Brainstorm a list of open-ended materials to begin collecting (e.g., papers, boxes, cardboard tubes, lids).	Yes	*We chose boxes paper towel tubes, newspapers, and yogurt containers.*
6. Brainstorm a list of child reference materials to begin collecting (e.g., children's reference books and nonfiction; adult manuals with diagrams and photos; and magazines or brochures).	Yes	*Asked to borrow books from other teachers. Found some books to use at the public library. Planning to collect brochures and other informational materials at the botanical center.*
7. Begin to collect materials and tools that children may use to gather information.	Yes	*Began to collect tools and materials that we can use to plant seeds and plants (pots, potting soil, seed packets, shovels, trowels, watering cans, etc.).*
8. Brainstorm a list of vocabulary words and/or terms children might learn as a result of participating in the project (e.g., words for topic-related tools, processes, objects, or jobs).	N/A	

Phase I		
	Record Yes, No, or N/A	Record notes about the activities and dates that you implemented these items
9. Identify an area of wall space at the large group meeting area where ongoing documentation of the project will be displayed on a Project History Board (e.g., low bulletin board or wall area that children can view and reference during class meetings).	Yes	We will use the bulletin board right behind where I sit at circle time.
10. Plan and implement an opening event to provoke discussion of the topic (e.g., simple story, topic-related book, presentation of topic-related object, or photograph or poster).	Yes	Planning to bring gardening tools in a paper bag. I have a riddle that gives them clues they can use to guess what is in the bag. Opening event will take place 4/22.
11. Begin recording children's knowledge of the topic in web format on large paper that is then posted on the Project History Board.	Yes	4/22 Tool activity worked well and got the children started on their web. Web is posted on bulletin board.
12. Explain the Project Approach to families (e.g., send home a written explanation, hold an informational meeting, and/or send e-mail informational links).	Yes	Sent home handout from Illinois State Board of Education on the Project Approach and the different phases.
13. Notify families that the project is beginning and suggest ways they can be helpful (e.g., contribute materials, props, or expertise).	Yes	Notified families with an introduction letter about beginning the project and how they can support the work.
14. Provide opportunities for children to reflect on and represent their prior knowledge or experience with the topic (e.g., drawing, painting, sculpting, pretending, or dictating).	Yes	4/24 We used an activity during center time where children were asked to draw "something you would see in a garden."
15. Begin to generate a list of possible guest experts and locations for fieldwork.	Yes	We know we are going to botanical center on 4/27.
16. Hold large- and/or small-group discussions to identify and record children's questions about the topic (e.g., "What do you want to find out?").	Yes	4/23 Generated questions for botanical center field experience during a large group discussion.

Phase I		
	Record Yes, No, or N/A	**Record notes about the activities and dates that you implemented these items**
17. Select one or two questions and ask children to make predictions about the answers.	N/A	
18. Select one or two questions and ask children how they can find out the answers to their questions.	N/A	
19. Continue to capture children's questions on an ongoing basis (e.g., large- and/or small-group discussions, opportunities in the natural course of everyday activities).	Yes	*Add questions to list as children think about them.*
20. Display children's web, questions, and samples of Phase I work on the Project History Board (e.g., artwork, photographs, emergent writing).	Yes	*4/23 through end of project* *We will continue to display work from the Garden Project.*

Phase II		
	Record Yes, No, or N/A	**Record notes about the activities and dates that you implemented these items**
21. Continue to inform families about the progress of the project on a regular basis (e.g., newsletter stories, notes home, phone calls).	Yes	*We sent a note home when we began Phase II.*
22. Provide materials that could help children better understand the topic through firsthand exploration (e.g., authentic objects related to the topic such as tools, accessories, components, and/or samples).	Yes	*4/28* *We continue to have tools in the dramatic play and science areas. We discussed tools today in small group.*
23. Provide topic-related materials that could help children better understand the topic through experimentation (e.g., mixing, touching, cutting, connecting, mashing, cooking, combining, taking apart).	Yes	*4/27* *Children got to pot plants at the botanical center.* *5/13* *We planted lima beans in baggies and hung them on the window.*

Phase II		
	Record Yes, No, or N/A	Record notes about the activities and dates that you implemented these items
24. Provide topic-related props that could help children better understand the topic through dramatic play in the housekeeping and block areas (e.g., hats, uniforms, equipment, tools, accessories, signs, components, photographs).	Yes	We have provided gardening tools, hats, gloves, and plastic flowers and pots for planting. There are photos of flowers displayed.
25. Provide open-ended art materials that children could use to represent their growing understanding of the topic (e.g., a variety of papers, cardboard, tape/glue, staplers, cardboard tubes, cardboard boxes, clay, paint).	Yes	Children use tubes, paint, papers, pipe cleaners, tape, glue, and staplers to create plants.
26. Prepare teacher- and/or child-made word cards that include illustrations for the class word wall and for the writing area (e.g., children can suggest new topic-related words, child or teacher copies the word onto the card, and child illustrates it).	Yes	4/28 We made word cards to label tools. 4/29 Children wrote thank-you letters and drawings to the botanical center.
27. Teach the children to use drawing as a way to record information.	Yes	4/27 Children used clipboards and pencils to make field sketches while on the field trip to the botanical center. 4/30 Small groups of children used cameras to take pictures of plants around the school building (red bud, flowering tree, flowers). 4/30 Used field sketches from the botanical center as a guide for paintings of plants. Made observational drawings of a flower during small group time.
28. Read children's books that provide factual information and introduce new vocabulary (e.g., children's reference books, nonfiction books, stories based on factual information).	Yes	Ongoing throughout project.
29. Teach the children to use clipboards and pens to record their observations.	Yes	Children knew how to use clipboards before visiting the botanical center on 4/27.
30. Teach children how to conduct surveys.	Yes	Children have prior experience with creating and conducting surveys. We revisited how to conduct surveys with tally marks.
31. Ask children to draw a plan for three-dimensional constructions they intend to build individually or as part of a small group.	Yes	5/14 Children in small groups brainstormed how to make a planter. 5/18 Children designed the planter by creating a blueprint. They measured and drew the plans.

Phase II		
	Record Yes, No, or N/A	**Record notes about the activities and dates that you implemented these items**
32. Encourage children to take advantage of their peers' help or expertise (e.g., ask a friend who is good at hammering to help you connect the boards, find someone to hold the tape so you can cut it).	Yes	5/13 Children helped each other collect natural items to add to class compost.
33. Ask open-ended questions to provoke deeper thinking about the topic (e.g., What makes you think so? How could you do that? What else could we try? What do you think will happen if . . . ?).	Yes	Ongoing.
34. Regularly invite children to suggest additions to the Project History Board (e.g., new words, graphs, samples, anecdotal notes, quotes, photos, artifacts, drawings).	Yes	One of the students added a new word to the board: compost.
35. Provide regular opportunities for children to review and add new knowledge of the topic to the class topic web.	Yes	Ongoing.
36. Provide regular opportunities to review the list of questions, record any findings, and add additional questions.	Yes	Ongoing.
37. Invite a guest expert or experts to visit the class. Provide them with background on the project and the children's questions.	Yes	5/20 Observed a parent using tools to plant. Invited a dad to help with the construction of the planter because of his experience with tools and building.
38. Provide opportunities for fieldwork (e.g., focused observations of the topic, whether on or off site).	Yes	4/23 We visited the botanical center.
39. Prepare children to ask questions during fieldwork (e.g., take dictation of each child's question and record it on an index card, provide children with opportunities to practice asking questions).	Yes	Practiced questions beforehand. Informed botanical center staff that the children would be asking questions from a student-generated list.

	Phase II	
	Record Yes, No, or N/A	**Record notes about the activities and dates that you implemented these items**
40. Involve children in a variety of methods to summarize and view their findings (e.g., charting, diagramming, graphing).	Yes	5/11 Children created a story and diagram of how a flower grows. Children created a web about vegetables. 5/20 Children created drawings for a book about vegetables
41. Ask children what the group would like to make to show what they have learned about the topic (e.g., large group construction, playscape, mural, other).	Yes	5/26 Small groups discussed how to share the project. Tool crews made labels for the tools (sentence strip and marker).
42. Ask children to dictate plans for their group representation (e.g., What exactly do they plan to make? How will they make it? What materials do they think they will need? Who will make what?).	Yes	5/27 Created an invitation for parents and Jefferson staff and classrooms (small group sitting at round table, taking turns writing words, added small flowers and hearts).
43. Revisit and invite the children to update their plans for the group representation regularly (e.g., two or three times per week).	Yes	Revisited the plan for group representation.
44. Provide time and space for production of the group representation (e.g., at least an hour of uninterrupted choice time, a designated project production area, and/or learning centers set up for small group work on components of the representation).	Yes	6/1 Small groups of children delivered invitations to each staff member. Made finishing touches to unfinished parts of project.
45. Provide a variety of open-ended materials that lend themselves to the construction being produced.	Yes	Ongoing.
46. Teach children new skills or strategies that will help them accomplish project-related tasks (e.g., writing, tracing, taping, measuring, drilling, nailing, sewing, gluing, and/or folding).	Yes	5/15 Planted plants outdoors. 5/26 Children helped construct, paint, and decorate the planter.
47. Scaffold when an aspect of producing the representation is beyond children's ability (e.g., sawing thick wood, cutting wire, sewing fabric).	Yes	*Many, including:* Writing invitations. Building a planter. Making compost. Planting outdoors.

Phase III		
	Record Yes, No, or N/A	**Record notes about the activities and dates that you implemented these items**
48. Ask children how they would like to celebrate their accomplishments (e.g., open house for families, inviting another class over, displaying their group representation in a public place).	Yes	5/26 Children discussed how to share what they have learned.
49. Invite children to help make specific plans for the culminating event (e.g., deciding who will be invited, deciding what will happen at the event, making displays, designing invitations, and/or creating posters).	Yes	5/26 Children signed up for different "crews" that would be in charge of areas at the culminating event.
50. Support the children's efforts to implement the culminating event (e.g., mail invitations, prepare refreshments, and/or communicate with administration).	Yes	5/27 Created invitations (small group sitting at round table, taking turns writing words, added small flowers and hearts). 5/28 Small groups of children delivered invitations to each staff member. 6/3 Parent volunteer helped small groups of children put together treats for classes that would visit.
51. Prepare a final documentation display summarizing important events in the project (e.g., How did the project start? What were the children's questions? What were the salient events? What were the challenges? Which children especially benefited from participation in the project? How did the class benefit from participation in the project? What standards were met?).	Yes	6/1 Small group of children helped Mrs. K. put botanical center photos on display board. Displayed videotape of children and their favorite part of the project or what they learned during the project. 6/3 Finished display boards.
52. Summarize and communicate information about the project with families and administrators (e.g., hallway documentation display and/or newsletters or notes to families).	Yes	6/3 Held open house for parents, staff, and classrooms from 10:00–2:00.

APPENDIX A.3

Ms. Harrison completed the Project Approach Implementation Checklist to demonstrate how the Library Project developed. Teachers can use the blank version of this checklist (included as an appendix with Chapter 1) to document and guide the development of their projects.

Project Approach Implementation Checklist

Phase I		
	Record Yes, No, or N/A	**Record notes about the activities and dates that you implemented these items**
1. Select a topic based on children's interests, district curriculum, or an unexpected event (e.g., topics of conversations among children, unexpected event such as a new baby, or a neighborhood construction project).	Yes	*Early September* *Several children discovered hotel key cards in purses in the family living area, and they began to pretend they were library cards. They have repeated this pretend play several times, and other children have joined in.*
2. Select a topic that meets the criteria for a topic.	Yes	*Definitely meets all criteria for topic selection.*
3. Generate a teacher topic web with co-teacher(s).	Yes	*10/4* *We were fairly certain the children's interest was strong enough to support a project, so we spent our planning time making a teacher web.*
4. Select an aspect of the topic to use as a starting point (e.g., an aspect of the topic that is most likely to interest the children and lend itself to firsthand investigation).	Yes	*10/8* *Some of the parents brought in pictures they took at their community library with their child. I also took pictures at my local library and printed them out. I spent time looking through the pictures and talking with the children about what they noticed. It seems like shelves are high interest.*
5. Brainstorm a list of open-ended materials to begin collecting (e.g., papers, boxes, cardboard tubes, lids).	Yes	*10/9* *I have begun to collect pieces of cardboard and boxes children might want to use to build shelves. Our director donated a really sturdy box. I have borrowed a set of tools and connectors that can be used with cardboard.*
6. Brainstorm a list of child reference materials to begin collecting (e.g., children's reference books and nonfiction; adult manuals with diagrams and photos; and magazines or brochures).	Yes	*9/27* *I made my first trip to the library to take pictures and to check out books related to libraries. I was amazed at how many books I found! One has a map of the layout of a library!*
7. Begin to collect materials and tools that children may use to gather information.	Yes	*10/8* *I brought out materials children could use to make their own books. I started a class book with photos from libraries and started displaying pictures on the Project History Board. I am looking for real shelves the children can study and use for observational drawing.*
8. Brainstorm a list of vocabulary words and/ or terms children might learn as a result of participating in the project (e.g., words for topic-related tools, processes, objects, or jobs).	Yes	*10/4* *When we did our teacher web, we came up with quite a few words and concepts we want to reinforce. We plan to have children label the photos of libraries that we are collecting.*

Phase I		
	Record Yes, No, or N/A	Record notes about the activities and dates that you implemented these items
9. Identify an area of wall space at the large group meeting area where ongoing documentation of the project will be displayed on a Project History Board (e.g., low bulletin board or wall area that children can view and reference during class meetings).	Yes	9/22 Today we began to take down the documentation from the Piano Project and replace it with lists and our beginning webs.
10. Plan and implement an opening event to provoke discussion of the topic (e.g., simple story, topic-related book, presentation of topic-related object, or photograph or poster).	N/A	Early September This really happened naturally when the children discovered the hotel key cards and began to pretend they were library cards.
11. Begin recording children's knowledge of the topic in web format on large paper that is then posted on the Project History Board.	Yes	9/26 I invited children to help me make a web, and two children began to make their own web about the library. I put their web and my version on the Project History Board. 9/27 I invited children to join me individually or in small groups during choice time to add to the web.
12. Explain the Project Approach to families (e.g., send home a written explanation, hold an informational meeting, and/or send e-mail informational links).	N/A	Most families at our center are familiar with the Project Approach from past projects. New families learn about it in their orientation to our center.
13. Notify families that the project is beginning and suggest ways they can be helpful (e.g., contribute materials, props, or expertise).	Yes	9/29 I sent home a note to families telling them that we are starting a project on the library. I encouraged them to take their child to visit their local library.
14. Provide opportunities for children to reflect on and represent their prior knowledge or experience with the topic (e.g., drawing, painting, sculpting, pretending, or dictating).	Yes	10/10 I invited children to draw a picture about the library and dictate narrative about their picture. Each child put his or her picture in a clear plastic sleeve in a binder. The binder is our first book about the library.
15. Begin to generate a list of possible guest experts and locations for fieldwork.	Yes	10/11 I met with our director today, and we talked about who I might invite to visit as a guest expert for the Library Project. She suggested Malavika. Malavika is a parent of a child who attended our center in the past, and she works at a library.
16. Hold large- and/or small-group discussions to identify and record children's questions about the topic (e.g., "What do you want to find out?").	Yes	10/4 I began to record a few questions on 9/22, and children were interested in adding to the list today.

Phase I		
	Record Yes, No, or N/A	**Record notes about the activities and dates that you implemented these items**
17. Select one or two questions and ask children to make predictions about the answers.	Yes	10/5 I selected several questions and recorded them on a chart. Then I asked children to make predictions and write them in the middle column. I posted it on the Project History Board.
18. Select one or two questions and ask children how they can find out the answers to their questions.	Yes	10/5 I did this as I asked them to make predictions about how bar codes are attached to books and other objects. I modeled strategies for figuring out how they put bar codes on books by running my fingers across the surface of the book and noticing the edge of the bar code label (using sense of touch).
19. Continue to capture children's questions on an ongoing basis (e.g., large- and/or small-group discussions, opportunities in the natural course of everyday activities).	Yes	I am keeping a running list of questions on the board.
20. Display children's web, questions, and samples of Phase I work on the Project History Board (e.g., artwork, photographs, emergent writing).	Yes	10/10 Yes! It looks messy, but the webs, children's questions, Phase I drawings, and photographs labeled by the children are on the Project History Board.

Phase II		
	Record Yes, No, or N/A	**Record notes about the activities and dates that you implemented these items**
21. Continue to inform families about the progress of the project on a regular basis (e.g., newsletter stories, notes home, phone calls).	Yes	Parents and other family members bring their children and pick them up, so they see the progress of the project firsthand. I send anecdotal notes home every day. They include information about the children's progress on the project.
22. Provide materials that could help children better understand the topic through firsthand exploration (e.g., authentic objects related to the topic such as tools, accessories, components, and/or samples).	Yes	10/17 Children are extremely interested in bar codes, so I have collected books with different types of bar codes and other labeling systems for the children to sort and tally.
23. Provide topic-related materials that could help children better understand the topic through experimentation (e.g., mixing, touching, cutting, connecting, mashing, cooking, combining, taking apart).	Yes	10/12 and ongoing Children fold, tape, and/or staple paper together to make their own books. 10/17 A child found a book with a ripped page. I showed him how to use tape to repair it. 11/14 Children used their senses of touch and sight to explore wooden stacking bookshelves.

Phase II		
	Record Yes, No, or N/A	**Record notes about the activities and dates that you implemented these items**
24. Provide topic-related props that could help children better understand the topic through dramatic play in the housekeeping and block areas (e.g., hats, uniforms, equipment, tools, accessories, signs, components, photographs).	Yes	11/1 *Malavika, a librarian who is a parent of one of my former students, loaned us a real scanner to use in dramatic play.* 11/14 *My Project Approach mentor loaned us real stacking bookshelves to examine as we build our own shelves.*
25. Provide open-ended art materials that children could use to represent their growing understanding of the topic (e.g., a variety of papers, cardboard, tape/glue, staplers, cardboard tubes, cardboard boxes, clay, paint).	Yes	*Ongoing. We are lucky to have an art studio within the school that is well stocked with recyclables as well as commercial art media and tools. We keep art materials that we are currently using in our portable art cart.*
26. Prepare teacher- and/or child-made word cards that include illustrations for the class word wall and for the writing area (e.g., children can suggest new topic-related words, child or teacher copies the word onto the card, and child illustrates it).	Yes	*Ongoing.* 10/19 *We worked on writing book-related words today. Words are on display in the writing area.*
27. Teach the children to use drawing as a way to record information.	Yes	*Ongoing.* 11/15 *Children used observational drawings of bookshelves to think about how to build them.*
28. Read children's books that provide factual information and introduce new vocabulary (e.g., children's reference books, nonfiction books, stories based on factual information).	Yes	*We began to collect these during Phase I and added to our collection throughout.*
29. Teach the children to use clipboards and pens to record their observations.	Yes	*Ongoing.*
30. Teach children how to conduct surveys.	Yes	10/19 *Children used clipboards and T-charts. They surveyed teachers and children in other classrooms and tallied responses.*
31. Ask children to draw a plan for three-dimensional constructions they intend to build individually or as part of a small group.	Yes	11/14 *Children drew individual plans for shelves.*

Phase II		
	Record Yes, No, or N/A	**Record notes about the activities and dates that you implemented these items**
32. Encourage children to take advantage of their peers' help or expertise (e.g., ask a friend who is good at hammering to help you connect the boards, find someone to hold the tape so you can cut it).	Yes	*Mid-November* *Children constructed bookshelves. They usually worked on them in small groups. Children had to help each other to saw the cardboard and to keep the pieces of cardboard close together so the screwdrivers could be used to screw them together.*
33. Ask open-ended questions to provoke deeper thinking about the topic (e.g., What makes you think so? How could you do that? What else could we try? What do you think will happen if . . . ?).	Yes	*Ongoing.*
34. Regularly invite children to suggest additions to the Project History Board (e.g., new words, graphs, samples, anecdotal notes, quotes, photos, artifacts, drawings).	Yes	*Ongoing.*
35. Provide regular opportunities for children to review and add new knowledge of the topic to the class topic web.	Yes	*Ongoing*
36. Provide regular opportunities to review the list of questions, record any findings, and add additional questions.	Yes	*Ongoing.*
37. Invite a guest expert or experts to visit the class. Provide them with background on the project and the children's questions.	Yes	*10/11* *I spent 45 minutes explaining our project to our guest expert, Malavika, answering her questions, and brainstorming about her visit.* *10/22* *Our guest expert visited. Children had prepared questions for her visit.* *11/6* *We revisited what we learned during our guest expert's visit.*
38. Provide opportunities for fieldwork (e.g., focused observations of the topic, whether on or off site).	Yes	*12/6* *Children visited the Bettendorf Library. I had previously talked with the children's librarian, Christine, and she talked about some of the children's high-interest topics, including book repair and bar codes.*
39. Prepare children to ask questions during fieldwork (e.g., take dictation of each child's question and record it on an index card, provide children with opportunities to practice asking questions).	Yes	*12/4 and 12/5* *We discussed our trip to the library and reviewed our questions.*

Phase II		
	Record Yes, No, or N/A	**Record notes about the activities and dates that you implemented these items**
40. Involve children in a variety of methods to summarize and view their findings (e.g., charting, diagramming, graphing).	Yes	10/17 We tallied bar codes. 10/19 Children tallied the results of their surveys.
41. Ask children what the group would like to make to show what they have learned about the topic (e.g., large group construction, playscape, mural, other).	Yes	12/7 Children discussed what they saw on the field trip. They reviewed photos from the field trip in informal small groups during choice time, and they discussed what they would like to make (book sorter).
42. Ask children to dictate plans for their group representation (e.g., What exactly do they plan to make? How will they make it? What materials do they think they will need? Who will make what?).	Yes	12/10 We began to talk about making the book sorter, and I showed them some of the materials they could use. One student, Henry, got us started.
43. Revisit and invite the children to update their plans for the group representation regularly (e.g., two or three times per week).	Yes	12/10 through 12/14 Children constructed, elaborated on, and revised the book sorting machine.
44. Provide time and space for production of the group representation (e.g., at least an hour of uninterrupted choice time, a designated project production area, and/or learning centers set up for small group work on components of the representation).	Yes	12/10 through 12/14 Children constructed the book sorter in the circle area. We were able to move it to one side to have large group meetings.
45. Provide a variety of open-ended materials that lend themselves to the construction being produced.	Yes	12/10 through 12/14 We had lots of cardboard, vinyl, plastic carry-out containers from a restaurant, collage materials, and packing tape.
46. Teach children new skills or strategies that will help them accomplish project-related tasks (e.g., writing, tracing, taping, measuring, drilling, nailing, sewing, gluing, and/or folding).	Yes	11/14 through 12/4 Children learned to saw, poke holes, and use the special screwdrivers to connect the cardboard pieces of the bookshelves. 12/4 One student, Addelyn, mastered using masking tape to create a fish tank like the one she had seen at the library. 12/10 through 12/14 We worked a lot on cutting packing tape.
47. Scaffold when an aspect of producing the representation is beyond children's ability (e.g., sawing thick wood, cutting wire, sewing fabric).	Yes	12/10 through 12/14 I needed to help children get past many small obstacles during the construction of the bookshelves and the book sorter.

Phase III		
	Record Yes, No, or N/A	**Record notes about the activities and dates that you implemented these items**
48. Ask children how they would like to celebrate their accomplishments (e.g., open house for families, inviting another class over, displaying their group representation in a public place).	Yes	1/24 We are back from winter break, and we had a discussion at circle time about all the things we learned during the Library Project. We decided that we want to make a big book about our Library Project. We have been exploring watercolors, and I was delighted when the children suggested we make our book with watercolors.
49. Invite children to help make specific plans for the culminating event (e.g., deciding who will be invited, deciding what will happen at the event, making displays, designing invitations, and/or creating posters).	Yes	1/25 through 1/30 Children worked on pages for the watercolor book about the Library Project. We discussed how we planned to share the book with the children in the Dragonfly Room.
50. Support the children's efforts to implement the culminating event (e.g., mail invitations, prepare refreshments, and/or communicate with administration).	Yes	1/24 I asked Lori, the teacher in the Dragonfly Room, if we could make a presentation about the Library Project to her preschool students. We decided we would do this on January 31.
51. Prepare a final documentation display summarizing important events in the project (e.g., How did the project start? What were the children's questions? What were the salient events? What were the challenges? Which children especially benefited from participation in the project? How did the class benefit from participation in the project? What standards were met?).	Yes	February I am working on formal documentation posters that will be printed, laminated, and displayed in the center entry.
52. Summarize and communicate information about the project with families and administrators (e.g., hallway documentation display and/or newsletters or notes to families).	Yes	I reported on the culminating event in our newsletter to families.

Training Activities

INTRODUCTION TO THE TRAINING MATERIALS

In-service and preservice teachers often receive training in a curricular approach without considering how they might actually integrate it into their own setting. Trainers and college instructors can use the training materials provided in this appendix to help practicing teachers and future teachers think more deeply about how they can use the Project Approach in their own early childhood settings. Teachers who want to form a Project Approach study group can use the materials to support their discussion about how to implement high-quality project work. The materials are intended to be used in conjunction with the book and the Project Approach Implementation Checklist, and they include PowerPoint slides, discussion questions, and activities.

PowerPoint Slides

Twenty-two sets of PowerPoint slides are available online. They include main ideas from the book and are organized in the order of the chapters:

Chapter 1: PowerPoints 1, 2, 3, 4, 5, and 6

Chapter 2: PowerPoints 7 and 8

Chapter 3: PowerPoints 9, 10, 11, 12, 13, 14, and 15

Chapter 4: PowerPoints 16, 17, 18, and 19

Chapter 5: PowerPoints 20 and 21

Chapter 6: PowerPoint 22

These slides introduce the Project Approach, explore the role of teachers and students in project work, and share how projects get started.

Discussion Questions

Three types of discussion questions are provided for each chapter. Questions for observation are intended to help readers connect with their own prior experience related to the chapter content. Questions for reflection are intended to help readers think about possibilities related to the chapter content. Questions for application are intended to help readers think about how they might apply the chapter content in their current or future early childhood setting.

Activities

One or more training activities are provided for each chapter. Trainers, college instructors, or teachers who form a Project Approach study group could use the instructions to lead these activities. They are intended to help readers integrate the chapter content by engaging actively in partner or small group work. Task sheets and other handouts needed to implement the training activities are provided.

CHAPTER 1
Getting Started With the Project Approach

DISCUSSION QUESTIONS

Use the discussion questions that follow to begin a discussion about the Project Approach and the usefulness of the Project Approach Implementation Checklist.

Observe

1. Discuss what you have observed about the Project Approach in the past.

   a. Have you ever observed a teacher implementing the Project Approach?

   b. What was the project?

   c. What were children doing?

   d. What things did you notice the teacher doing?

   e. What questions do you have about what you observed?

Reflect

1. When you were a child, did you ever engage in an in-depth investigation of something that interested you? This could have been an investigation you did on your own, or you might have had assistance from an adult. What do you remember about the experience? How did it feel to be involved in the investigation?

2. Look over the Project Approach Implementation Checklist. What do you notice about how it is organized? What kinds of things does it guide teachers to do? How might it help you during project work?

3. Many people know how to use a cell phone but do not understand how it works. Can you think of something you encounter in your everyday life but do not really understand how it works? What would it take for you to understand it?

Apply

1. Identify the most successful learner in your class of children and list dispositions that child uses that help him or her succeed (i.e., the disposition to be persistent). Now think of a child in your class who is less successful. Can you list dispositions that contribute to the child's lack of success (i.e., the disposition to be argumentative)?

2. Teachers often struggle with the tension between implementing what they know to be recommended practices and the expectations of their school system. Do you anticipate that this struggle will apply to you as you begin to implement the Project Approach? How might you resolve this tension?

3. In Chapter 1, we discuss universal design for learning. After reading the chapter, list the components of universal design for learning. Describe one way in which each component is present in your classroom.

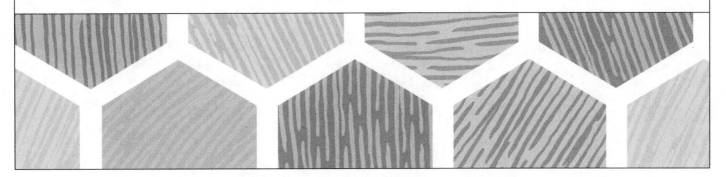

CHAPTER 1 **TRAINING ACTIVITIES**

Activity 1: Using the Project Approach Implementation Checklist to Analyze a Project

Concept: In the following activity, educators will engage with the Implementation Checklist within a low-stress, small-group activity.

Materials:

- Blank copy of the Project Approach Implementation Checklist (printed in the appendix to Chapter 1) for each participant

- Copy of the Project Approach Implementation Checklist that was completed by the teachers in the Dog Project for each small group (see Appendix A)

- Computer and Internet access

Directions:

1. Work in small groups of five to six people.

2. Open the link to the project examples on the Illinois Early Learning (IEL) web site on the computer (https://illinoisearlylearning.org/resources/pa/projects/).

3. Browse through the various project topics on the site.

4. Choose a project example with your group. Take a few minutes to read the chosen project report on the web site.

5. Using your copy of the Project Approach Implementation Checklist, evaluate the fidelity of implementation of the Project Approach in your assigned project.

6. Ask one member of your group to be the official recorder. The recorder will note how each checklist item was met on the blank Implementation Checklist. You may use the completed checklist from the Dog Project as an example.

7. When you are finished, discuss your findings with your small group. Were there some checklist items that were not met? Why? What else could the teacher have done?

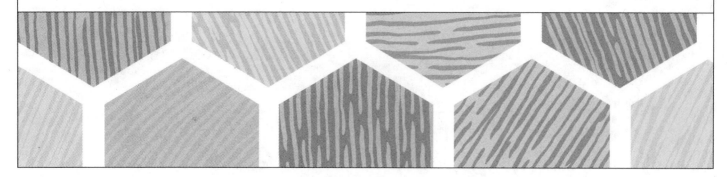

The Project Approach for All Learners: A Hands-On Guide for Inclusive Early Childhood Classrooms,
by Sallee J. Beneke, Michaelene M. Ostrosky, and Lilian G. Katz.

CHAPTER 2
Defining the Role of the Teacher

DISCUSSION QUESTIONS

Use these questions to begin a discussion about the role of the teacher in project work.

Observe

- Watch Video A.1 on the book's web page. What do you notice about the way the teacher, Ms. Harrison, positions her body as she listens to the child, Bianca? How is this helpful to Ms. Harrison?

- Active listening involves paying attention not just to what children say, but also to what they are trying to say. Watch Video A.2. Review the section in Chapter 2 that describes active listening. What active listening strategies do you notice the teacher, Ms. Harrison, using with her student Henry?

Reflect

- Rather than planning in advance what the children will do and what they will learn in a given week, implementing the Project Approach requires flexibility and frequent adjustments to one's plans in response to children's interests. How do you feel about this way of teaching? Does it make you anxious, or can you imagine being this flexible quite easily? In your view, what are the potential pros and cons?

- In Chapter 2, the teacher's role is described as that of a researcher, as they assess children's knowledge and skills and then develop and revise teaching strategies based on these ongoing assessments. How does this compare to the way you currently assess children's knowledge and skills? What resources (e.g., knowledge, materials, personnel, professional development) might you need to assess children in this way?

Apply

- Three types of questions are described in Chapter 2: "big" questions, clarifying questions, and questions about alternatives. Imagine that many of the children in your class are interested in the ants that have recently appeared on the playground and you are considering starting a project on ants. What are three big questions you might ask the group to get the conversation about ants going?

- The topic of documenting children's learning for display is introduced in Chapter 2. One way in which this is done is through a working documentation board that is dynamic and not static. Where can you set up this type of documentation board in your classroom? How would you introduce it to the children?

Activity 1: Practicing Wait Time

Concept: Experts recommend that teachers wait 3–5 seconds before repeating or rephrasing a question. The following activity is designed to raise educators' awareness of the value of wait time.

Materials:

- Task Sheet: List of Questions handout, which follows on the next page

Directions:

1. Find a partner to work with on this activity. Each of you will need a copy of the Task Sheet: List of Questions on the page that follows.

2. First, one partner will ask the other partner Questions 1–5 on the list, allowing only 1 second between questions for the other partner to answer. Then, the first partner will ask Questions 6–10, allowing 5 seconds between questions for the other partner to answer.

3. Next, switch roles with your partner so that you both have the opportunity to answer the questions with varying wait times.

4. Join others in your small group to discuss your experience.

    a. Which questions were most frustrating when only 1 second was provided for an answer? Why?

    b. Which questions were the easiest to answer when only 1 second was provided?

    c. How will this experience impact your teaching?

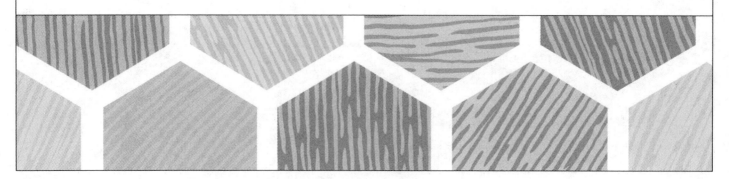

The Project Approach for All Learners: A Hands-On Guide for Inclusive Early Childhood Classrooms,
by Sallee J. Beneke, Michaelene M. Ostrosky, and Lilian G. Katz.

List of Questions

Instructions: You will ask the questions below to a partner. For Questions 1–5, allow 1 second between questions for your partner to answer. For Questions 6–10, allow 5 seconds between questions for your partner to answer. After all of the questions are completed, switch roles with your partner so that both of you have an opportunity to experience the impact of various wait times.

Questions:

1. What is your name?

2. What day is it?

3. Why did you become a teacher?

4. How many years have you been a teacher?

5. Do you like teaching?

6. What are your three favorite things about teaching?

7. What is the name of your school or center?

8. How many children are in your class?

9. What makes a great teacher?

10. Did you like answering these questions?

CHAPTER 3
Implementing With Fidelity

DISCUSSION QUESTIONS

Use these questions to begin a discussion about implementing the Project Approach with fidelity.

Observe

- Teachers often get ideas for topics for projects from observing children's pretend play. If you think about what your students like to pretend about in their indoor and outdoor play, what possible topics come to mind?

- Sometimes project topics emerge from unanticipated events. Can you remember an event encountered by your students or their families that could have launched a project?

- Chapter 3 highlights the importance of making open-ended materials and real objects available to children. What open-ended materials do you have available in your classroom that children could use for representation? What materials do you need to collect?

Reflect

- Why is it important for teachers to gather reference materials that children can use to do their own research?

- Chapter 3 recommends that teachers make webs with children to reflect their current knowledge about the topic. What experience, if any, do you have with webbing? How do you feel about using webs versus lists? Do you have any concerns?

- How do you think families will feel about their children engaging in project work? What are some ways you might help them to react positively to this approach?

Apply

- In what ways might a child's or the program's cultural context affect the topic that is selected for project work?

- The younger the children in the class, the nearer in proximity the topic of the project should be to them. This allows children the opportunity for firsthand investigations, and they are able to revisit the topic frequently. What are some potential topics in or near your school or center that might be worth investigating?

- In Chapter 3, you learned that teachers may choose to meet with children in small groups if meeting in large groups is challenging for them. Given your current context, how do you plan to meet with children to add to the web and to gather their questions? Why?

CHAPTER 3 **TRAINING ACTIVITIES**

Activity 1: Identifying High-Interest Topics

Concept: In this activity, educators will gain hands-on experience actively listening to children to identify project topics. As adults engage in casual conversations with children and enter into their play, these topics start to present themselves.

Directions:

- Create a list of all the students in your class. You will use this to record your observations during this activity.

- Observe the children in your class during choice time, with the goal of identifying topics that are of high interest to them. If you do not have a class of your own, arrange to observe in another teacher's classroom during choice time.

- While observing, use active listening skills. Find out about children's interests by engaging in casual conversations and joining them in dramatic play. Pay special attention to children who have limited communication skills, carefully observing their nonverbal behaviors.

- On your class list, note student interests that you noticed while observing.

- Postobservation discussion: When you meet with your fellow educators again, discuss the following in small groups:

  - What was your observation experience like?

  - Was it difficult to ascertain high-interest topics?

  - Were you able to identify high-interest topics for children with disabilities?

  - What were the challenges? How did you overcome these challenges?

  - Were you able to find topics that were of shared interest among the children? Do these topics meet the criteria for topic selection described in Chapter 3?

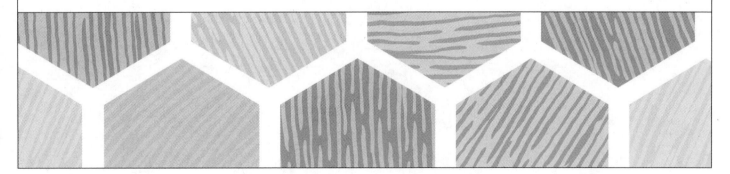

Activity 2: Identifying Topics for Projects

Concept: This activity is designed to provide educators with experience using the criteria for topic selection to evaluate the potential of topics.

Materials:

- A copy of Task Sheet: Identifying Topics for Projects

Directions:

- Review the sections in Chapter 3 that discuss criteria for topic selection.

- Think of three project topics that teachers at your center or school might investigate.

- Guess which topic would likely be most successful.

- Record three potential topics at the top of Columns 2, 3, and 4 on your copy of the Task Sheet.

- Read the criteria for topic selection in the left-hand column of the task sheet. Evaluate each of your topics based on the criteria, checking off the applicable boxes.

- Discuss the experience in small groups. Were you surprised at the results of this activity?

Identifying Topics for Projects

Instructions: Think of three topics for projects that children and teachers at your school or center might investigate. Use the criteria for topic selection in the first column to evaluate the potential topics. If the topic meets the criterion, place a checkmark in that box.

Criteria for topic selection	Topic #1: _____	Topic #2: _____	Topic #3: _____
1. Directly observable			
2. Within most children's experiences			
3. Firsthand direct investigation is feasible			
4. Local resources are available			
5. Has potential for representation			
6. Parental participation is likely			
7. Sensitive to local culture			
8. Interesting to many children			
9. Related to curriculum goals			
10. Opportunities to apply basic skills			
11. Not too narrow or broad			
12. Interesting to the teacher			

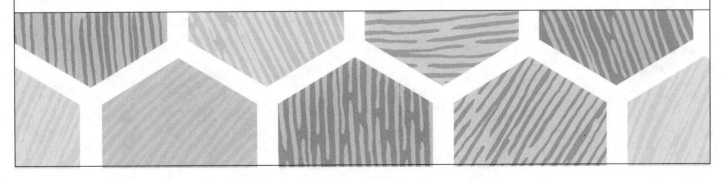

CHAPTER 3 **TRAINING ACTIVITIES**

Activity 3: Brainstorming Phase I Activities

Concept: In this activity, educators will generate ideas for Phase I project activities. Educators will brainstorm activities for three projects: shoes, bicycles, and the hardware store.

Materials:

- A copy of Task Sheet: Brainstorming Phase I Activities and Materials

Directions:

- Find a partner for this activity.

- Look over your copy of Task Sheet: Brainstorming Phase I Activities and Materials.

- Work with a partner to complete the task sheet, brainstorming activities and materials for three projects: shoes, bicycles, and the hardware store.

- When you and your partner have completed your task sheet, compare your work with that of some fellow educators.

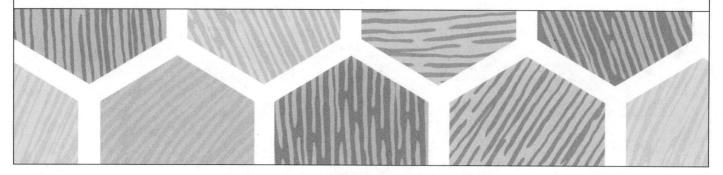

Brainstorming Phase I Activities and Materials

This activity is intended to provide you with experience in planning Phase I activities. Work with a partner to plan for these three topics.

Topic: Shoes

Ideas for an opening event:

Ideas for reflecting on past experience:

Helpful materials:

Topic: Bicycles

Ideas for an opening event:

Ideas for reflecting on past experience:

Helpful materials:

Topic: The Hardware Store

Ideas for an opening event:

Ideas for reflecting on past experience:

Helpful materials:

Activity 4: Phase I—Planning Accommodations for Case Studies

Concept: This activity helps educators think about how they can help children with disabilities successfully participate in project work. Case studies are introduced and will be revisited in Phases II and III.

Materials:

- A copy of Task Sheet: Case Study Activity I

Directions:

- This activity is intended to help you think about how you will tailor project work so that children with disabilities get optimal benefit from it.

- Read the nine brief case students on your copy of the Task Sheet: Case Study Activity I.

- Select three students from the worksheet.

- Answer the following questions for each of the three children:

  ◦ How could Phase I project work benefit this child (e.g., selecting a high-interest topic, expressing and representing prior knowledge about the topic, posing initial questions about the topic)?

  ◦ What strengths could this child use?

  ◦ What accommodations could you make to support the child's successful participation in Phase I?

- Share your ideas with the group. Discuss each of the nine case studies, and share your thoughts on the children you chose. Activities in Phases II and III will return to these same case studies.

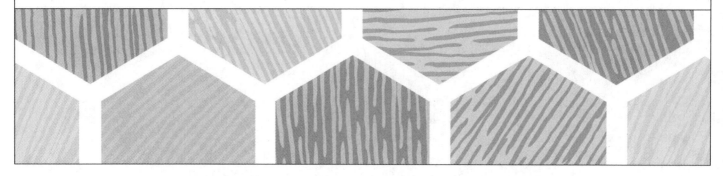

CHAPTER 3 **TASK SHEET**

Case Study Activity I

How could participation in project work benefit this child?

What strengths could this child use?

What accommodations could you make to support the child's successful participation in Phase I?

Case Study A

Ajari, a 3.5-year-old boy, has increased his use of eye contact, smiles, giggles, and vocalizations and is a more willing participant in activities. He has made progress interacting with toys and tasks for longer periods of time before reverting to self-directed activities (e.g., books, blocks, magnets, vibrating toys, bells, climbing, structures). Ajari sometimes shows interest in his peers' activities during center time. He is good at running and climbing. He now communicates his wants and needs by getting items himself and bringing them to adults if he needs assistance. He often talks aloud and repeats lines from movies or television shows.

Case Study B

Baylee, age 4.5 years, has a lot of energy and plays well with other students. She is able to respond to questions vocally or with the assistance of an augmentative and alternative communication (AAC) device. She knows her shapes and letters and can count from 1 to 15. Baylee likes to jump and be hugged. She enjoys nursery rhymes and will often sing them out loud. Baylee likes to count, especially when she seems upset. She enjoys coloring with markers and crayons, and she likes to line up the markers or crayons on a table. She really enjoys animals and will often draw pictures of dogs and cats.

Case Study C

Cameron is 3 years old. After 2 years in foster care, he was recently adopted. He was born addicted to methamphetamines, and as a result, he has developmental delays in almost every area. He has significant vision loss and is almost completely blind in his left eye. Cameron also has some physical delays. He uses one-word phrases to communicate his needs, and he will sometimes imitate words. Cameron enjoys playing with shape sorters and three-piece inset puzzles. He loves the classroom sensory table (especially water, sand, and rice) and is very interested in his peers.

Case Study D

Devin is 4 years old. He has an intellectual disability. He uses some short phrases to communicate (i.e., two-word combinations). He likes to match colors and shapes, and he is beginning to point to some shapes when named. He also is beginning to point to pictures in familiar books when prompted. Devin is very interested in cars, trucks, blocks, and buildings, although he typically likes to play by himself.

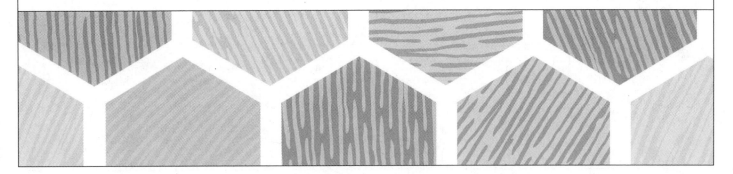

Case Study E

Evelyn is 5 years old. She was (for the most part) typically developing until she was 18 months old, when her parents noticed she was losing her language skills and regressing in some skills, such as toileting. Initially doctors were not sure why this happened; however, Evelyn was subsequently diagnosed with Rett syndrome. She was nonverbal and displayed significant challenging behaviors when she began preschool at age 3. Now, at age 5, Evelyn is communicating using some signs and interacting occasionally with peers, and her challenging behaviors have decreased. She needs adult support when completing tasks that she is not interested in, and she needs adult support for self-regulation (e.g., when she becomes frustrated, angry, or sad). Evelyn does not like fine motor tasks such as drawing. She enjoys playing in the kitchen area and with magnetic tiles, especially if her friends are nearby.

Case Study F

Frankie, a kindergartner, is 6 years old and has been diagnosed with attention-deficit/hyperactivity disorder. He engages in some challenging behaviors. He uses full sentences and has very strong receptive language skills. He ignores adult requests to clean up, grabs toys from peers, and runs away from adults on the playground. Frankie needs visual supports to understand expectations in the classroom. For example, for large group, he uses visual supports that explain: "It's circle time. I sit in my cube chair. I listen to the teacher. It is time to read a book." Frankie needs breaks during structured class periods to help keep his attention on the task at hand. He loves to be outdoors.

Case Study G

Garret is 5 years old and was recently diagnosed with autism spectrum disorder. He engages in challenging behaviors when presented with activities that he does not like. He uses some language, which typically consists of "phrases" that he has heard, although these may or may not be used appropriately (e.g., he will say "I want pig" when he sees a picture of a pig in a book). Garret is very motivated by the toy farm and zoo animals. He also enjoys music. When a teacher prompts Garret to use different materials in the classroom, he often screams and needs supports (visual and verbal); he calms down when told that he can have his small plastic animals back after he finishes the activity. Garret typically plays by himself and gets upset if a peer comes near his space.

Case Study H

Helen, a nonnative English speaker, is a 4-year-old girl who loves to ride her toy tractor and tricycle. She also enjoys one-on-one time with adults. In the classroom, she has been observed touching and grabbing others, talking loudly to peers, and often entering into her classmates' personal space. Helen typically responds to verbal cues after two or three times. She enjoys any activities with the teaching staff, especially music and movement. Helen also does better in one-on-one situations with peers, but she needs reminders to keep her hands to herself.

Case Study I

Iona is a 3-year-old student who was diagnosed with a traumatic brain injury after a car accident. She uses a wheelchair, has visual impairments, and requires adult support for most daily activities. Iona benefits from consistency in her days, loves to be held and bounced on exercise balls, and enjoys music. She likes to engage with items that light up, such as shape sorters and light tables. She can participate in parallel play using the same materials as her peers if an adult is sitting directly next to her and uses hand-under-hand to help her interact with materials.

CHAPTER 4
Supporting the Investigation

DISCUSSION QUESTIONS

Use the questions that follow to discuss the many ways in which teachers can support children's engagement in firsthand investigations.

Observe

- How is the way of learning that was described in Chapter 4 similar or different from the way you currently teach? What aspects of active investigation do you look forward to adopting?

- Chapter 4 explains the value of integrating authentic resources, such as topic-related artifacts and tools, into the classroom environment. What kinds of authentic resources have you brought into your classroom, and for what purpose? What was the impact on children of using authentic resources versus pictures of the items?

- Think of a child with a disability who you currently have or have had as a student. How might project work impact this student?

- Chapter 4 contrasts drawing something from memory with drawing to collect data. How are these two activities similar or different from the way you have instructed children to use drawing in your class?

Reflect

- In what ways does the Project Approach provide a context for learning?

- Chapter 4 explains that the heart of the Project Approach is authentic child research aimed at helping children find answers to their questions. Why is this way of learning important?

- Does the type of learning that takes place through project investigations support or detract from addressing children's individualized education program goals or readiness skills? Why?

- Chapter 4 lists many strategies that teachers can share with children so that they can investigate independently (e.g., using new vocabulary, using drawing as a way to collect information, finding information in reference books). What are some strategies that you look forward to teaching children? Why?

- Which of the following is most effective: planning to meet standards or planning based on the interests of the children? What makes you think so?

Apply

- When are regular times during your daily schedule that you could meet with children to revisit and revise the questions that they have posed?

- What are the potential benefits of participating in a project investigation for all children? What are the potential benefits of participating in a project investigation for children with disabilities? What accommodations or adaptations might you need to consider in order to fully engage all of your students in project work?

Activity 1: Planning to Use Authentic Resources

Concept: The following activity is designed to help educators think resourcefully about authentic materials that can be incorporated into the classroom for use in project work.

Note: This activity is planned for a group of 24 educators. You can increase or decrease the number of project topics discussed depending on the size of the group.

Materials:

- Chart paper for six charts
- Six different dark- or bright-colored markers
- Timer

Directions:

- Form groups of four to five people. Each group needs a chart paper and a colored marker.
- Identify a leader for your group. That leader should make a T-chart with two columns on your chart paper.
- Title the chart with one of the following six project topics: Bread, Shoes, Cars, Bicycles, Farm, Cats.
- Label Column 1 with the header "Material." Label Column 2 with the header "Location."
- Hang your poster on the wall or place it on a table so that it is easily viewed by the other groups. Then stand in front of your group's poster.
- Set the timer for 3 minutes.
- In the 3 minutes allotted, brainstorm ideas for topic-related authentic materials that a teacher could bring into the classroom. These ideas are to be recorded in the first column. In the second column, note where this item might be located in the classroom environment (e.g., science area, block area).
- After 3 minutes, rotate clockwise to the next poster. Take your group's marker with you as you rotate.
- Repeat the brainstorming activity for each poster.
- Once your group has had a chance to rotate through all the posters, take 5 minutes to visit each poster and view the ideas of your peers. Then return to your seat.
- Engage in a whole-group discussion about the activity. What was easy, difficult, or surprising about the experience? Which ideas did you think were especially helpful?

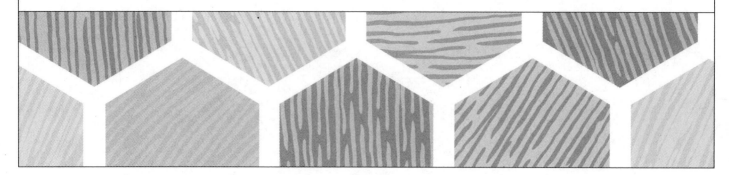

CHAPTER 4 TRAINING ACTIVITIES

Activity 2: Planning for Next Week

Concepts: The following activity engages educators in planning Phase II activities in response to children's questions.

Materials:

- A copy of Task Sheet: Lesson Planning in Phase II, which follows these directions

Directions:

- Form small groups to engage in Phase II lesson planning. Each educator will need a copy of Task Sheet: Lesson Planning in Phase II.

- One way that projects can be child initiated is through teacher-planned activities that help children answer their questions. In your small group, work together to complete the plan for either the project on shoes or the project on bicycles, as explained on the Task Sheet.

- When all educators are finished with the sheet, hold a group discussion on the experience.

  ◦ Was it difficult to plan based on children's questions? Why? Why not?

  ◦ How was this way of planning different from the way you typically plan?

165

Lesson Planning in Phase II

Part of lesson planning for Phase II is planning experiences in response to the questions children have posed at the end of Phase I. In this activity, you will have an opportunity to generate plans based on children's questions.

Project Topic #1: Shoes

Questions from Phase I:

- Where do you buy shoes?
- Why do some dogs wear shoes?
- What kinds of shoes are there?
- How do they put lights inside of some shoes that blink?
- How do you make a shoe?
- What sizes are shoes?

Next Week

Ideas for Centers

Blocks	Dramatic Play	Fluid Materials	Science	Easel
Manipulatives	Writing	Books	Cooking	Art
Computers	Outdoors	Quiet		

Ideas for Circle Time

Monday	**Tuesday**	**Wednesday**	**Thursday**	**Friday**

Ideas for Special Activities

Monday	**Tuesday**	**Wednesday**	**Thursday**	**Friday**

Project Topic #2: Bicycles

Questions from Phase I:

- Where do you buy bicycles?
- How do you ride a bicycle?
- How do you put on the wheels?
- I saw a monkey at the circus ride a bike. How is a monkey taught to do this?
- Do bikes break?

Next Week

Ideas for Centers

Blocks	Dramatic Play	Fluid Materials	Science	Easel
Manipulatives	Writing	Books	Cooking	Art
Computers	Outdoors	Quiet		

Ideas for Circle Time

Monday	Tuesday	Wednesday	Thursday	Friday

Ideas for Special Activities

Monday	Tuesday	Wednesday	Thursday	Friday

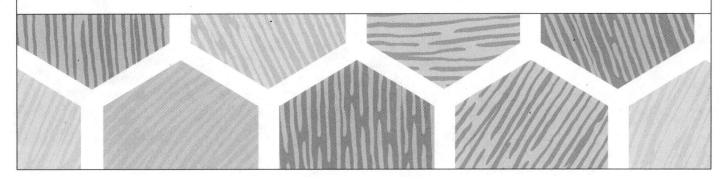

Activity 3: Planning for Data Collection

Concepts: In this activity, educators will think creatively about the many ways that young children who cannot yet read or write can collect data about their project topic.

Materials:

- A copy of the Task Sheet: Strategies for Data Collection

Directions:

- In this activity you will consider the idea of children as data collectors. Try thinking "outside the box" about ways children can collect data.

- Find a partner and work together to complete the Task Sheet: Strategies for Collecting Data. List strategies that young children can use to collect data.

- When everyone at your table is finished, compare your ideas with those of others at your table.

- Participate in a whole-group discussion, sharing someone's idea that challenged you to think differently, that you had not considered, or that you thought was a good one.

Strategies for Collecting Data

As young children investigate a project topic in depth, they discover new ideas and information (data). However, because they do not yet know how to write words, they cannot collect and record these discoveries as an adult would. Therefore, it is important to teach children strategies and provide them with materials that will help them collect data.

Task:

Work with your partner to answer the following question by listing ideas in the table below: What strategies might children use to collect data?

1.	Draw a picture of an experience they have had with the topic.
2.	
3.	
4.	
5.	
6.	
7.	
8.	

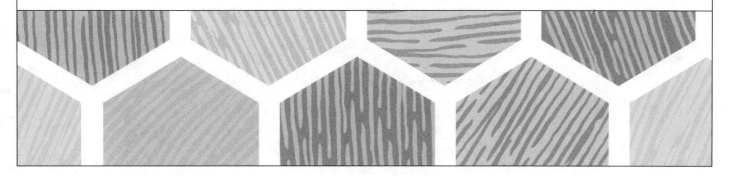

Activity 3: Phase II—Planning Accommodations Using the Case Studies

Note: This activity assumes that participants have previously engaged with the case studies in the Phase I version of this activity (see Chapter 3 section of Appendix B).

Concept: The purpose of this activity is for educators to think about how they can help children with disabilities successfully participate in project work. You will revisit the case studies that you read in the Phase I activity. The case studies will be revisited in Phase III as well.

Materials:

- A copy of Task Sheet: Case Study Activity II

Directions:

- This activity is intended to help you think about how you will tailor project work so that children with disabilities can optimally benefit from it.

- Read the case studies from your copy of the Task Sheet: Case Study Activity II.

- Form small groups and choose three children to focus on.

- Answer the following questions for each of the three children:

  ◦ How could Phase II project work benefit this child (e.g., firsthand investigation to find answers to questions, representing new understanding, interviewing guest experts, fieldwork)?

  ◦ What strengths could this child use?

  ◦ What accommodations would you make to support the child's successful participation in Phase II?

- Once all educators have completed the assignment, engage in a large group discussion, talking through each of the nine case studies. Share your thoughts on the particular children that you focused on.

- You will revisit these case studies as you read about Phase III.

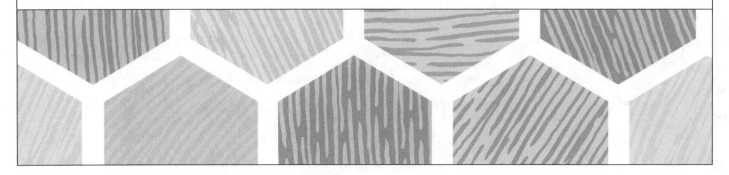

Case Study Activity II

How could participation in project work benefit this child?

What strengths could this child use?

What accommodations would you make to support the child's successful participation in Phase II?

Case Study A

Ajari, a 3.5-year-old boy, has increased his use of eye contact, smiles, giggles, and vocalizations and is a more willing participant in activities. He has made progress interacting with toys and tasks for longer periods of time before reverting to self-directed activities (e.g., books, blocks, magnets, vibrating toys, bells, climbing, structures). Ajari sometimes shows interest in his peers' activities during center time. He is good at running and climbing. He now communicates his wants and needs by getting items himself and bringing them to adults if he needs assistance. He often talks aloud and repeats lines from movies or television shows.

Case Study B

Baylee, age 4.5 years, has a lot of energy and plays well with other students. She is able to respond to questions vocally or with the assistance of an augmentative and alternative communication (AAC) device. She knows her shapes and letters and can count from 0 to 15. Baylee likes to jump and be hugged. She enjoys nursery rhymes and will often sing them out loud. Baylee likes to count, especially when she seems upset. She enjoys coloring with markers and crayons, and she likes to line up the markers or crayons on a table. She really enjoys animals and will often draw pictures of dogs and cats.

Case Study C

Cameron is 3 years old. After 2 years in foster care, he was recently adopted. He was born addicted to methamphetamines, and as a result, he has developmental delays in almost every area. He has significant vision loss and is almost completely blind in his left eye. Cameron also has some physical delays. He uses one-word phrases to communicate his needs, and he will sometimes imitate words. Cameron enjoys playing with shape sorters and three-piece inset puzzles. He loves the classroom sensory table (especially water, sand, and rice) and is very interested in his peers.

Case Study D

Devin is 4 years old. He has an intellectual disability. He uses some short phrases to communicate (i.e., two-word combinations). He likes to match colors and shapes, and he is beginning to point to some shapes when named. He also is beginning to point to pictures in familiar books when prompted. Devin is very interested in cars, trucks, blocks, and buildings, although he typically likes to play by himself.

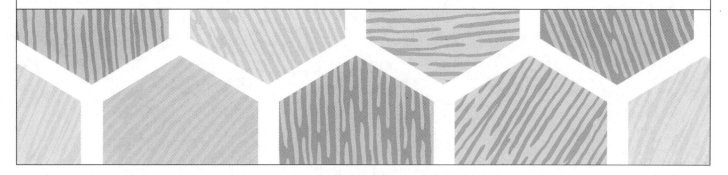

Case Study E

Evelyn is 5 years old. She was (for the most part) typically developing until she was 18 months old, when her parents noticed she was losing her language skills and regressing in some skills, such as toileting. Initially doctors were not sure why this happened; however, Evelyn was subsequently diagnosed with Rett syndrome. She was nonverbal and displayed significant challenging behaviors when she began preschool at age 3. Now, at age 5, Evelyn is communicating using some signs and interacting occasionally with peers, and her challenging behaviors have decreased. She needs adult support when completing tasks that she is not interested in, and she needs adult support for self-regulation (e.g., when she becomes frustrated, angry, or sad). Evelyn does not like fine motor tasks such as drawing. She enjoys playing in the kitchen area and with magnetic tiles, especially if her friends are nearby.

Case Study F

Frankie, a kindergartner, is 6 years old and has been diagnosed with attention-deficit/hyperactivity disorder. He engages in some challenging behaviors. He uses full sentences and has very strong receptive language skills. He ignores adult requests to clean up, grabs toys from peers, and runs away from adults on the playground. Frankie needs visual supports to understand expectations in the classroom. For example, for large group, he uses visual supports that explain: "It's circle time. I sit in my cube chair. I listen to the teacher. It is time to read a book." Frankie needs breaks during structured class periods to help keep his attention on the task at hand. He loves to be outdoors.

Case Study G

Garret is 5 years old and was recently diagnosed with autism spectrum disorder. He engages in challenging behaviors when presented with activities that he does not like. He uses some language, which typically consists of "phrases" that he has heard, although these may or may not be used appropriately (e.g., he will say "I want pig" when he sees a picture of a pig in a book). Garret is very motivated by the toy farm and zoo animals. He also enjoys music. When a teacher prompts Garret to use different materials in the classroom, he often screams and needs supports (visual and verbal); he calms down when told that he can have his small plastic animals back after he finishes the activity. Garret typically plays by himself and gets upset if a peer comes near his space.

Case Study H

Helen, a nonnative English speaker, is a 4-year-old girl who loves to ride her toy tractor and tricycle. She also enjoys one-on-one time with adults. In the classroom, she has been observed touching and grabbing others, talking loudly to peers, and often entering into her classmates' personal space. Helen typically responds to verbal cues after two or three times. She enjoys any activities with the teaching staff, especially music and movement. Helen also does better in one-on-one situations with peers, but she needs reminders to keep her hands to herself.

Case Study I

Iona is a 3-year-old student who was diagnosed with a traumatic brain injury after a car accident. She uses a wheelchair, has visual impairments, and requires adult support for most daily activities. Iona benefits from consistency in her days, loves to be held and bounced on exercise balls, and enjoys music. She likes to engage with items that light up, such as shape sorters and light tables. She can participate in parallel play using the same materials as her peers if an adult is sitting directly next to her and uses hand-under-hand to help her interact with materials.

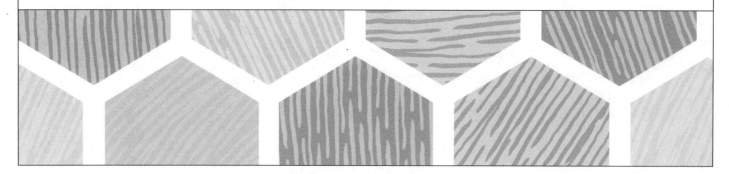

Representing and Sharing Project Work

DISCUSSION QUESTIONS

Use the questions that follow to begin a discussion about the final activities of Phase II and the activities of Phase III, which culminate the project.

Observe

- What kinds of group projects or representations have students done in your class? How were they similar or different from the types of group representations described in Chapter 5?

  - Were guests invited? If so, who decided on the guests to be invited? What was the process that went into making this decision?

  - Who decided on the program of events? What was the process that went into making this decision?

  - Who decided what would be displayed? What was the process that went into making this decision?

- What types of visual organizers have your students created? Have you seen other visual organizers created by different preschoolers?

Reflect

- How might children with disabilities enjoy, benefit from, or struggle with participating in the construction of group representations? What could you do, as the teacher, to ensure this is a positive experience?

- Chapter 5 recommends that teachers help children reflect on what they have learned from their in-depth investigation (e.g., observational drawing, interviewing guest experts, fieldwork). Is this a useful practice? Why or why not?

- Children in the Library Project created a model of the book sorter. Given no explanation, would a visitor to the classroom recognize the construction as a book sorter? If you were the classroom teacher, how would you make the purpose of this construction apparent to visitors?

- What challenges might you face in giving up some of the control for planning the culminating event?

Apply

- Where might students work together on a group construction in your classroom?

- What types of materials would you need to collect so that children could use them to construct group representations for a project on 1) shoes, 2) bicycles, and 3) cell phones?

- How could you involve families in the construction of group representations?

CHAPTER 5 TRAINING ACTIVITIES

Activity 1: Reviewing Project Summaries

Concept: The following activity will raise educators' awareness of how experienced project implementers have helped children summarize their learning.

Materials:

- Access to the Internet

Directions:

1. Review project examples on the Project Approach page of the Illinois Early Learning web site (https://illinoisearlylearning.org/resources/pa/projects/).

2. List the ways that teachers helped children to summarize their learning in the project examples that you reviewed.

3. Write a paragraph in which you react to the variety of ways children summarized their learning in the project examples. Indicate whether the techniques could be implemented in your classroom and provide reasons for your answers.

4. Share your reactions in a group discussion.

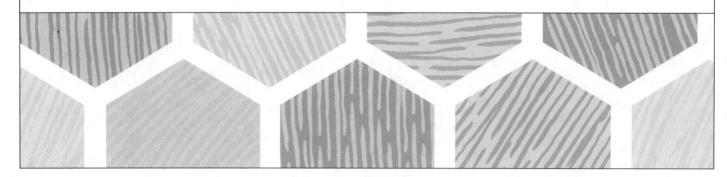

Activity 2: Planning for the Future

Concepts: In the following activity, educators will think through the key events in a potential project.

Materials:

- A copy of Task Sheet: Planning for Next Week, which follows this page

Directions:

1. Chapter 5 concludes the overview of the Project Approach. In this activity, you will have a chance to use your new knowledge to think about implementing your first project. You will need a copy of Task Sheet: Planning for Next Week.

2. Think of a project topic you are considering implementing with your students, given what you know about your students' interests. Use the Task Sheet to brainstorm ideas for implementing the project. What resources do you have that might contribute to this project? What will you do first to get project work going in your class?

3. You may work independently or with co-teachers or assistants.

4. When you have completed the form, share your ideas with others at your table.

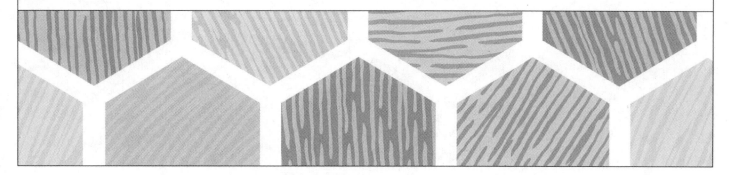

Planning for Next Week

Now that you have learned about the three phases of the Project Approach, what project can you envision doing with your class? What resources do you have that might contribute to this project? What will you do first to get project work going in your class? Use this form to brainstorm ideas.

Ideas

Topic
Opening Event
Authentic Materials
Guest Experts
Sites for Fieldwork
Things to Check On

Notes:

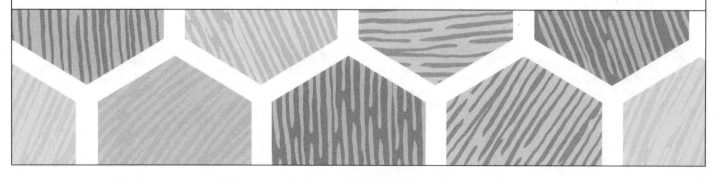

CHAPTER 5 TRAINING ACTIVITIES

Activity 3: Phase III—Planning Accommodations Using the Case Studies

Note: This activity assumes that participants have previously engaged with the case studies in the Phase I and II versions of this activity (see the Chapters 3 and 4 materials in Appendix B).

Concept: In this activity, educators will think about how they can support children with disabilities in successfully participating in project work through Phase III.

Materials:

- A copy of Task Sheet: Case Study Activity III

Directions:

- This activity is intended to help you think about how you will tailor project work to allow children with disabilities to get optimal benefit from Phase III. You will need a copy of the Task Sheet: Case Study Activity III.

- In small groups, review the case studies on the sheet and choose three children to focus on.

- Answer the following questions for each of the three children:

  - How could Phase III project work benefit this child (i.e., by organizing their learning and communicating it to others)?

  - What strengths could this child use?

  - What accommodations would you make to support the child's successful participation in Phase III?

- Once all educators have completed the assignment, engage in a large group discussion, talking through each of the nine case studies. Share your thoughts on the particular children that you chose.

Case Study Activity III

How could participation in project work benefit this child?

What strengths could this child use?

What accommodations would you make to support the child's successful participation in Phase I?

Case Study A

Ajari, a 3.5-year-old boy, has increased his use of eye contact, smiles, giggles, and vocalizations and is a more willing participant in activities. He has made progress interacting with toys and tasks for longer periods of time before reverting to self-directed activities (e.g., books, blocks, magnets, vibrating toys, bells, climbing, structures). Ajari sometimes shows interest in his peers' activities during center time. He is good at running and climbing. He now communicates his wants and needs by getting items himself and bringing them to adults if he needs assistance. He often talks aloud and repeats lines from movies or television shows.

Case Study B

Baylee, age 4.5 years, has a lot of energy and plays well with other students. She is able to respond to questions vocally or with the assistance of an augmentative and alternative communication (AAC) device. She knows her shapes and letters and can count from 0 to 15. Baylee likes to jump and be hugged. She enjoys nursery rhymes and will often sing them out loud. Baylee likes to count, especially when she seems upset. She enjoys coloring with markers and crayons, and she likes to line up the markers or crayons on a table. She really enjoys animals and will often draw pictures of dogs and cats.

Case Study C

Cameron is 3 years old. After 2 years in foster care, he was recently adopted. He was born addicted to methamphetamines, and as a result, he has developmental delays in almost every area. He has significant vision loss and is almost completely blind in his left eye. Cameron also has some physical delays. He uses one-word phrases to communicate his needs, and he will sometimes imitate words. Cameron enjoys playing with shape sorters and three-piece inset puzzles. He loves the classroom sensory table (especially water, sand, and rice) and is very interested in his peers.

Case Study D

Devin is 4 years old. He has an intellectual disability. He uses some short phrases to communicate (i.e., two-word combinations). He likes to match colors and shapes, and he is beginning to point to some shapes when named. He also is beginning to point to pictures in familiar books when prompted. Devin is very interested in cars, trucks, blocks, and buildings, although he typically likes to play by himself.

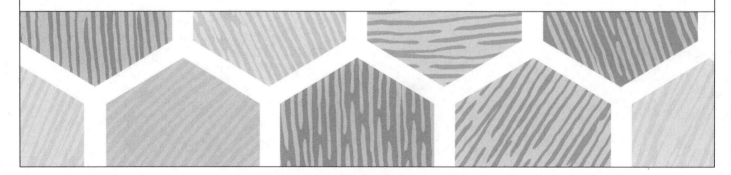

Case Study E

Evelyn is 5 years old. She was (for the most part) typically developing until she was 18 months old, when her parents noticed she was losing her language skills and regressing in some skills, such as toileting. Initially doctors were not sure why this happened; however, Evelyn was subsequently diagnosed with Rett syndrome. She was nonverbal and displayed significant challenging behaviors when she began preschool at age 3. Now, at age 5, Evelyn is communicating using some signs and interacting occasionally with peers, and her challenging behaviors have decreased. She needs adult support when completing tasks that she is not interested in, and she needs adult support for self-regulation (e.g., when she becomes frustrated, angry, or sad). Evelyn does not like fine motor tasks such as drawing. She enjoys playing in the kitchen area and with magnetic tiles, especially if her friends are nearby.

Case Study F

Frankie, a kindergartner, is 6 years old and has been diagnosed with attention-deficit/hyperactivity disorder. He engages in some challenging behaviors. He uses full sentences and has very strong receptive language skills. He ignores adult requests to clean up, grabs toys from peers, and runs away from adults on the playground. Frankie needs visual supports to understand expectations in the classroom. For example, for large group, he uses visual supports that explain: "It's circle time. I sit in my cube chair. I listen to the teacher. It is time to read a book." Frankie needs breaks during structured class periods to help keep his attention on the task at hand. He loves to be outdoors.

Case Study G

Garret is 5 years old and was recently diagnosed with autism spectrum disorder. He engages in challenging behaviors when presented with activities that he does not like. He uses some language, which typically consists of "phrases" that he has heard, although these may or may not be used appropriately (e.g., he will say "I want pig" when he sees a picture of a pig in a book). Garret is very motivated by the toy farm and zoo animals. He also enjoys music. When a teacher prompts Garret to use different materials in the classroom, he often screams and needs supports (visual and verbal); he calms down when told that he can have his small plastic animals back after he finishes the activity. Garret typically plays by himself and gets upset if a peer comes near his space.

Case Study H

Helen, a nonnative English speaker, is a 4-year-old girl who loves to ride her toy tractor and tricycle. She also enjoys one-on-one time with adults. In the classroom, she has been observed touching and grabbing others, talking loudly to peers, and often entering into her classmates' personal space. Helen typically responds to verbal cues after two or three times. She enjoys any activities with the teaching staff, especially music and movement. Helen also does better in one-on-one situations with peers, but she needs reminders to keep her hands to herself.

Case Study I

Iona is a 3-year-old student who was diagnosed with a traumatic brain injury after a car accident. She uses a wheelchair, has visual impairments, and requires adult support for most daily activities. Iona benefits from consistency in her days, loves to be held and bounced on exercise balls, and enjoys music. She likes to engage with items that light up, such as shape sorters and light tables. She can participate in parallel play using the same materials as her peers if an adult is sitting directly next to her and uses hand-under-hand to help her interact with materials.

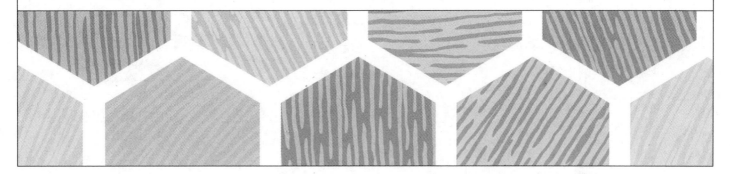

CHAPTER 6
Sustaining the Project Approach

DISCUSSION QUESTIONS

Use the questions that follow to discuss the barriers and supports that impact a teacher's ability to sustain the Project Approach.

Observe

- What are some ways that children currently make meaningful decisions or choices in your class?

- Share a time when you were able to successfully scaffold a child's learning.

Reflect

- How do you think offering children opportunities to make meaningful decisions will impact the students in your class?

- Administrative support for project work can help you access materials and resources. How might you convince your administrator to support your use of the Project Approach?

- Do you think the Project Approach will help prepare children for kindergarten? If so, how?

- What are some challenges you think you may face as you incorporate the Project Approach into your curriculum?

- In Chapter 6, Dawn Johnson shares her experience with forming a regional Project Approach group. Would a regional group be helpful to you? Why or why not?

Apply

- What are some *new opportunities* you can offer children to make meaningful decisions or choices in your class?

- What are some decisions that you currently make that could be decided by a vote among your students?

- Do you have any students who you believe will not be able to participate in project work? Why? How could you support their participation?

- If you are a teacher in a part-day or variable-attendance class, what are some strategies you could use to make the Project Approach work for two or more classes?

- How will you use the Project Approach Implementation Checklist (e.g., on your own, with a colleague who is also starting a project, with your whole team filling it out together as you begin implementing a project)?

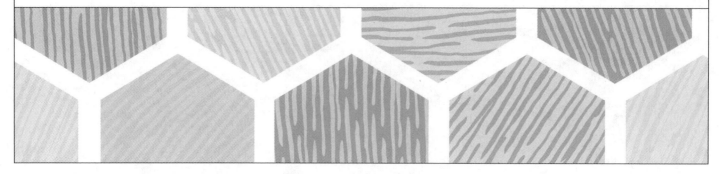

CHAPTER 6 TRAINING ACTIVITY

Activity 1: Identifying Barriers and Solutions to Implementing the Project Approach

Concept: The following activity is designed to help educators identify barriers and solutions to implementing the Project Approach.

Materials:

- Markers
- Timer
- Ten pieces of chart paper, each titled with one of the following barriers:
  - Trusting Children to Share Planning and Decision Making
  - Flexible Planning
  - Supporting Children With a Range of Abilities
  - Garnering Peer Support for This Way of Teaching
  - Implementing Project Work in Part-Day or Variable-Attendance Classes
  - Fitting the Project Approach in With Existing Curricula
  - Raising Administrative Support
  - Accessing Financial Support for Materials and Field Trips
  - Finding Guest Experts, Volunteers, and Locations for Field Trips
  - Responding to Pressure to Get Children Ready for Kindergarten

Directions:

1. Divide into small groups. In your small group, choose one of the 10 chart papers. Each paper lists a different barrier to implementing the Project Approach.

2. Set a timer for 5 minutes.

3. In the 5 minutes allotted, brainstorm solutions to the barrier listed at the top of your chart paper.

4. At the end of the 5 minutes, rotate clockwise to the next chart paper with your group. Your group will again have 5 minutes to brainstorm solutions for that barrier.

5. Continue rotating until you have listed solutions for all 10 barriers.

6. When all the groups are finished working, visit each poster to consider the barriers and solutions that the groups identified.

7. Engage in a large-group discussion, sharing your reflections on the activity.

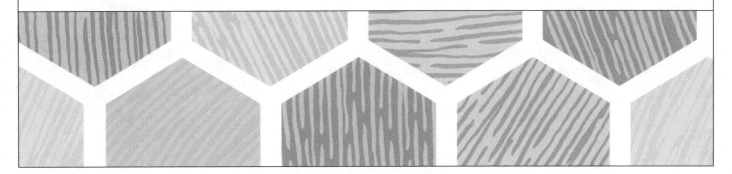

Index

~~~~~~